Maria Pascuzzi's *Paul: Windows on His Thought and His World* explores . . . Paul and his writings in light of his historical and social contexts. It eschews the common format of letter-by-letter review, opting for a topical introduction that better explores reoccurring themes and synthesizes Paul's thought. A good introduction for those beginning their Pauline studies or those ready to renew their acquaintance with the Apostle to the Gentiles.

—Laurie Brink, OP
Associate Professor of New Testament Studies
Catholic Theological Union

In her book *Paul: Windows on His Thought and His World*, Maria Pascuzzi provides a helpful and accessible introduction for students who want to understand the Apostle Paul. . . . She gives students easy access to Paul's Christology, soteriology, ecclesiology, and ethics [and] . . . students will also find interesting her concise treatments of Paul's position on homosexuality and the role of women in church and society. Pascuzzi's book is a first-rate orientation to the field of Pauline studies that should be used as a required textbook in introductory courses on Paul.

—Troy W. Martin, PhD
St. Xavier University

This helpful book takes a fresh approach to the enormously challenging (and rewarding) task of studying the life and legacy of Paul. After providing a sound, nuanced picture of Paul's historical world and his place in it, before and after his transforming encounter with the risen Jesus, . . . Pascuzzi guides readers in an encounter with the foundation and superstructure of Paul's thought. . . . Students and teachers alike will profit immensely from this work.

—Marion L. Soards
Professor of New Testament Studies
Louisville Presbyterian Theological Seminary

Dr. Pascuzzi has succinctly presented the history of Pauline interpretation, summarizing a wide variety of opinions without being dismissive of any tradition. Well-researched but not wordy, this book explores competing views on sensitive subjects such as same sex relationships and Paul's attitudes toward women, in a balanced manner without promoting her personal opinion. Pascuzzi brilliantly offers a comprehensive but nuanced view of Paul's life and thought, which leads to an appreciation of Paul as a complex person of his time.

—Eugenia Constantinou
University of San Diego

Author Acknowledgments

The idea for this book developed after several years of teaching Introduction to Pauline Studies to undergraduates at the University of San Diego. Its production involved a number of persons whose contribution must be recognized.

In the first place, I am indebted to many people at Anselm Academic, especially Kathleen Walsh, development editor; Maura Hagarty, managing editor; Angie Kaelberer, copy editor; and Laurie Nelson, production coordinator. Anselm Academic is a creative and attentive publisher, and at every level the collaboration was always professional and cordial.

I am also indebted to generous colleagues, John Clabeaux, Florence Gillman, John Gillman, Stephen Lampe, Seamus O'Connell, and Robert O'Toole, who read various chapters or sections of this book and offered helpful advice and insights for improving it. I am especially thankful for the invaluable support and contribution of Patricia Burke Brande, who read each chapter along the way and helped in the final reading and editing.

This book began on the West Coast and was completed on the East Coast. I am most grateful to Elizabeth Hill, CSJ, JD, president of Saint Joseph's College, Brooklyn, New York, and to the faculty and staff, for the hospitality and resources that allowed for the completion of this book. Since Saint Joseph's College is my alma mater, I was also able to renew friendships and enjoy the encouragement of former professors whose pursuit of academic excellence has been a lifelong inspiration.

Finally, I also extend heartfelt thanks to family and friends, especially Attilia, Willie, and Stella, who were immensely supportive while I was engaged in this project. I will consider the days and months dedicated to the writing of this book to have been well spent if readers come away with a better understanding of Paul's thought and the world that shaped it.

Maria Pascuzzi, STD, SSL
January 25, 2014
Feast of the Conversion of Saint Paul, Apostle

Publisher Acknowledgments

Thank you to the following individuals who reviewed this work in progress:

Kevin McCruden
Gonzaga University, Spokane, Washington

Jeffrey Siker
Loyola Marymount University, Los Angeles, California

Created by the publishing team of Anselm Academic.

Cover image: Saint Paul escapes Damascus in a basket. Mosaic from the twelfth century Cathedral of Monreale, Palermo, Italy. © The Bridgeman Art Gallery

The scriptural quotations contained herein are from the New Revised Standard Version of the Bible with the Apocrypha. Copyright © 1989 by the Division of Christian Education of the National Council of the Churches of Christ in the United States of America. All rights reserved.

Copyright © 2014 by Maria Pascuzzi. All rights reserved. No part of this book may be reproduced by any means without the written permission of the publisher, Anselm Academic, Christian Brothers Publications, 702 Terrace Heights, Winona, Minnesota 55987-1320, *www.anselmacademic.org*.

Printed in the United States of America

7060

ISBN 978-1-59982-214-3

PAUL

WINDOWS ON HIS THOUGHT AND HIS WORLD

MARIA PASCUZZI

Contents

Preface

Windows on the Thought and World of Paul

One day while sitting at my computer, I typed "Paul Apostle" into my browser. In less than a second, there were more than 18 million results. Even if only 1 percent of those links contained worthwhile information, that would still be more than 180,000 results. So I limited my search terms to "Paul, impact on Christianity," but still got almost 29,000 hits. Clicking any one of those links opens a new window filled with information about Paul. The first information accessed usually contains multiple embedded links leading to other windows with further information about Paul. A person interested in Paul can open successive windows all day and discover an almost endless supply of information. Add to this all the print publications pertaining to Paul produced over the centuries, and you realize that a mountain of information stands before you.

The information about Paul and his writings is extensive because, after Jesus, Paul was arguably the most important and certainly the most controversial figure in the movement that eventually became Christianity. Paul is usually referred to as Christianity's "first theologian," meaning that he made the first attempt to explain the significance of the life, death, and Resurrection of Jesus. Christians recognize that in grappling with the meaning of Christ's death and Resurrection and its implications for all of God's creation, Paul provided most of the insights at the heart of the faith they share. Among Christians, however, Paul is also a lightning rod for controversy. Some hold Paul responsible for anti-Judaism, the subordinate role of women in the church, disregard for ethnic diversity, and other oppressive situations. Others see him as a faithful Jew and liberator of women. Still others charge him with distancing Christianity from the simple preaching of Jesus, who by word and example called his fellow Jews to religious renewal. No one who reads Paul comes away without forming an opinion about him. It's hard to be indifferent about him!

The purpose of this book is to sort through the vast literature about Paul and provide the information needed to understand who Paul was, what he thought, what was important to him, and why. Fortunately, a fair amount of Paul's thought is available in letters that he wrote to some of the first communities of believers in Jesus. These letters, written between ca. 49 and 60 ce, are the earliest Christian writings contained in the New Testament and, while they are helpful to have, they have never been easy to understand (see 2 Pet 3:15–17). Like all letters, they are part of conversations between *two* parties who both possess and presume information about people and issues that does not need to be stated or explained. Third-party readers do not share that information and, therefore, remain at a disadvantage. Second, Paul wrote his letters two millennia ago during the Greco-Roman period to people who lived around the Mediterranean basin. Their daily reality differed greatly from ours, as did their concerns, fears, goals, social structures, customs, notions of success and failure, honor and shame—just to name a few differences. Moreover, Paul wrote to them in Greek. Reading Paul's letters in English can obscure the fact that when we open them, we really enter a foreign conceptual world. Like all travelers to foreign places, getting a feel for the culture and thought of the people to whom Paul wrote, and with whom he sometimes clashed, requires windows onto the world in which he worked. So think of each chapter in this book as one of a select number of windows that you can open to find information about Paul, his world, and the key themes and issues that thread through his letters. Within each chapter, there are a number of footnotes. In addition to referencing the sources used in the composition of this book, many footnotes function as links to further scholarly literature and debate on a topic. This book is not a substitute for reading the letters of Paul, which are the *primary source* where the reader encounters Paul in his own words. Rather, it is intended to *help* readers explore those letters and make the most out of that encounter by providing the background information and insights needed to make sense of Paul.

How This Book Works

Most introductory books on Paul begin with a few chapters of basic information about his life and work, followed by a chapter-by-chapter examination of each of his letters according to the order in which they were written. This book will proceed somewhat differently. After dealing with indispensable introductory material in the first three chapters, it will examine clusters of texts that focus on a particular topic. Thus rather than treating each letter individually, this text takes a synthetic approach to Paul. It deals with important recurring themes and issues that cut across the letters and examines why these issues mattered to Paul and why he was in dialogue—and sometimes conflict—with others over them. In the course of this study, readers will be introduced to contemporary scholarship on these issues, which continue to elicit debate.

Each chapter will begin with an overview of its contents. Beginning in chapter 4, immediately after the overview, various scripture passages are listed under "Recommended Reading." Reading these scriptural passages *in advance* of the chapter prepares one to better understand the issues considered in the chapter. Each chapter ends with a summary of key points and suggested resources to consult for further information. In keeping with the subtitle of this book, the resources for further study go beyond print material to suggest various websites that provide trustworthy information not only about Paul but also about his world. These sites are solid electronic resources intended to help readers move beyond reliance on popular websites that may not contain reliable information.

Putting Paul in His Place

Overview

This chapter considers the emergence and development of the Jesus movement within the context of first-century CE Judaism, as well as Paul's place within that movement. Next, it examines the sources of information about Paul and their relative value. Finally, the text discusses what is known about Paul's life before and after the event that led him to accept Jesus, the crucified and Risen One, as God's messiah.

The Jesus Movement before Paul

Paul's name is attached to almost half the documents in the New Testament, and his missionary work dominates the account in the Acts of the Apostles of how the gospel spread. Because of this, one can easily overlook the fact that the Jesus movement began before Paul, in Palestine, among devout Jews. Paul, also a devout Jew, was one of the Jesus movement's fiercest opponents before becoming one of its strongest advocates. Before examining his relation to the Jesus movement, it is important to consider the Jewish world of Palestine, where the movement began.

By the turn of the first century ce, the daily reality for Jews such as Jesus was Roman control of Palestine, the Jewish homeland, with all the oppression and violence that occurs when one nation imposes its will and presence on another. The Roman takeover began in 63 bce when Pompey conquered Palestine, put an end to Hasmonean rule, and brought Palestine under Roman control. Before

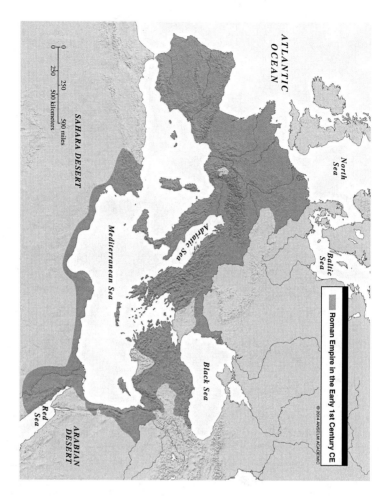

the Romans, Palestine had been occupied by the Greeks and, before that, by a succession of foreign powers as far back as the sixth century bce.[1] The imposition of Greek thought, language, and culture—a process begun by Alexander the Great ca. 332 bce and referred to

1. The period of Jewish history from 519 bce (when the Jews built a second temple to replace the first, which the Babylonians destroyed in 587 bce) through 70 ce (when the Romans destroyed that second temple), is known as the Second Temple Period. A concise review of this period is provided by Lester Grabbe in, *An Introduction to Second Temple Judaism: History and Religion of the Jews in the Time of Nehemiah, the Maccabees, Hillel and Jesus* (New York: Continuum, 2012).

as Hellenization—had transformed the entire Mediterranean world. Palestine had also been Hellenized, but not without Jewish opposition. Because Greek language and culture remained pervasive, even after the Roman conquest of the Mediterranean world, the period of Roman hegemony from ca. the second century bce to the fourth century ce is commonly referred to as the Greco-Roman era.

First-century-ce Jews longed for liberation from foreign rule. Segments of the population banded behind various messianic figures who emerged at different times to lead popular uprisings, largely unsuccessful, against the Romans.[2] Others attached themselves to prophetic figures leading renewal movements.[3] Some hoped for the coming of a new "anointed one" (Hebrew *mashiach*/messiah; Greek *Christos*/Christ), from David's line, who would restore the kingdom to Israel (see Ps 89: 20–29; further 2 Sam 7:8–17) and be both king and shepherd (see *Pss. Sol.* 17:21–46).[4] Some first-century Jews came to believe that the crucified and Risen One, Jesus of Nazareth, was the hoped-for messiah, or *christ*, from the line of David (see Acts 2:29–36; Rom 1:1–6). Most Jews did not. Among other things, the messiah was expected to bring about the political liberation of the Jewish nation now oppressed by Rome.[5] Jesus had not done this.

---

2. For example, Simon, former slave of Herod, was acclaimed king by some Jews and led an unsuccessful revolt (see Josephus, *Antiquities of the Jews (hereafter Ant.)*, 17.10:6), as did Anthronges, a shepherd, who declared himself king (*Ant.* 17:10.7). Concerning Judas, see *Ant.* 17.10:5. In this book all citations from Josephus are from William Whiston, trans., *The Works of Josephus: Complete and Unabridged One Volume*, new updated edition (Peabody, MA: Hendrickson, 1988). Josephus' writings can be accessed at *www.ccel.org/ccel/josephus/complete*. Original language editions of Josephus' works with translations are available in multi volumes in the Loeb Classical Library Series published by Harvard University Press.

3. For example, in the 40s ce, Theudas, a self-declared prophet, saw himself as a new Moses, leading a new Exodus. The Romans beheaded him; see Josephus, *Ant.*, 20.5:1.

4. The *Psalms of Solomon* (*Pss. Sol.*) are hymns written by pious Jews in the first century bce in response to the Roman capture of Jerusalem. They are part of a corpus of valuable Jewish religious writings not included in the canon of the Hebrew Bible. The hymns, along with other noncanonical Jewish writings, are available in translation in James H. Charlesworth, ed., *The Old Testament Pseudepigrapha*, 2 vols. (New York: Doubleday, 1983, 1985).

5. The idea of the messiah as a warrior king and liberator from the Davidic line was widespread in first-century Judaism. However, it was only one of four main ways Jews conceived the Messiah. An excellent discussion of messianic paradigms and expectations is provided by John J. Collins, *The Scepter and the Star: Messianism in Light of the Dead Sea Scrolls*, 2nd ed. (Grand Rapids, MI: William B. Eerdmans, 2010).

In fact, the Romans had executed him. For the majority of Jews, this served as decisive evidence that Jesus was not the messiah.

The small Jewish group that formed around Jesus, at first known simply as "the way" (Acts 9:2), or the Nazarenes (Acts 24:1), was only one of a number of Jewish groups at the time. Other groups had come into existence during the brief period of Jewish self-rule that began in ca. 164 bce with a successful revolt against the Seleucid Greeks. A family of pious Jews, the Hasmoneans, led the revolt.[6] Before self-rule ended in 63 bce when the Romans seized power, the Jews were governed by the Hasmonean kings for almost eighty years (ca. 142–63 bce). However, not everyone recognized them as legitimate kings or agreed with their policies and practices, which led to further splintering of the population.[7] By the time the Romans seized control, there were four main groups: the Sadducees, Pharisees, Essenes, and Zealots. These groups shared some core convictions; for example, the beliefs that there was only one God and that they were God's elect people who expressed their love for God by obedience to the Torah. However, beyond a core of shared beliefs, each group had different ideas about what it meant to be a true Jew, what practices and beliefs were essential, and how to respond to the Roman occupation.

From the limited ancient sources available, one can glean a few broad insights about each group.[8] The Sadducees comprised the elite strata of Jewish society. Some may have been priests associated with the Jerusalem Temple or members of the Sanhedrin, the ancient Jewish court system. To protect their interests, they apparently collaborated with the Romans, which did not put them in good standing with the rest of the Jews. The Sadducees rejected the resurrection of the dead, whereas the Pharisees believed in it. Moreover, the

---

6. This revolt is also referred to as the Maccabean Revolt. "Maccabee," which means "hammer," was the nickname give to Judah Hasmonean. He and his brothers continued the revolt started by their father, Mattathias. For information, see Uriel Rappaport, "Maccabean Revolt," in *The Anchor Bible Dictionary*, ed. David N. Freedman (New York: Doubleday, 1992), vol. 4, 433–39.

7. On the Hasmoneans, see Tessa Rajak, "Hasmonean Dynasty," in *The Anchor Bible Dictionary*, ed. David N. Freedman (New York: Doubleday, 1992), vol. 3, 67–76.

8. The main source of information about Jewish groups in the first century ce is the Jewish historian, Flavius Josephus. See *Ant.* Bk. 18.1:1–6

Sadducees rejected the Pharisees' innovative interpretations of the Torah and adhered to the text as written.[9]

Though portrayed negatively in the New Testament (see, e.g., Matt 23:1–39), the Pharisees were a widespread social and religious reform movement of laypersons who, unlike the Sadducees, enjoyed great popular appeal.[10] In response to the upheaval the Roman occupation caused, they worked to maintain and reform Jewish identity around strict observance of the Torah, which they continuously interpreted and applied to their current circumstances. The Pharisees aimed to sanctify everyday domestic life and live the same holiness required of priests. According to Josephus, they were ascetic in their eating habits. They believed in God's preordained will, which, in their view, did not preclude human freedom. They also believed in a system of postmortem rewards and punishments based on how one lived. Josephus says they were admired for their virtuous conduct. The New Testament portrays the Pharisees as preoccupied with purity concerns and adherence to the Torah (see, e.g., Mark 2:18; 7:1–15; Matt 12:1–8). Within the Pharisaic movement, there were divergent views on the Roman occupation. Some advocated tolerance, while others inclined more toward revolution.

The Essenes, who flourished from the mid-second century bce to the time of the failed Jewish Revolt against Rome (66–70 ce), opted out of mainstream urban life and society and formed intentional communities where members lived according to a set code of conduct. One could think of the Essenes as a kind of ancient religious commune whose members withdrew from what they perceived as a corrupt world in order to focus on the spiritual life. They were opposed to the priesthood and ritual system of the Jerusalem temple and were especially attentive to purity regulations and strict adherence to the written Torah. A major Essene settlement was located on the shores of the Dead Sea at Qumran. Most scholars maintain that this community produced the Dead Sea Scrolls, a collection of ancient texts and text fragments dating from ca. third century bce to the first century ce, written in Hebrew, Aramaic,

---

9. See Josephus, *Ant.* 13.10:6.

10. Ibid.

and Greek and discovered near the western shore of the Dead Sea beginning in 1947.[11]

Essenes referred to themselves as the "sons of righteousness" or "sons of light" (see 1QS III.13; 1QM 1:1, 8)[12] and believed they alone were the elect who represented the truest form of Judaism. Based on some text evidence from Qumran literature (e.g., 1QS 9:11; CD 9:b29), many scholars hold that the Essenes awaited two distinct "anointed ones," or messiahs: a military leader from God who would intervene and destroy their enemies and a priestly messiah who would restore proper worship in the Temple. Finally, the Zealots seem to have been a heterogeneous group of fervent Jewish nationalists who sought to end Roman occupation through armed rebellion. The Zealots tolerated no ruler or lord but God, which meant the Romans had to be vanquished.[13]

It was within this world, where various ways of being Jewish coexisted, that the Jesus movement emerged as another reform movement in Judaism. This occurred sometime between 30 and 33 ce. The first followers of Jesus continued to understand themselves as Jews and to follow Jewish traditions, which they now reinterpreted in light of Christ's death and Resurrection.[14] Their movement, whose central proclamation was that the crucified and Risen Jesus was God's messiah, started in Jerusalem among Jews, with James and Peter as its leaders. Within a short time, the Jesus movement spread beyond Jerusalem to other parts of Palestine, where even some Gentiles (a generic term for non-Jewish people), came to believe in the

---

11. On the scrolls, their provenance, content, and significance, see John J. Collins, "The Dead Sea Scrolls," in *The Anchor Bible Dictionary*, ed. David Noel Freedman (New York: Doubleday, 1992), vol. 2, 85–101.

12. References to texts from Qumran generally mention the number of the cave in which a text was found, then a descriptive name or a number that identifies the text, and then the column of the text and lines. In the citation above, 1QM 1:1, 8, "1Q" means the scroll was found in Qumran cave 1; "M" is the designation for the "War Scroll" and 1:1, 8 means Column 1, lines 1 and 8. On how texts are designated, and for an index of titles, see Florentino García Martínez and Eibert J. Tigchelaar, eds. *The Dead Sea Scrolls: Study Edition* (Leiden, The Netherlands: Brill, 1998), vol. 2, 1325–59.

13. See Josephus, *Ant.* 18.1:6.

14. The resemblance of the early Jesus movement to other Jewish groups is discussed by Daniel C. Harlow, "Early Judaism and Early Christianity," in *Early Judaism: A Comprehensive Overview*, ed. John J. Collins and Daniel C. Harlow (Grand Rapids, MI: William B. Eerdmans, 2012), 391–419, esp. 397–400.

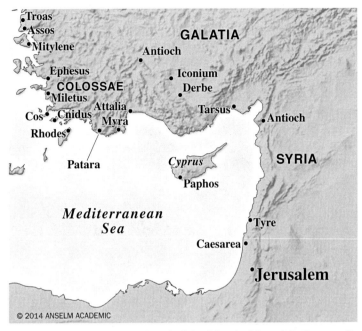

The Jesus movement emerged within Palestinian Jewish society. However, its diffusion across Asia Minor led to its rapid growth and increased diversity. The community at Syrian Antioch supported missions throughout Asia Minor.

gospel proclamation (Acts 10:40). The inclusion of the Gentiles and the terms of their inclusion were a major source of contention among the earliest followers of Jesus and had significant implications for the development of Christianity.

The movement also spread beyond Palestine. One of the largest and most important communities of believers flourished in Antioch, Syria, the third major city of the Roman Empire. At Antioch, according to Acts 11:19, Jews were the first to receive the gospel. Then Gentiles were evangelized and joined Jews in accepting the gospel proclamation that Jesus was God's messiah. This mixed community of Jewish and Gentile believers advocated and financed a mission to the Gentiles. Eventually Paul was invited into the community at Antioch, where he lived and worked for one year. The Antioch community then sent Paul out on a mission team led by Barnabas to bring the gospel west, into Asia Minor (see Acts 13:2–3).

Though the pre-Paul period of the Jesus movement was relatively brief—perhaps no more than three or four years from the death and Resurrection of Jesus until Paul's entry into the movement—it was a time of growth and development. During this period, the movement had spread not only beyond the physical borders of Palestine but also beyond the religious border of Judaism to include Gentiles. The practices and ideas that developed during this period influenced Paul's own formation in the faith. In fact, he states in some of his own letters that he was passing on traditions that he had received from the Christ-believers who came before him (see, e.g., 1 Cor 15:3).

Where to Find Information about Paul

Paul's own letters in the New Testament are the most important source for information about his life, thought, and work. Thirteen New Testament letters name Paul as author. However, based on some notable differences in style, vocabulary, and theological outlook, most scholars agree that not all of these letters were authored by him.

Few scholars believe that Paul authored 1 and 2 Timothy and Titus, known together as the Pastoral Epistles. Most assume they were written in Paul's name *after his death* by one or more followers to promote Paul's legacy and to gain his authority for their own teaching. With regard to Ephesians, Colossians, and 2 Thessalonians, scholars continue to debate whether Paul is the author of these letters or whether they postdate Paul's life. In recent years, more scholars have come to accept that Paul authored Colossians during his lifetime.[15] However, this is still far from a majority. If these six letters, collectively referred to as the deutero-Pauline letters, were authored by others after Paul's death, then they do not contain Paul's own theological thought or his responses to questions and issues that arose during his lifetime among the communities of believers he knew or knew about. For these reasons, scholars rely on the seven letters universally considered to have been authored by Paul during his lifetime as the primary source of knowledge about him.

---

15. See Maria Pascuzzi, "Reconsidering the Authorship of Colossians," *Bulletin for Biblical Research* 23.2 (2013): 223–46.

The Primary Evidence: The Seven Undisputed Letters of Paul

No one disputes that Paul was the author of the following seven letters: Romans, 1 and 2 Corinthians, Galatians, Philippians, 1 Thessalonians, and Philemon. With the exception of Romans and Philemon, addressed to communities Paul had not founded, his other authentic letters were written to communities of Christians among whom he had lived and worked. However, Paul hoped to pay a visit to Philemon and the church that met in his house (see Phlm 22) and planned to stop in Rome on his way to Spain. Among other reasons, he wrote the letter to the Romans to announce his planned visit (Rom 15:22–24).

The seven undisputed letters were written in the span of a decade or so, sometime between ca. 49–50 and 60 ce. Unlike typical modern letters, Paul's letters are not dated; moreover, the location from which he writes a particular letter is not always evident. Both the dates of the letters and their places of origin have to be established using clues within the letters and information from Acts, which helps establish a chronology for Paul's life and work. In terms of the chronological order of Paul's letters, scholars generally agree that First Thessalonians came first, written ca. 49–50 ce, and Romans last, written perhaps as late as 58 ce.

Paul's Gospel

The four New Testament texts, Matthew, Mark, Luke, and John, referred to as Gospels, were written between 70 and 100 ce; that is, after Paul had died. When Paul used the Greek term *euangelion* (English "gospel" or "good news"), it was not yet a technical term for the four written narratives about Christ's life, death, and Resurrection. By "gospel," Paul meant his proclamation or teaching about the significance of Christ's life, death, and Resurrection. In Galatians, for example, Paul insists only his gospel, or preaching, which was "not of human origin" (Gal 1:11), and which was received "through a revelation of Jesus Christ" (Gal 1:12), is valid.

The letters vary in length, ranging from sixteen chapters (Romans and 1 Corinthians) to just one (Philemon). In the letters, Paul is often involved in passionate arguments over controversial issues and is insistent that his gospel, and no other, is the right one (see Gal 1:6–9). Therefore, it is important to keep in mind that even though the letters are primary sources and offer the best access to Paul's thought, they are not dispassionate, objective accounts of what went on among the earliest communities of believers. They are Paul's presentation of what others said and did. They give Paul's point of view and were written with the expectation that his first readers would agree with him.

The Acts of the Apostles

After Paul's seven undisputed letters (Romans, 1 and 2 Corinthians, Galatians, Philippians, 1 Thessalonians, Philemon), scholars consider Acts of the Apostles the next most important resource for the study of Paul. Luke, whose name is attached to the third Gospel, is also considered the author of the Acts of the Apostles. In Acts, which is presented as a sequel to the Gospel of Luke, the author tells the story of how the small Jewish Jesus movement grew to include Gentiles and spread from Palestine throughout the Mediterranean region as far as Rome. Though entitled Acts of the Apostles, the work is mostly about Paul. The author of Acts briefly recounts Paul's activity as a zealous Pharisee, as well as his life-changing encounter with the Risen Jesus, and then provides extensive coverage of Paul's life as a traveling missionary, including the suffering he heroically endured in order to spread the gospel.

When reading Acts, one can get the impression that Luke provides an unbiased, factual history of the spread of earliest Christianity, with special attention to Paul's contribution. However, readers should exercise caution when using Acts to construct a picture of Paul's life. First, unlike the undisputed letters, which provide Paul's firsthand accounts of his own life and work, Acts is a third-person account *about* Paul, written perhaps two or more decades after his death. Second, when Luke speaks in the first person plural "we" in Acts (see, e.g., Acts 21:1–17), he portrays himself as Paul's traveling companion, someone who knew Paul well and was an eyewitness to the events he narrates. But certain things do not square with Luke's self-portrait as a close associate of Paul. For example, Luke omits mention of Paul's letter-writing activity, while featuring Paul as a miracle worker and powerful orator. By contrast, Paul only once makes a general reference to having done "signs, and wonders and mighty works" (2 Cor 12:12). Further, he distances himself from powerful speechmaking (1 Cor 2:1–4) and admits to being an unskilled speaker (2 Cor 11:6). Although Paul is the hero of Acts, Luke only twice (Acts 14:4,14) refers to him as an apostle, a title Paul claimed and fiercely defended throughout his letters (see, e.g., 1 Cor 9:1–2). One of Paul's key projects had been a collection for the poor in Jerusalem. In narrating Paul's final journey to Jerusalem (Acts 21:1–26), Acts omits mention of the delivery of the collection, which was the purpose of this visit (see Rom 15:25–29). Moreover, Luke seems to suggest that after failing to persuade Jews to accept the gospel, Paul invested himself in a mission directed exclusively to the Gentiles. Yet even in Romans, his last letter, Paul remains concerned about the salvation of both Jew and Gentile. These observations raise doubts about Luke's actual knowledge of Paul. In fact, many now believe that the presentation of Paul in Acts as a perfect Jew, Roman citizen, and Hellenist, who is perfectly comfortable with non-Jews, has more to do with Luke's own theological purposes than facts about Paul.[16] In addition, Acts contains biographical data Paul never mentions in his own letters, such as Roman citizenship (Acts 22:25–29) and birth in Tarsus of Cilicia (cf. Acts 21:39; 22:3). Paul's silence about these details does not mean that Luke's data should be rejected as undependable. In fact, sometimes Luke's account confirms what is found in Paul (see, e.g., Acts 9:23–25 and 2 Cor 11:32–33). However, for these reasons and others, the information in Acts needs to be used with caution when constructing a portrait of Paul's life and work.

---

16. There is no scholarly consensus regarding the literary genre of Acts or its precise theological purpose. For more on these matters, see Luke Timothy Johnson, "Luke–Book of Acts," in *The Anchor Bible Dictionary*, ed. David Noel Freedman (New York: Doubleday, 1992), vol. 4, 403–20; see also, Joel B. Green, "Acts of the Apostles," in *Dictionary of the Later New Testament and Its Developments*, ed. Ralph P. Martin and Peter H. Davids (Downers Grove, IL: InterVarsity Press, 1997), 7–24.

Other Useful Resources outside the New Testament

Resources other than those directly related to Paul shed light on the social, religious, and cultural contexts in which he and the first believers lived. One can learn about the world of Jewish thought in Paul's day from many sources including the writings of the Jewish intellectual Philo, the Jewish historian Flavius Josephus, and the Dead Sea Scrolls. An abundance of literature about Greco-Roman culture exists, ranging from the works of great statesmen and orators such as Cicero to those of philosophers such as Seneca and satirists such as Juvenal. The *Geography*, a work by the Greek writer Strabo, is a first-century-ce travel guide to the major cities and cultures of the Greco-Roman world. In addition, frescoes, inscriptions, mosaics, statues, pagan temples and sanctuaries, jewelry, coins, and a host of other material remains offer insight into Paul's world. That world was dominated by the Roman Empire. Among the abundant primary sources about the empire are the histories of Suetonius and Tacitus and the patriotic poetry of Horace and Virgil. Material remains of the empire can still be seen across Europe, Asia Minor, the Middle East, and North Africa.

Pauline scholars regularly go outside the texts of the New Testament to study extant writings and material culture that can help in understanding Paul's letters. This activity is not unique to Pauline scholars or even to New Testament scholars. Just as students of Charles Dickens better understand his writings by reading about the social, cultural, and political conditions of nineteenth-century

© The Trustees of the British Museum / Art Resource, NYImage Reference:ART306112

Silver coin, Ephesus ca. 50–51 ce, British Museum, London, featuring Emperor Claudius and the goddess Diana (Greek Artemis). Artemis' cult flourished in Ephesus, where Paul's successful evangelization incited a riot (see Acts 19:21–41).

Remains of a Roman aqueduct that carried fresh water from Mt. Carmel to Caesarea Maritima, Rome's provincial headquarters in Palestine beginning in 6 BCE.

Victorian England, so do students of Paul gain insight into his writings by examining the extant literary and material evidence of his world.

Paul's Life before and after the Damascus Road Experience

Paul was probably born sometime in the first decade of the first century ce in Tarsus, located in Southeast Asia Minor, which is now southeast Turkey. Tarsus was a heavily Hellenized city that the Romans later made the capital of the province of Cilicia. In addition to Paul, a Latin name, he was also known by his Jewish first name, Saul. As a native of Tarsus, Paul was a diaspora Jew. His first language was Greek, and, like other Greek-speaking Jews, Paul's Bible was the Septuagint, the Greek translation of the Hebrew Scriptures. In his *Geography*, Strabo wrote that Tarsus rivaled Athens and Alexandria as one of the great centers of learning and that Rome was filled with educated Tarsians.[17] No one can be certain whether Paul was educated in the Greco-Roman educational system of his day, but it seems likely. Besides reading and writing, that education would have included rhetoric, the study and practice of how to argue persuasively.

---

17. Strabo, *The Geography*, trans. Horace L. Jones (Cambridge, MA: Harvard University Press, 1960), 14.5:12–15.

Diaspora Jews

The Greek word *diaspora* means "scattered" or "dispersed." It is used to distinguish Jews of Palestine from Jews who forcibly or voluntarily left Palestine and resettled in other locations in and around the Mediterranean basin. They and their descendants are called diaspora Jews. By Paul's day, more Jews lived outside Palestine than within. In most of the major cities where they settled, diaspora Jews represented a distinct minority. However, they were visible and cohesive enough to impact the social and political order. Diaspora Jews, like their fellow Jews in Palestine, had different attitudes toward the surrounding culture. Some were more open to Hellenistic influences; others were less receptive and focused on strict adherence to the Law of Moses.

In one of his few autobiographical statements, Paul says he was a Pharisee (Phil 3:5; Acts 23:6, 26:5), and certain Pharisaic influences are notable in his letters. For example, throughout his letters Paul has recourse to scripture to sustain his arguments. Like the Pharisees, he believes in the resurrection of the dead and interprets Jesus' Resurrection as the guarantee of the future resurrection of believers (see 1 Cor 15:20). He exhibits Pharisaic concern for holiness (see, e.g., 1 Cor 5:1–13) and, like the Pharisees, believes that true worship of God does not consist in performing rituals in the temple but in doing what is right and acceptable according to God's standards (see, e.g., Rom 12:1–3).

Paul mentions nothing about being a son of Pharisees, as indicated in Acts 23:6. Nor does he ever state that he was educated according to the strict manner of the law in Jerusalem under the supervision of Gamaliel, a Pharisee and expert in the interpretation of Jewish religious law, as reported in Acts 22:3. Beyond self-identifying as a Pharisee, he says only that he outdid his peers when it came to being a devoted Jew (Gal 1:14), was blameless with regard to observing the law (Phil 3:6), and was extremely zealous with regard to Jewish tradition (Gal 1:14). From these few remarks, it is clear that Paul was a conscientious, Torah-observant Jew, passionately committed to Jewish law and tradition. In these same texts where Paul speaks about his fervor for the law and Jewish tradition, he also discusses his role in persecuting Christ-believers. This fervor apparently drove Paul to persecute the church, which he says he wanted to destroy. His self-description as a zealous persecutor of believers, at Galatians 1:13 and Philippians 3:4, squares with information at Acts 8:1–3, 9:1–2, 22:4–5, and 26:9–11.

The fact that Paul felt so compelled to stamp out the Jesus movement exposes at least two important considerations:

1. The first believers were still recognized as a group within Judaism and therefore subject to Jewish authority. Otherwise Paul, with the backing of Jewish authorities (see Acts 9:1), would have had no reason to take action against them. Despite the widespread and incorrect assumption to the contrary, at this stage of persecution, in the early to mid-30s ce, believers in Christ were not looked upon as a separate, new religion called Christianity. Even after Paul joined the Jesus movement and had been evangelizing for more than a decade, it was still viewed as a group within Judaism (see Acts 18:12–16; see further 2 Cor 11:24).

2. In contrast to the other groups within Judaism, this particular group was apparently perceived as radically departing from acceptable Jewish beliefs and practices. This required disciplinary action to bring the group back into line or even suppress it.

Paul never states exactly what he found so objectionable about the Jesus movement. Among other things, Paul, a devout Jew, would have rejected the movement's claim that a man the Romans crucified as a common criminal could be the Jewish messiah.[18] Deuteronomy

---

18. The offense to Jews by the proclamation of a crucified messiah is frequently cited as a motive for Paul's persecuting activity. The Jesus movement's relaxation of Torah requirements for pagans has also been cited as a possible motive. See, e.g., John Dominic Crossan and Jonathan L. Reed, *In Search of Paul: How Jesus' Apostle Opposed Rome's Empire with God's Kingdom* (San Francisco: Harper, 2004), 6. It has also been suggested that Paul sought to stamp out the Jesus movement to avert Roman reprisal against the Jews because of the political claims made about Jesus by his followers. See, e.g., Pamela Eisenbaum, *Paul Was Not a Christian: The Original Message of a Misunderstood Apostle* (New York: Harper Collins, 2009), 146. These reasons are not mutually exclusive.

21:23 states anyone hung from a tree—that is, a sinner executed for transgressing the law—was under God's curse. In Jewish thought, therefore, it would be simply inconceivable that Jesus, or anyone deemed deserving of crucifixion, could ever be God's messiah. But this is exactly what Jesus' followers believed and proclaimed: Jesus the crucified and Risen One was messiah and Lord. At Galatians 1:23 Paul says he was known among believers as the one "now preaching the faith he once tried to destroy." From a Jewish perspective, this faith rested on a claim both false and offensive, and Paul was bent on stopping its spread. In fact, later in life when Paul was preaching "Christ-crucified," he acknowledged that Jews could not conceive of a crucified messiah. To Jews, he says, it was a "stumbling block" (1 Cor 1:23). And Paul would know. For a long time, it was a huge stumbling block for him until the revelatory event that changed his perspective.

Paul's Revelatory Experience

In the detailed account of Paul's life-changing experience in Acts (9:1–19), the author narrates how, as Paul traveled to Damascus to persecute Christians, the Risen Jesus revealed himself. After this event, Paul came to believe. Over the centuries, Luke's dramatic presentation of the event with sound and blinding light has been the source of countless renderings from Renaissance masters to contemporary artists. Paul, by contrast, offers few details about why he stopped persecuting Christ-believers, embraced the faith he sought to destroy, and became one of its strongest advocates and fiercest defenders.

In only three places in his letters does Paul very briefly refer to the event that changed his heart and mind: Galatians 1:15–17, Philippians 3:7–11, and 1 Corinthians 15:8–11. From these three texts, a few important ideas emerge about his life-changing experience. First, Paul owed his changed mind and heart to God, who graced Paul with the revelatory opportunity enabling him to understand that Jesus, crucified and risen, was the Christ. Second, Paul was graced with this revelation for the purpose of spreading his newly acquired knowledge of Christ to others. As Paul understood it, his commission to preach the gospel to the Gentiles was intrinsically linked to this revelatory event. Third, as one commissioned by God to preach the gospel, Paul considered himself to be an apostle by the will of

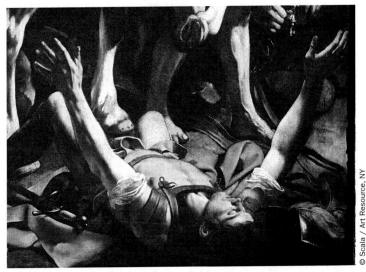

Caravaggio's 1601 painting of Paul's conversion for a chapel in Rome's Santa Maria del Popolo church features a supine Paul blinded by a heavenly light. Countless artists have embellished the Acts narrative by showing Paul thrown from a horse.

© Scala / Art Resource, NY

God. He stresses this point in the opening verses of Romans, 1 and 2 Corinthians, and Galatians, all of which begin with the notice that he is an apostle, called by God.

The Impact of Paul's Revelatory Experience

The word most often used to describe Paul's change of heart and mind is "conversion," a word that this text has so far avoided. For many people, *conversion* connotes, with reference to Paul, something like this: Paul was a Jew, who as a result of his God-initiated revelatory experience, rejected Judaism and became a Christian. This understanding of conversion is imprecise on two counts. First, historically speaking, when Paul received his revelation, estimated to be as early as 34 and possibly as late as 36 or 37 ce, there was no distinct entity called Christianity to which he could convert. As previously discussed, the Jesus movement existed as a movement within Second Temple Judaism. Second, Paul did not reject Judaism. This misperception has allowed both Christians and Jews to consider Paul the father of anti-Judaism and to lay the blame for the subsequent history of Christian anti-Judaism at his feet. Like Jesus, Paul was born, raised, lived, and died a Jew. Before his revelatory experience, he rejected the idea that the crucified Jesus was the Jewish messiah or *christos*. After the revelatory experience, Paul accepted this and, as a result, can be considered a Christ-believing Jew.

Paul's faith remained centered in the One God of Israel, the source of all creation, who had promised to redeem and save that creation. However, Paul's thought about God and how God was acting to redeem creation underwent a significant change in a number of areas. First, Paul's Christology radically shifted. As a result of his revelatory experience, Paul came to understand that God's plan to redeem creation was being accomplished through the life, death, and Resurrection of Jesus. By accepting this, Paul acknowledged that the crucified and Risen One, Jesus, was indeed God's messiah/*christos*. This required Paul to reassess everything he believed about the messiah's identity and role and to grapple especially with the scandal of the cross. Second, like so many Jews in his day, Paul awaited that moment when God would intervene through the agency of his messiah to vanquish Israel's enemies, bring an end to the old age of evil and oppression, and inaugurate a new age. Paul now understood that Jesus was God's messiah and that he and other Jews were actually witnessing the inauguration of the long-awaited new age of redemption, which would be complete when the messiah returned again. Third, Paul's view of the law changed. While he continued to believe that the law was given by God through Moses, that it was holy, and that the commandments of the law were good and just (see Rom 7:12), Paul came to understand that the law had no power to save. Its function was to guide people (see Gal 3:23–26) until the coming of Christ, through whom God brought about redemption.

It remains uncertain whether all of Paul's views immediately changed as a result of this one revelatory experience or whether that initial experience began a process of personal and theological transformation that continued over time. Some, following Paul's own language of "call" (see Gal 1:15), prefer to describe Paul's revelatory experience as a call or commission to bring the knowledge of the God of Israel to the Gentiles, in fulfillment of the Old

Testament prophecy that all nations would one day know Yah-weh.[19] In fact, in a number of texts Paul seems to cast himself in the role of prophet, asserting that his purpose was to bring the Gentiles to worship the God of Israel (see, e.g., Rom 1:5, 11:13; cf. further 1 Thess 1:9). Others prefer the term *conversion*, which they believe bet-ter expresses the radical shift in Paul's thinking. Regardless of the term adopted, scholars agree that Paul, the Jew, joined other Jews, as well as pagans, in becoming a Christ-believer. Both before and after the revelatory event through which he came to know Christ, Paul remained a Jew. He never turned his back on his fellow Jews or abandoned his ancestral religion in order to join a completely new one.

Perceptions of Paul

Paul in His Own Eyes

Paul insisted that both his apostolic calling and the content of his gospel came directly from God. He was aware that he was called *after* the twelve apostles who had accompanied Jesus during his lifetime. Paul also knew that his activity as a persecutor of the fol-lowers of Jesus made him unworthy of this call (see 1 Cor 15:8–9). However, Paul never considered himself a second-class apostle, nor did he believe that the gospel message entrusted to him to preach to the Gentiles was inferior or deficient. On the contrary, he was not only proud of his apostolic calling but considered himself the best, "having worked harder than any of them" (1 Cor 15:10). Like-wise, he considered the gospel he preached the only true gospel (Gal 1:6–7) and traveled thousands of miles throughout the Med-iterranean, suffering physical and emotional hardship, in order to preach it.

If Paul believed others had compromised the truth of the gospel or excluded anyone from the salvation offered in Christ, he fought to defend the truth of the gospel and the rights of both Jew and Gentile to belong to the community of God in Christ (see Gal 1–2).

---

19. See, e.g., Krister Stendahl, *Paul among Jews and Gentiles and Other Essays* (Phil-adelphia: Fortress Press, 1976), esp. 7–23.

Paul saw himself as a rather flexible and transparent person. In his own words, he became "all things to all people" to save whomever he could (1 Cor 9:22b). He considered his own life so conformed to that of Christ that he proposed himself as a model to imitate, exhorting believers, "Be imitators of me as I am of Christ" (1 Cor 11:1; Phil 3:17). His name, Paul, from the Latin *Paulus*, means humble or insignificant. Paul was neither, although he always credited God with giving him the grace and strength to preach the gospel (see, e.g., 1 Cor 15:10).

Paul as Others Saw Him

Some New Testament writings that postdate Paul's death, as well as later Christian writings from the first few centuries ce, embellish Paul's reputation. They showcase his miracle-working (see, e.g., Acts 14:8–13, 28:7–9), acclaim his fidelity to orthodox doctrine (see, e.g., 1 Tim 2:5–7; 2 Tim 3:10) and hold him up as a model of Christian perfection.[20] However, not all of Paul's contemporaries who knew him and heard his message liked him or what he had to say. In fact, he often found himself at the center of controversy. Within circles of Jewish Christ-believers, Paul's outreach to the Gentiles caused great disagreement. Jews did not allow pagans full participation in Jewish religious life unless pagans adopted the Jewish religion and its customs and agreed to live under its laws. Many Jewish Christ-believers insisted on maintaining some distance from pagans who had not converted to Judaism. Paul disagreed, and this caused him to clash with other Jewish Christ-believers—including, most notably, Peter (cf. Gal 2:1–14).

In addition to their concerns about his message, Paul's contemporaries also questioned his credentials as an apostle. Rival apostles were quick to disparage him (see, e.g., 2 Cor 10:10–11). He had been a violent persecutor of the church, but he now insisted that his apostolic calling and gospel message were as valid as that of the twelve and their associates. Moreover, although Paul claimed to be a genuine apostle,

---

20. Among the Apostolic Fathers, Clement of Rome considered Paul a hero and the greatest example of endurance (*1 Clement* 5:6–7; cf. further Ignatius, *Letter to the Ephesians* 12); Polycarp likewise considered him an example of endurance (cf. *Letter to the Philippians* 9:1) as well as a teacher of orthodoxy (3:2).

his apostolic practice failed to convince many of his contemporaries. True apostles received financial support from the communities. This expectation apparently derived from Jesus' own statements about a preacher's right to compensation for the work of preaching the gospel (see Luke 10:7 and Matt 10:8–10). Paul apparently refused such support (see 2 Cor 11:7, 12:13–16). Especially among Gentiles, the expectation was that true apostles would preach eloquently, powerfully, and persuasively. Paul, by his own admission, was an ineloquent speaker who preached what most Jews and pagans considered an absurd message about a crucified messiah (see, e.g., 1 Cor 2:1–5; 2 Cor 11:5–6). These and other aspects of Paul's practice raised suspicions about his apostolic credentials. Finally, to Jews who refused to accept Jesus as the Messiah and supported Paul's efforts to stamp out the Jesus movement, his sudden turn from persecutor of that movement to its staunchest defender branded him as an apostate, a traitor to the Jewish faith.

While Paul saw himself as a dedicated apostle, committed to bringing Christ's salvation to all, his contemporaries had some serious reservations about his credentials, message, and apostolic methods. In their view, Paul was a conundrum: Jews considered him an apostate; many Jewish Christ-believers thought him too "Gentile-friendly"; and some Gentile Christ-believers probably perceived Paul as a bit too Jewish! Christian history has transformed Paul of Tarsus into Saint Paul, with all the positive connotations the term *saint* conjures, perhaps blurring the reality that Paul was something of a misfit who often found himself opposed and unwelcomed.

Summary

Any study of Paul must consider a number of factors. First, Paul must be considered within the trajectory of the development of the Jesus movement. Although Paul strongly advocated for the movement, it emerged within the context of Judaism and had its beginning before Paul. Second, any attempt to construct a Pauline biography depends on the cautious use of sources. Among sources, the most important are Paul's own letters, followed by Acts of the Apostles. Sources outside the New Testament also are necessary to understand the society and culture that formed the framework of

Paul's life and work. Third, at some point while engaged in stamping out the Jesus movement, Paul had a revelatory experience that brought him to accept the crucified and Risen Jesus as Lord and Messiah and initiated a transformation in his thinking about a number of Jewish beliefs and practices. On account of both the content of his gospel and his apostolic practice, Paul attracted some and alienated others. He was a sincere but complicated man, and many tried, although ultimately unsuccessfully, to counter his impact within the early Jesus movement.

Questions for Review and Discussion

1. Was Jesus accepted by all Jews as the Messiah? Why or why not?

2. Name a few characteristics of the four main Jewish groups active during the first century ce and indicate how each group responded to Roman rule. To which group did Paul belong, and how do you know?

3. What are the sources for the study of Paul? What is the value of each source?

4. Which letters are considered "indisputably" Pauline and why?

5. On what did Paul base his belief that he was an apostle commissioned to preach to the Gentiles? What are a few reasons that caused some in the movement to disagree with him?

6. In what sense is it correct to say that Paul was not a Christian?

Opening Other Windows

Carter, Warren. *Seven Events That Shaped the New Testament World.* Grand Rapids, MI: Baker Academic, 2013.

Collins, Raymond F. *Letters That Paul Did Not Write: The Epistle to the Hebrews and the Pauline Pseudepigrapha.* Wilmington, DE: Michael Glazier, 1988.

Fitzmyer, Joseph A. *The One Who Is to Come.* Grand Rapids, MI: William B. Eerdmans, 2007.

Greenspoon, Leonard J. "Between Alexandria and Antioch: Jews and Judaism in the Hellenistic Period," in *The Oxford History of the Biblical World,* ed. Michael D. Coogan. New York: Oxford University Press, 1998, 317–51.

Harlow, Daniel. "Early Judaism and Early Christianity," in *Early Judaism. A Comprehensive Overview,* ed. John J. Collins and Daniel C. Harlow. Grand Rapids, MI: William B. Eerdmans, 2012, 391–419.

Levine, Amy-Jill. "Visions of Kingdoms: From Pompey to the First Jewish Revolt," in *The Oxford History of the Biblical World,* ed. Michael D. Coogan. New York: Oxford University Press, 1998, 352–87.

Richards, E. Randolph. *Paul and First-Century Letter-Writing: Secretaries, Composition and Collection.* Downers Grove, IL: InterVarsity Press, 2004.

Saldarini, Anthony J. *Pharisees, Scribes and Sadducees in Palestinian Society: A Sociological Approach.* Grand Rapids, MI: William B. Eerdmans, 2001.

Chapter 2

What Did Paul Do?

Overview

This chapter begins by considering the chronology of Paul's missionary career. Though his travels and letter-writing activity cannot be sequenced with absolute precision, there are important reasons for attempting to do so. Next, the chapter examines Paul's missionary strategy, his preaching, and his view of his key ministerial role. This is followed by a discussion of the form and function of Paul's letters as well as a consideration of how others were involved in their composition. Finally, Paul's letters are considered in relation to ancient rhetoric, which was concerned with persuasive speech.

Missionary Preacher

At Galatians 1:15–16, Paul writes that the revelatory experience through which he came to know the Risen Christ was intrinsically linked to his mission to preach to the Gentiles. The experience helped Paul understand that the story of God acting in Christ to redeem creation was the gospel or "good news" and that he had to share with others. At 1 Corinthians 9:16, Paul describes the task of preaching the good news as a duty entrusted to him to make Christ known to as many people as possible. For the next thirty or so years of his life, until his death in ca. 64 ce, Paul would devote himself exclusively to this task.

When and Where Did Paul Preach?

One of the most challenging tasks in the study of Paul is sequencing the unfolding of his missionary career—figuring out where he was when and then trying to fit his letters into this sequence. The task proves difficult for a number of reasons, not least of which is that the sources are limited to Paul's letters and the book of Acts. The letters themselves present a number of challenges. First, Paul's undisputed letters were not written in the order in which they appear in the New Testament. For example, although the New Testament lists Romans first among Paul's letters, it was the last of his letters and contains information about missionary plans late in his career. Second, rearranging the order of the letters would still not yield a sequenced account of Paul's missionary career because Paul's aim in his letters was not to chronicle his career but to respond to pressing issues that arose among the first believers. In a few places, Paul mentions his beatings, imprisonments, and even shipwrecks (see, e.g., 2 Cor 6:4–5, 11:23–26; Phil 1:12–14), which attest to his travels by land and sea as well as his numerous hardships, including multiple incarcerations. Given the variety and number of experiences, one can reasonably assume Paul's missionary travels took place over a number of years. However, the exact years cannot be established with certainty. Third, even when Paul makes a temporal reference, he does not supply a fixed chronological framework by which to date it. For example, in Galatians 1 Paul speaks of his conversion (15–17) and his first visit to Jerusalem (18). The letter's next chapter begins, "Then after fourteen years . . ." (2:1) but does not clarify which event happened fourteen years prior.

In contrast to Paul's own writings, the Acts of the Apostles sequences all of Paul's missionary travels. Based on this ordering, scholars have traditionally envisioned Paul's travels in terms of three great missionary campaigns. Acts 13:4–14:28 describes Paul's first campaign, which covered Cypress and southern Asia Minor in the company of Barnabas. While Paul confirms that he and Barnabas were approved co-missionaries to the Gentiles (see Gal 2:1; 9), he never details their travels. According to Acts, although their first journey was a success, the partnership was short-lived. After the two disagreed about travel companions (Acts 15:36–41), Paul went his own way, taking Silas and Timothy on his second and third missionary campaigns (Acts 16:1–18:22, 19:1–20:38).

The Acts account, which traces Paul's travels and chronicles his failures and successes at each stop along the way, provides extensive detail. However, scholars disagree about the extent of its historical

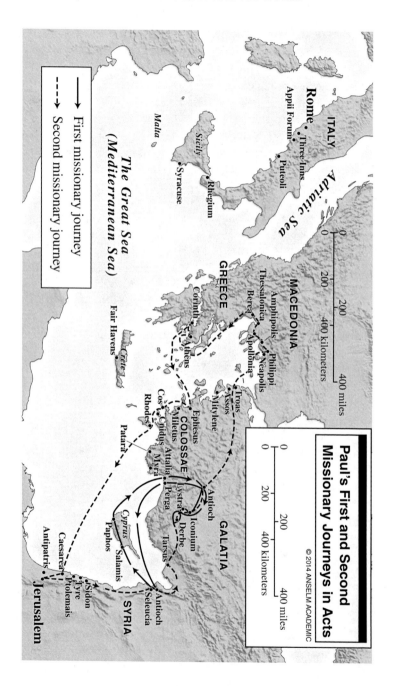

Paul's First and Second Missionary Journeys in Acts

© 2014 ANSELM ACADEMIC

First missionary journey

Second missionary journey

The Great Sea (Mediterranean Sea)

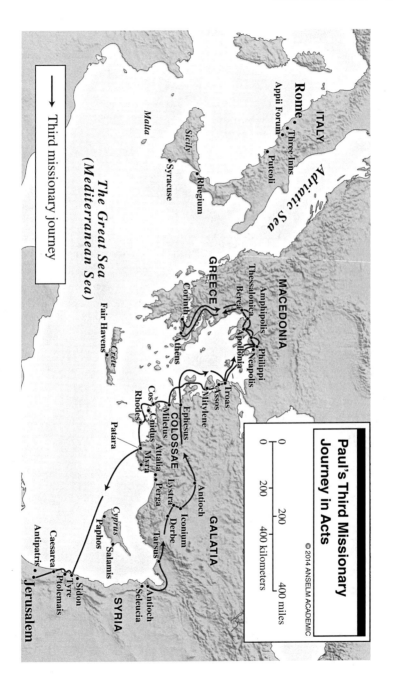

Paul's Third Missionary Journey in Acts

© 2014 ANSELM ACADEMIC

→ Third missionary journey

reliability and recognize that it differs or even conflicts with information Paul provides. For example, Paul mentions that he had taken two trips to Jerusalem (see Gal 1:18 and 2:1–10) and anticipated taking a third, which he mentions in both 1 Corinthians (16:3–4) and Romans (15:25, 31). Acts, on the other hand, reports that Paul went to Jerusalem five times: twice (9:26–30, 12:25) before going to the Apostolic Council (15:1–29) and twice after it (18:22, 21:17). Further, Paul reports that immediately after his conversion, he left Damascus for Nabatea in Arabia (Gal 1:15–18) and then returned to Damascus. It is likely that Paul had already begun evangelizing in Nabatea.[1] As a Jew preaching to non-Jews about a Jewish messiah, Paul would have been perceived as engaging in Jewish proselytism; the Nabateans would have looked unfavorably upon Paul's activity.[2] This probably explains his return to Damascus, where he was later pursued by the Nabatean king Aretas IV after the Nabateans regained rule over Damascus ca. 37 ce. Based on Paul's account, it seems he fled Damascus sometime after 37 ce, but before Aretas IV's death, which probably occurred in 39 ce. Paul describes his escape at 2 Corinthians 11:32–33. By contrast, Acts has Paul remaining in Damascus after his conversion and presents him as initiating his ministry among Jews there. Paul's preaching incited the Jews against him, forcing his disciples to arrange his stealthy departure from the city (Acts 9:23–25). The Acts account contradicts what Paul says at 2 Corinthians 11:32–33 about the role of the Nabateans in his forced departure from the city. It also omits any mention of Paul's evangelizing activity in Arabia and focuses all of his initial evangelizing in Damascus. These few examples illustrate the challenge of trying to establish a Pauline chronology.

Some help is provided by historical references in the texts, which scholars can link to established dates and data outside the New Testament. Except for 2 Corinthians 11:32–33, the only textual clues that

---

1. As pointed out by Jerome Murphy-O'Connor, *Paul: A Critical Life* (New York: Oxford University Press, 1996), 80–84.

2. The Nabateans and Jews had a long, turbulent history. One piece of that history, familiar from the Gospels, concerns Herod the Great's son, Herod Antipas. His marriage to Phasaelis, daughter of Aretas IV, was meant to cement peaceful relations between Judea and Nabatea. But Antipas divorced her and married his brother Philip's wife, Herodias. The divorce reignited political hostilities between the two kingdoms. John the Baptist condemned Antipas' action, which led to John's execution (Mark 6:17–28; Matt 14:3–12).

can be linked to external chronology are found in Acts.[3] Two pieces of data prove especially important. The first concerns the pro-consulship of L. Junius Gallio. Acts reports that, during his eighteen-month ministry in Corinth, Paul was arraigned before Gallio, who refused to hear the case against Paul (18:12–16). Inscriptional evidence from Delphi in Greece dates Gallio's pro-consulship over the region of Achaia, whose capital was Corinth, from 51–52 ce.[4] This inscription does not prove Paul appeared before Gallio, but if Acts is correct, the inscription allows scholars to accurately date Paul's presence in Corinth to sometime between 50 and 52 ce. A second text clue at Acts 24:27 concerns the transfer of power over Judaea from Felix to Festus. This transfer took place in Caesarea, the capital of Roman Judaea and a large port city on the Mediterranean coast, where Paul reportedly was imprisoned for two years before his departure for trial in Rome (see Acts 23:23–26:1–30). During this time, Paul had hearings before Felix and then Festus. The transfer of power from one to the other cannot be dated with the same precision as Gallio's pro-consulship. However, using information from Josephus, scholars date Festus' replacement of Felix to ca. 59 or 60 ce.[5] Thus Paul's two-year imprisonment in Caesarea likely occurred between 57–59 ce or 58–60 ce. According to Acts, Paul was arraigned before Festus within two weeks of his arrival (25:1–12), when it was determined that he would be allowed to appeal his case in Rome. Paul could have arrived in Rome as early as 60 or 61. If his conversion occurred ca. 34 ce, as most scholars hold, and his death occurred under Nero, sometime between 64–68 ce,[6] then Paul's work and letters need to fit within these thirty to thirty-five years, with one or two pivotal dates anchoring the rest of the reconstruction. The following reconstruction hinges around the sure dating of Gallio's pro-consulship and integrates data from the undisputed letters and Acts.

---

3. The text clues are found at Acts 11:27–30, 12:20–23, 13:7, 18:2, 18:12–16, 23:2, 25:1.

4. A thorough discussion of the inscriptional fragments was provided by Adolf Deissmann, *Paul: A Study in Social and Religious History*, 2nd rev. ed., trans. William E. Wilson (New York: Harper and Row, 1926), Appendix 1, 261–86.

5. See, e.g., Robert Jewett, *A Chronology of Paul's Life* (Philadelphia: Fortress, 1979), 40–44.

6. This is the traditional view based on Eusebius, *Church History*, 2.25. This text is available in English language translation at *www.newadvent.org/fathers/250102.htm*.

A Reconstruction of Paul's Missionary Career

ca. 34 CE	Paul has a life-changing experience on the road to Damascus (Acts 9, 22, 26; Gal 1:12–15).
ca. 37–38 CE	Paul flees Damascus, visits Cephas in Jerusalem, and evangelizes in Syria and Cilicia (2 Cor 11:32–33; Gal 1:17–18).
ca. 37–38 through 47–49 CE	Paul is active in Syria and Cilicia and then joins Barnabas for a missionary campaign (ca. 46–49). According to Acts, this trip included evangelizing in Seleucia, Cyprus, Salamis, Paphos, Perga, Antioch in Pisdia, Iconium, Lystra, and Derbe (13:4–14:24). When the mission was over, Paul and Barnabas returned to Antioch in Syria.
ca. 49–50 CE	Paul takes a second trip to Jerusalem for the Council according to Acts (15:1–21). This may be the visit that Paul refers to in Galatians (2:1–10). Shortly after this trip, Paul and Peter faced off in Antioch (Gal 2:11–14).
ca. 49–50 through 52–53 CE	Paul takes a second missionary journey, accompanied by Silas and Timothy, according to Acts (15:36–18:17). Acts portrays Paul again evangelizing in Asia Minor and then crossing the Aegean Sea to Greece, where he continued evangelizing in Philippi, Thessalonica, Beroea, Athens, and Corinth.
ca. 50–52 CE	Paul's 18-month ministry in Corinth overlapped with the pro-consulship of Gallio, before whom Paul was brought for trial. After the case against him was dismissed, Paul went to Ephesus before returning to Antioch in Syria. Paul probably wrote 1 Thessalonians from Corinth in ca. 51, after Timothy arrived with good news about that community (cf. 1 Thess 3:6).

Continued

Continued

A Reconstruction of Paul's Missionary Career

ca. 53 through 58 CE	Paul takes a third missionary journey, according to Acts (18:23–20:38), mostly through the regions of north Galatia, with a two- to three-year stay in Ephesus (20:31), during which time he was imprisoned for the first time (ca. 57 CE). This is likely the imprisonment Paul refers to in 1 Corinthians 15:32; 2 Corinthians 1:8–9, and Philippians 1:26. Shortly after arriving in Ephesus, Paul probably wrote Galatians (53–55 CE) and 1 and 2 Corinthians (55–56 CE). While imprisoned there, he may have also written the letters to Philemon and the Philippians. After his release, he headed to Jerusalem (Rom 15:25) to bring an "offering" before traveling to Rome and Spain.
ca. 58 CE	Before going to Jerusalem, Paul revisited Corinth, and in all likelihood, the nearby town of Cenchreae (cf. 1 Cor 16:5–6; 2 Cor 1:16; Acts 20:2–3). Paul probably composed Romans during this brief stay in Corinth or nearby Cenchreae (see Rom 16:1).
ca. 58 CE	Paul was arrested in Jerusalem (Acts 21:1–23:22). His plans to visit Rome and Spain (see Rom 15:22–29) are thwarted.
ca. 58–60 CE	Paul's second imprisonment was in Caesarea under Felix (Acts 23:23–24:27).
ca. 60 CE	Paul was arraigned before the new procurator, Festus, and then King Agrippa (Acts 25:1–26: 32).
ca. 61 CE	Paul arrived in Rome (Acts 27:1–28:16).
ca. 61–63 CE	Paul lived under house arrest in Rome (Acts 28:16–31).
ca. 64–68 CE	According to tradition, Paul was martyred in Rome sometime within this four-year period.

Most reconstructions of Paul's chronology work within the same broad contours of the chronology presented here. However, one finds variations within them. For example, some scholars argue that Paul composed Galatians before 1 Thessalonians,[7] and some date the Jerusalem conference (see Acts 15 and Gal 2:11) after Paul's stay in Corinth.[8] While absolute precision cannot be achieved, the attempt to establish the chronology of Paul's missionary career affords some important insights about his letters. First, while Paul's evangelizing work took place over three or more decades, his letter-writing work was concentrated in one decade, within which he composed the seven undisputed letters. Second, Paul's decade of literary activity dates to the latter part of his career. That means the letters reflect the thought of a man who had fifteen to twenty years of missionary experience, whose faith had matured, and whose theological insights had been honed by the questions and needs of the communities to whom he ministered. Therefore, it is important to recognize that Paul was not an abstract thinker who retreated to a quiet corner to systematically develop a theology disconnected from the pastoral realities of his ministry. Rather, Paul was a practical theologian whose theological thought was fashioned in the encounter of faith, tradition, and human experience. Third, while Paul's letters reflect the thought of a mature man, they do not necessarily give Paul's definitive last word on every subject. Paul's letters continue to be (mis)cited as the last word on the Jews and the law, the role of women, and homosexuality, to name just a few examples. Yet Paul could never have anticipated that his writings would shape the thought and historical development of Christianity, much less be applied to twenty-first-century pastoral situations he could never have envisioned.

Paul's Missionary Strategy

Jesus ministered in rural areas among a largely agrarian populace. Paul's ministry was urban. During most of the 50s ce, his ministry

---

7. The variations on the dating of Galatians are concisely discussed by Frank Matera, *Galatians*, Sacra Pagina, 9 (Collegeville, MN: Liturgical Press, 1992), 19–26. Matera's solution involves dating Paul's first missionary journey after the Apostolic Council.

8. See example, Murphy-O'Connor, *Paul: A Critical Life*, 24–31, and Jewett, *A Chronology of Paul's Life*.

was centered in large cities along the Aegean Coast that, like Thessalonica and Philippi, were located on or near major Roman roads. Paul's longest sojourns were in Corinth and Ephesus. Corinth served as the major conduit for all east-west shipping and the commercial capital of the Mediterranean. Ephesus was also a prominent and prosperous port city on the west coast of Asia Minor. Paul's choice to work in large urban centers was probably calculated. In addition to being accessible by land and sea, these cities had large, diverse populations accustomed to the flux and flow of ideas that came with the traveling merchants, sailors, soldiers, and philosophers. Paul could expect to get a hearing for his proclamation about the Risen Jesus, which would spread rapidly via the human traffic moving in and out of these major cities. He would also likely find opportunities to practice his tent-making trade (Acts 18:3) in order to support himself and his ministry. Moreover, Paul had grown up in Tarsus, a center of international exchange, and returned there after his conversion. Thus he had ample exposure to diverse philosophical and religious ideas, which no doubt equipped him for the challenges of cosmopolitan life and ministry.

The accounts in Acts feature Paul as foremost an apostle to the Jews, directing his evangelizing efforts first to them. According to Acts, Paul had a consistent mission strategy. When he arrived in a new place, he went first to the synagogue to persuade the Jews that Jesus was the Jewish messiah (see, e.g., 13:13–42; 14:1–3; 17:1–3,10,17; 18:5). In each case, Acts describes Paul as having only limited success among the Jews. The majority rejected his preaching about Jesus, and in some cases reacted with hostility and violence (17:5–9). Acts 18:6 identifies the Jews' hostility as the reason Paul redirects his evangelizing to the Gentiles (see further 22:17–21). Acts' depiction of Paul's mission strategy seems both logical and practical. Paul considered Jesus to be the Jewish messiah, so it makes sense Paul would go to the Jews first. Moreover, Paul went to unevangelized cities without a Christian network on which he could depend. Practically speaking, the synagogue offered the only religious infrastructure familiar to Paul that might provide a platform for his ministry.

Acts' depiction, however, contrasts with Paul's insistence that he had been entrusted with a mission to the Gentiles. Evidence from the letters appears to confirm that he directed evangelization efforts

© 2014 ANSELM ACADEMIC

With the exception of Athens, Paul labored successfully to establish small Christian communities in major cities along the Aegean Coast.

to Gentiles, not Jews. For example, Paul refers to the pagan past of his addressees, contrasting that past with their current relationship to God through Christ (see, e.g., 1 Cor 6:9–11; 12:2–3; Gal 4:8–9; 1 Thess 1:9–10). Though Paul does not reference the pagan past of the Philippians, the majority of Christ-believers in Philippi were likely Gentiles. Philippi apparently had no synagogue (Acts 16:11–15), suggesting the city's Jewish population was negligible in Paul's day.[9] In Romans, Paul's last letter, he does discuss the fate of his fellow Jews who have failed to embrace the gospel (Rom 9–11). However, apart from that, his letters are not concerned with unbelieving Jews and their evangelization but with Gentiles and their fidelity to the gospel he preached to them.

---

9. There is no evidence of a synagogue in Philippi before the third century ce. See Chaido Koukouli-Chrysantaki, "Colonia Iulia Augusta Philippensis," in *Philippi at the Time of Paul and after His Death*, ed. Charalambos Bakirtzis and Helmut Koester (Eugene, OR: Wipf and Stock, 1998), 5–35.

What Did Paul Preach?

No independent record exists of the content of Paul's preaching during the period of his initial evangelizing among the communities he founded.[10] What he preached, which he most frequently refers to as "the gospel," can be known only from his letters. Paul's use of the term "my gospel" at Romans 2:16 and 16:25, and his insistence at Galatians 1:11–12 that his gospel came directly via revelation—was not of "human origin" or received from a "human source"—can create the impression that Paul preached something fundamentally different from all other evangelizers. But that was not the case. The heart of the gospel Paul preached had been handed on to him by others, "For I handed on to you as of first importance, what in turn I had received" (1 Cor 15:3). After stating this, Paul repeats the basic content of the gospel, which consists of four affirmations: "that Christ died for our sins . . . that he was buried . . . that he was raised on the third day . . . and that he appeared to Cephas, then to the twelve" (1 Cor 15:4–5). Elsewhere, Paul cites shorter creedal statements (1 Thess 4:14; Rom 4:24–25), confessions (Rom 10:9), hymns (Phil 2:5–11), liturgical formulas (Gal 3:27–29), and other pieces of tradition. Clearly, Paul's gospel was the same as that preached and believed by the first Christians. What is unique to Paul is the way he understands the "Christ-event" (shorthand for the whole triad of Christ's life, death, and Resurrection) as the fulfillment of God's plan to save and reconcile humans to himself, to each other, and to all of creation, as well as the way he elaborates the benefits issuing from the Christ-event for all who now belong to God in Christ.

To most of Paul's contemporaries, Jesus' humiliating death by crucifixion added up to nothing more than defeat and powerlessness. Yet Paul proclaimed that the gospel was God's initiative and that through it—that is, through Christ crucified and raised—God's power to save and God's righteousness were made manifest

---

10. The speech at Acts 13:16–39 may approximate what Paul preached at Antioch in Pisidia, but ultimately the speeches in Acts were the author's creation. Creating speeches was a typical feature of historical writing in antiquity. The Greek historian Thucydides wrote, "my habit has been to make the speakers say what was in my opinion demanded of them by the various occasions" cf. *The History of the Peloponnesian War*, Bk I. 1 at *classics.mit.edu/Thucydides/pelopwar.1.first.html*.

to everyone who believes (Rom 1:16–17). Though Jesus' death impressed many as inefficacious and even scandalous (see 1 Cor 1:22–23), Paul says it was actually the power and wisdom of God (see 1 Cor 1:18), a part of God's plan to right the relationship between humans and God and save them from destruction. Those with faith understood this. Those without could not (see 1 Cor 1:18–25). According to Paul, God's relationship with humanity was compromised through humans who had sinned and fallen short of what it means to be an authentic human created in God's image (Rom 3:23). In his kindness, God took the initiative and, through Christ's death on behalf of humans, restored right relations (see Rom 3:24–26).

Paul's letters indicate that he preached extensively about the many benefits humans gained because of what God had done in Christ. Those in Christ will be spared God's wrath and destruction when it is visited on the godless in the future (1 Thess 1:9–10). Their sins are expiated (Rom 3:25); they enjoy peace with God (Rom 5:1). They are no longer enslaved to the power of Sin, a force that keeps people from doing what is good (Rom 6:17–18; 7:13). Through baptism, they enter into the community of the saved in Christ, receive the same one Spirit of God (1 Cor 12:13), and walk together in the newness of life (Rom 5:6) in anticipation of being raised with Christ to the fullness of new and eternal life (1 Cor 15:22). The Spirit—God's presence residing in each believer individually and in the community that is one body in Christ—empowers and guides believers to lead lives worthy of their reconciled life in Christ. All these benefits are a grace—that is, gifts freely given by God, out of love, through Christ and sealed with the Spirit.

In a nutshell, Paul's gospel is the good news of God's faithful love. On account of love, God, acting in Christ-crucified, has saved people from their own destructive ways and offered them the opportunity to be created anew in his own image by being conformed to Christ, the image of God (2 Cor 4:4), who gave his life to make this new life possible. Announcing this joyous news of what God had done in Christ was no doubt the easier part of Paul's ministry. The harder part, as clear from Paul's letters, was getting believers to live as God-loved, Christ-redeemed, and Spirit-filled people once the newness of the good news wore off and old ways and customs incompatible with new life in Christ began to reassert themselves.

Community Builder and Pastor

Acts presents Paul as a persuasive public speaker and debater who addressed large audiences. However, Paul admitted that he was an unskilled public speaker (2 Cor 11:6) and was apprehensive about how his message would be received (see 1 Cor 2:3–4; 2 Cor 10:10). It is probable that when he entered a new city, Paul began a modest ministry among people he saw daily in the workplace. These were the socially and economically disadvantaged, who, like Paul, sustained themselves through manual labor.[11] Eventually, Paul converted the heads of small households. A household was more than a nuclear family. It also included extended family, workers, and slaves. A small household might number anywhere from ten to twenty people. These households comprised the first cells of believers. In his letters, Paul mentions some, including that of Stephanus (1 Cor 16:15), Prisca and Aquila (1 Cor 16:19), Philemon (Phlm 1–2), and Gaius (Rom 16:23). In each city, the houses of such individuals, which varied in size according to individual means, provided the physical space where the first believers met to pray and eat the Lord's Supper (1 Cor 11:17–22). Because most of the cities where Paul evangelized were large, each had a number of "house-churches." Paul's ministry evolved with and within them. In addition to Paul's modest earnings, support for his ministry came from these households, some of which were headed by women such as Phoebe (see Rom 16:1) and Lydia (Acts 16:40).

In his letters, Paul never provides anything such as a daily journal or description of the activities that composed his ministry. In one of the few places where he mentions a ministerial role familiar to all Christians, "baptizer," he says he baptized only a small number of people (1 Cor 1:13–15). Rather than thinking in terms of pastoral roles familiar to Christians today, it is important to listen to Paul's language, which can provide insight about what he actually did.

---

11. On the social significance of Paul's manual labor, see Ronald F. Hock, *The Social Context of Paul's Ministry: Tentmaking and Apostleship* (Philadelphia: Fortress Press, 1980). By the same author, see also, "The Workshop as a Social Setting for Paul's Missionary Preaching," *Catholic Biblical Quarterly* 41.3 (1979): 438–50.

The House-Church

The church as a public building exclusively dedicated to Christian worship, completely separate from domestic space, did not appear until the fourth century CE. Its emergence coincided with Emperor Constantine's imperial endorsement of Christianity. New large public worship spaces, based on the model of the basilica, were constructed to reflect Christianity's new status. When Christianity was in its infancy in the first century CE, Christians met in individuals' houses. These "house-churches" were modest in size and no different from other first-century-ce houses. In addition to living quarters for the nuclear and extended family, slaves, and animals, many houses included shops for the household's commercial activities. Some house-churches may have been little more than apartments in the tenement blocks, or *insulae*, that were part of the landscape of major urban centers such as Rome and Ephesus. By the third century CE, archeological evidence shows that individual houses were remodeled to better accommodate Christian worship. The most famous example is the remodeled "house-church" excavated at the city of Dura-Europos in Syria. This house, dating from perhaps the first century CE, was remodeled in the mid-third century CE. The volume of literature on the early house-church attests to the importance of domestic space for the emergence of the Christian assembly.

Paul emphatically asserts at 1 Corinthians 1:17 that Christ sent him to evangelize (Grk. *euangelizein*). Thus wherever Paul went, he proclaimed that God, through the life, death, and Resurrection of Jesus, was reconciling the world to himself and saving those in Christ from the wrath to come. In addition to his role as proclaimer, Paul founded communities and used construction language such as "master-builder" and "foundation-layer"(see 1 Cor 3:10–14) to describe his role. What Paul built was a living temple, consisting of people among whom God would dwell (1 Cor 3:16). Just as each building is constructed on a foundation that determines its size and shape, so would God's temple be determined by the only foundation possible for God's people, Jesus Christ. Paul established and built each community on Christ and, throughout his ministry, worked to ensure that each community's character and shape conformed to its foundation. Paul recognized that others would minister after him. However, he insisted that the validity of their pastoral work be judged on whether it built upon the foundation he had already laid. Clearly, Paul believed that his God-given ministry to found new communities had primacy over the ministry of others. Even where he switches to agricultural metaphors, recognizing that God gives the growth, Paul understands his role as primary. He is the "planter," while others "water" (1 Cor 3:6).

In brief, in each place where he evangelized, Paul also established communities of believers. Together they would be the new people of God—a new holy space where God would dwell. This explains why in his letters, especially but not exclusively in 1 Corinthians, Paul speaks so urgently about maintaining the holiness and unity of these communities (see also 1 Thess 4:1–8; 2 Cor 6:14–7:2; Phil 2:1, 2:14–16; Rom 12:1–5). If either were compromised, the community would no longer be the spiritual temple—the holy place of God's dwelling. Thus Paul's task was not only to build but also to continue to pastor his communities so they maintained their unity and holiness. He did that in at least two important ways. When actively evangelizing among them, he led by example and expected others to imitate him as he imitated Christ (cf. 1 Cor 11:1). After he left, he exhorted them through his letters to maintain themselves in holiness and unity.

Another set of terms offering insight about Paul's ministry revolves around "family" language. Paul did not intend the Christian assemblies to be mere aggregates of individuals. Rather, he worked to create a sense of kinship among believers, who together formed a new family in Christ. This becomes clear from his letters, where Paul's most frequent term for believers is *adelphoi*. Although its English equivalent is "brothers," it is better translated "brothers and sisters" to reflect the inclusiveness of Paul's communities. They are also God's "children" and thus heirs of God and co-heirs with Christ (Rom 8: 14–17). As part of his ministry to foster familial identity, Paul educated believers about the responsibilities of belonging to this family. Certain choices and actions,

© Zev Radovan / www.biblelandpictures.com

Remains of the earliest known Christian church excavated at ancient Dura-Europos, located in modern Syria. The building, originally a private home, was remodeled, ca. 240–50 CE, to serve as a church. Small rooms used for assembly, instruction, and worship flanked the central courtyard. One small, fresco-decorated room served as the baptistery.

which might otherwise seem unremarkable apart from this family context, would have to be reconsidered (see, e.g., Rom 14:1–15; 1 Cor 8:9–13). In the family rooted and built on Christ, Paul urged the brothers and sisters to prefer humility to self-aggrandizement and joyful, generous sharing to self-interest (see, e.g., Phil 2:1–5; 2 Cor 8–9). Paul also related to communities he founded in a parental way, referring to himself as a "father" to his children (see, e.g., 1 Cor 4:15; 1 Thess 2:11). In Paul's day, the "father" of a household not only exercised authority over its members but also was responsible for their physical, social, and moral well-being. The terms also suggest that Paul understood himself to have a unique generative role vis-à-vis these communities, and hence a unique claim to their allegiance: "For though you might have ten thousand guardians in Christ, you do not have many fathers. Indeed, in Christ Jesus I became your father through the gospel. I appeal to you, then, be imitators of me" (1 Cor 4:15–16). As "father" of the household of believers, Paul provided the example of his own life, praised those living up to family standards, admonished those who were not (see, e.g., 1 Cor 5–6), and at all times urged everyone to continue to lead lives worthy of their calling in Christ (1 Thess 2:11–12; Phil 2:1). While actively evangelizing within the communities he founded, Paul gently nourished the faith of believers (1 Thess 2:6–18). After leaving, he remained actively concerned about their well-being (1 Thess 2:17; 2 Cor 11:28).

In summary, as an apostle—that is, "one sent" by God—Paul's task consisted of three aspects. First, he proclaimed God's salvation, which was effectuated through the life, death, and Resurrection of Jesus. Second, he founded communities of believers. Third, he molded and shaped believers into communities whose lives, individually and communally, witnessed their adherence to Christ Jesus, the foundation and source of their new life. Paul's ministry was primarily about building and sustaining relationships of individuals with Christ and of all those in Christ with each other. While Paul served as a chief agent in founding the first Christian communities, he recognized God, by whom "you were called into the fellowship of his Son" (1 Cor 1:9) as the ultimate originator of the communities of men and women joined together in Christ.

Letter Writer and Pastor

Paul's extended stays in Corinth and Ephesus seem to have been exceptions in a missionary career mostly spent traveling to bring the gospel to as many as possible. When issues later arose in the communities he founded, he was not always able to return to address them in person. Fortunately, the practice of letter-writing was a well-established convention in Greco-Roman society. There was a well-developed theory concerning the form and purpose of the letter, which was to substitute for personal presence when that was not possible. Paul used this medium to great advantage to deal with issues that arose in the communities after he left. Because the letters, with the exception of Romans and Philemon,[12] were Paul's responses to

---

12. During one of his imprisonments, Paul sent a short 335-word letter to Philemon and the assembly of believers who met in his house (Phlm 1–2). Scholars locate this small house-church in Colossae. Colossae, as well as Laodicea and Hierapolis, the three cities of the Lycus Valley, were evangelized as part of Paul's missionary expansion in Asia Minor. However, Paul left the evangelization and founding of the Lycus Valley communities to his associate, Epaphras (see Phlm 23; further Col 2:1, 3:12–13).

issues and problems arising in the communities he founded, scholars refer to them as "occasional letters." The term underscores the fact that Paul wrote when an occasion or situation demanded his response, not because he wanted to leave a compendium of his theological thought. Paul dealt with issues ranging from discord and lax living to pragmatic questions regarding food consumption, marriage, the necessity of circumcision, and a host of other questions that arose among believers in this formative stage of Christianity. Thus through his letter correspondence, Paul was able to remain present despite his physical absence (1 Cor 5:3) to pastor, guide, and instruct these communities and reinforce their distinct Christian identity.

In Paul's day, letters served a variety of purposes, just as they do today. In a work from antiquity entitled, "Epistolary Types," the author cataloged twenty-one types of letters for different occasions.[13] Among these were letters of friendship and letters of advice and exhortation (also called *paraenetic* letters). There were letters written to praise, shame, or rebuke. Others were written to recommend or introduce one person or party to another. There were also apologetic letters written to defend a person or a position.

Letter correspondence was a form of communication used at every level of society: between equals, superiors and inferiors, business associates, or government officials dealing with matters of state. Even a superficial reading of Paul's letters reveals that he writes both as an equal and superior, that is, to his brothers but also to his children, and that he freely combines elements of many letter types in a single letter. In 1 Corinthians alone he praises (1 Cor 11:2), shames (1 Cor 5:1–13), recommends (1 Cor 16:15–18), and defends his own position concerning self-support (1 Cor 9:1–27). While these elements are notable throughout the letters, Paul's letters are largely *paraenetic* or hortatory. As the founder and father of communities with responsibility for their growth in Christ, Paul wrote with paternal authority to exhort and encourage believers to remain faithful to the gospel and lead lives visibly transformed by its values. Thus scholars understand Paul's writings as part of his *ongoing work of community*

---

13. The author is unknown. The work has been dated anywhere from the second century bce to the third century ce, cf. Abraham Malherbe, *Ancient Epistolary Theorists* (Atlanta, GA: Scholars Press, 1988), 30–41.

formation, a process that began when he was physically present and continued via letters when he was absent. There is no indication that Paul considered his own writings "sacred scripture," as happened within a few generations after his death (see 2 Pet 3:15b–16), but he did expect his letters to be read aloud to all in the community (1 Thess 5:7). Moreover, given his self-understanding as God's apostle and ambassador (2 Cor 5:20), he no doubt expected his advice and exhortations to be taken as authoritative (1 Cor 4:14–16, 5:3–5).

The Form of an Ancient Letter

In Paul's day, as is also the case today, a letter had standard parts and a standard order. It began with the identification of the letter's sender and then its recipient. Next came a greeting followed by a thanksgiving or prayer. After these introductory features, the body of the letter began. Here the writer disclosed the reason for writing and laid out the matter. At the end of the body, the writer added final wishes, greetings, and exhortation before a formal conclusion, which contained a brief word of farewell.

The letter to Philemon, outlined on the next two pages alongside an ancient secular letter in the chart "Paul's Letter to Philemon Compared to an Ancient Secular Papyrus Letter," illustrates Paul's general adherence to the letter-writing conventions of his day. However, even in this briefest of Paul's undisputed letters, he clearly adapts these conventions for his own pastoral and theological purposes. Beyond his name as sender, he adds that he is a "prisoner of Christ Jesus," which indicates that he writes while imprisoned because of his work on behalf of Christ. In other letters, his self-identification is even more elaborate to underscore his apostolic credentials and divine commissioning and the authority stemming from them (see, e.g., Gal 1:1–5). As illustrated by Philemon v. 2, Paul theologically inflects and expands the standard secular "greetings" by offering "grace and peace from God our Father and the Lord Jesus Christ" (v. 2). In the conclusion at v. 25, Paul replaces the simple "farewell" with a grace benediction. In other letters, he expands the conclusion to include a "holy kiss" (1 Thess 5:26; 2 Cor 13:12) or a peace wish (2 Cor 13:11). By introducing these variations at the beginning and end of his letters, Paul sets their content within a liturgical framework.

Paul's Letter to Philemon Compared to an Ancient Secular Papyrus Letter

	A letter of admonition from one brother to another[14]	Paul's Letter to Philemon ca. 55–56 CE
Sender	From Theon	Paul, a prisoner of Christ Jesus, and Timothy (v. 1)
Recipient	To Heraclides, his brother	To Philemon our dear friend and co-worker, and to Apphia our sister, to Archippus our fellow soldier and to the church in your house. (v. 2)
Greeting	Warmest Greetings!	Grace to you and peace from God our Father and the Lord Jesus Christ. (v. 3)
Thanksgiving	Before I pray for your welfare . . . Though aware that a thanksgiving or prayer was in order at this point in the letter, the ancient writer chose to omit it. When a situation was urgent and writers were anxious to address it immediately, they might omit the opening thanksgiving or prayer. In addressing the urgent situation in Galatians, Paul omitted the thanksgiving.	When I remember you in my prayers, I always thank God because I hear of your love for all the saints and your faith toward the Lord Jesus. I pray that the sharing of your faith may become effective when you perceive all the good we may do for Christ. I have indeed received much joy and encouragement from your love, because the hearts of the saints have been refreshed through you, my brother. (vv. 4–17)
Body	. . . I learned that you are treating our revered mother harshly. Please, sweetest	For this reason, though I am bold enough to command you to do your duty, yet I

Continued

14. Papyrus letter SB3, 62643 found in Neill Elliott and Mark Reasoner, eds. *Documents and Images for the Study of Paul* (Minneapolis, MN: Fortress Press, 2011), 79.

Continued

Paul's Letter to Philemon Compared

Body	brother, do not cause her grief in any way. If any of the brothers talk back to her, you ought to hit them. For now you should be called father. I know you are able to please her without me writing this letter but do not take my letter of admonition in the wrong way. For we ought to worship her who bore us as a god, especially since she is good. I have written these things to you knowing the sweetness of our revered parents.	would rather appeal to you on the basis of love—and I Paul do this as an old man, and now also as a prisoner of Christ Jesus. I am appealing to you for my child Onesimus, whose father I have become during my imprisonment. Formerly, he was useless to you, but now he is indeed useful both to you and to me. I am sending him, that is, my own heart, back to you. I wanted to keep him with me that he might be of service to me in your place during my imprisonment for the gospel; [14] but I preferred to do nothing without your consent, in order that your good deed might be voluntary and not something forced . . . [21] Confident of your obedience, I am writing to you knowing that you will do even more than I say. One thing more—prepare a guest room for me, for I am hoping through your prayers to be restored to you. (vv. 8–22)
Conclusion	Please write to me about your welfare. Farewell, brother.	Epaphras, my fellow prisoner in Christ Jesus, sends greetings to you and so do Mark, Aristarchus, Demas, and Luke, my fellow workers. The grace of the Lord Jesus Christ be with your spirit. (vv. 23–25)

This indicates that he expected them to be read in the context of a worship service where blessings, prayers, and a ritual act such as a "holy kiss" would be appropriate.[15]

Paul's elaboration on the basic letter outline is most notable in the body of his letters. He uses typical formulas to introduce the body, such as "I want you to know" (Gal 1:11). He includes features that were typically used at the end of a letter, including confidence that the letter's recipients will heed his instructions and requests, as well as mention of his travel plans (see Phlm vv. 21–22.). However, the main body of Paul's letters, unusually long compared to ancient letters (with the exception of Philemon), are theological treatments of a variety of issues. Paul often marshals scripture and tradition to back up his points. His letters contain dialogic features, such as direct address, question and answer, and other argumentative features associated with Greco-Roman rhetoric.

Letters as Collaborative Projects

With the exception of Romans and Galatians, Paul names one or more persons as co-senders of his letters. Besides co-senders, it is clear that Paul employed at least one scribe to actually write his letters. In Paul's day, most people who sent letters used a secretary, or scribe—a literate, professional writer who did the actual writing. At Romans 16:22, the scribe says, "I, Tertius, the writer of this letter, greet you . . ." Elsewhere, Paul betrays his use of a scribe by emphasizing the addition of something in his own handwriting, for instance, "See what large letters I make when I am writing with my own hand!" (Gal 6:11); "I, Paul, write this greeting with my own hand" (1 Cor 16:21); "I, Paul, am writing this with my own hand . . ." (Phlm 19). These autographs added a personal quality to Paul's letters and likely reinforced their authority.

Until relatively recently, scholars did not consider either Paul's co-senders or the scribe to have made any contribution to a letter's content. They regarded the scribe as a mere copier, who committed Paul's thought to paper word for word. Named co-senders were

---

15. On the liturgical character of Paul's letters, see John Paul Heil, *The Letters of Paul as Rituals of Worship* (Eugene, OR: Cascade Books, 2011).

thought of simply as companions who happened to be present when Paul was sending his letters. It was widely assumed that Paul was solely responsible for the content of his letters and that he wrote alone in private. However, as noted in a recent study, the image of "Paul the lone writer" is actually indebted to modern, Western notions of authorship as a highly individualistic activity.[16] In Paul's day, scribes were not mere transcribers of dictation; they were known to edit, making changes in phrasing, style, and syntax. Many scribes actually composed entire letters for their clients.[17] Moreover, unlike the ruggedly individualistic society of today, Paul lived in a group-oriented society where letter-writing was a collaborative activity. Paul never worked alone, and there is no reason to assume he wrote alone, uninfluenced by anyone. In addition to numerous coworkers, he had close disciples such as Timothy, who is listed as a co-sender in four of the five letters where Paul names co-senders (2 Cor 1:1, Phil 1:1; 1 Thess 1:1, Phlm 1). In light of these considerations, more scholars are recognizing a more extensive role for the co-senders and admitting the possibility that they were actually coauthors.[18] If Paul sometimes wrote with one or more coauthors, it could explain the notable changes in style, syntax, and vocabulary in some of the letters attributed to him. Furthermore, recognizing how others influenced and contributed to the letters serves a reminder that far from being an autocrat, Paul was a team player. While as team leader his voice may have carried the greatest weight, it does not necessarily mean that only his voice is present in the letters ascribed to him.

Paul's Letters and Rhetoric

In antiquity, as today, a letter expressed what a writer would have said in person. So while a letter and a speech were not identical,

---

16. See E. Randolph Richards, *Paul and First-Century Letter Writing: Secretaries, Composition and Collection* (Downers Grove, IL: InterVarsity Press, 2004; see further, Jerome Murphy-O'Connor, *Paul the Letter-Writer: His World, His Options, His Skills* (Collegeville, MN: Liturgical Press, 1995), 16–19.

17. Richards, *Paul and First-Century Letter Writing*, 59–80.

18. See example, Michael J. Gorman, *Apostle of the Crucified Lord: A Theological Introduction to Paul's Letters* (Grand Rapids, MI: William B. Eerdmans, 2004), 87; see further Murphy-O'Connor, *Paul the Letter-Writer*, 19.

the letter substituted for speech. In Paul's day, speech served as the foundation of civic life—the critical tool that allowed society to develop according to reason rather than brute force.[19] Therefore, the ability to speak well was of utmost importance. Political leaders, as well as teachers of religious and philosophical truths, were expected to speak eloquently and persuasively. Rhetoric, the study of how to argue persuasively in a given situation, was a main component of Greco-Roman education and the mark of an educated person. Persons most adept at persuasion enjoyed great prestige and were deemed *sophoi*, or wise persons.

By Paul's day, there were a number of important handbooks on rhetoric, which are still extant and have been translated into English.[20] These handbooks explained how to research, construct, and order the parts of a speech, and also provided instruction on style, memorization, and techniques for delivering a winning speech. Rhetoric was essentially concerned with persuasive speech, but given the obvious overlap between speech and the letter, its aims and conventions also affected how people wrote. Because Paul designed his letters to be read aloud (Phlm 1:2; 1 Thess 5:27) and meant them to convey his own speech in absentia, it is reasonable to think Paul used contemporary argumentation techniques to make as persuasive a case as possible. In fact, the study of Paul's letters as persuasive arguments has yielded interesting insights into their composition. For example, rhetorical analysis of 1 Corinthians, a letter usually thought to contain just a series of disconnected treatments of a hodgepodge of topics, has shown that the letter has unity and coherence.[21] In addition, awareness of rhetorical devices (e.g., the diatribe, the rhetorical question, boasting, hyperbole), and how Paul uses them in his letters allows the contemporary reader to better comprehend the contours of his argument.

---

19. See Marcus Tullius Cicero, *De Inventione*, trans. H. M. Hubbell (Cambridge, MA: Harvard University Press, 1949), Bk. 1, ch. 2; cf. also *classicpersuasion.org/pw/cicero/dnv1-1.htm*, trans. C. D. Jonge.

20. The most important extant handbooks are those of the Greek philosopher, Aristotle (fourth century bce), and two Latin writers, Cicero (first century bce) and Quintilian (first century ce).

21. See, e.g., the study by Margaret Mitchell, *Paul and the Rhetoric of Reconciliation: An Exegetical Investigation of the Language and Composition of 1 Corinthians* (Tübingen, Germany: J. C. B. Mohr/Paul Siebeck, 1991).

Diatribe

While people today think of a diatribe as angry, abusive speech, in Paul's day the diatribe actually functioned as a teaching tool. It was a dialogic exchange between a teacher and an imaginary student. In Greco-Roman schools of philosophy, teachers created diatribes to teach a point. Paul made use of the diatribe especially in the letter to the Romans. In the dialogue at Rom 3:1–9, one can see some of its typical features: rhetorical questions and rejection of false conclusions, followed by reasons for the rejection. As with the letter form itself, Paul adapted rhetorical devices for his own purposes.

The handbooks of rhetoric classified speeches, or arguments, according to three species or types, each ordered to a distinct purpose and appropriate to a different setting. The forensic or judicial speech, proper to the courtroom, was used to defend or accuse someone in view of a past action. Lawyers still use this type of argument in courtrooms today. The deliberative speech, for use in the assembly, sought to persuade or dissuade those assembled about future courses of action. Finally, epideictic speech, appropriate to a variety of public occasions, employed praise or blame to affirm important values and reinforce the audience's current adherence to them. The standard template for any speech had four parts: the introduction; the presentation of the facts and the point the speaker wished to prove; the proofs; and the conclusion, which usually included a recap of key points. Additional parts were added to this basic template, depending on the type and purpose of a particular speech.

With regard to the species of rhetoric, it is difficult to categorize Paul's letters because he did not rigidly follow the template of any one particular type of speech. In fact, he seems to employ forensic rhetoric at 1 Corinthians 1–4, but later in the same letter he invites the community to deliberate about what action to take in light not only of what is good but what is more advantageous (see, e.g., 1 Cor 6:12–20, 8:1–13). As many scholars now recognize, rhetorical analysis of Paul's letters is most valuable when used not merely to classify a letter's genre but to identify and understand the two essential parts of any argument: the point to be proved and the proofs.[22] Without these, there is no argument.

Persuasion, regardless of the speech type, ultimately depended on three kinds of proofs: those based on the moral character of the speaker, known as proofs based on *ethos*; those based on the emotions of the audience, or proofs based on *pathos*; and finally, those based on the logical strength of what is said, or proofs based on *logos*. These three types remain important aspects of speech today. An audience has to trust the speaker, be disposed to agree with what is being promoted or rejected, and be convinced by the merit of the speaker's arguments. Paul uses all three types throughout his letters. He can rely on his own sincerity, trustworthiness, sufferings, and tireless dedication to ground his argument (cf., e.g., 1 Thess 2:3–8; 2 Cor 11:16–29); or he can appeal to the emotions of his audience to move them to change their behavior (cf., e.g., Gal 4:2; 2 Cor 11:7); or he can string together a series of logical arguments based on scripture, tradition, Christian praxis, nature, or any combination of these (cf., e.g., Rom 9:6–29; 1 Cor 15:1–58).

Some argue, in view of Paul's rejection of sophisticated speech (1 Cor 2:1–4) and his admission that he was an inept speaker (2 Cor 11:6), that he had neither formal training in rhetoric nor any interest in persuasive speech. As there is no direct evidence that Paul was a well-educated person with formal training in rhetoric, this issue will no doubt continue to be debated. However, most scholars today recognize Paul's letters as carefully crafted arguments aimed at persuasion and understand Paul's protestations of rhetorical ineptitude as illustrating his rhetorical strategy and skill. Read as arguments aimed at persuasion—not simply as static ancient letters to people now long dead—the persuasive power of Paul's letters can still be experienced today.

---

22. See example, Murphy-O'Connor, *Paul the Letter Writer*, 83–86.

Summary

A number of key points can help those studying Paul for the first time avoid many common misconceptions about his mission and his letters. First, it is important to bear in mind that Paul started small. He was nothing like a Sunday morning televangelist addressing arenas full of people, despite the impression one might get from Acts. He operated within the context of house churches and formed small networks of believers that served as the building blocks of an emerging church. Second, Paul's letters were not theological treatises written in a vacuum. Rather, he wrote them to address specific situations and issues arising in particular communities. Recognizing the occasional nature of Paul's letters will prevent the reader from taking his comments out of context and applying them to situations for which they were not written and to which they really do not respond. Third, Paul's letters constitute an essential part of his missionary activity. Through them, he continued his work of community formation and encouraging adherence to the gospel. Fourth, Paul was no "lone ranger," but the head of a mission team who collaborated with others. Finally, whether Paul had a formal education or not, his letters suggest that he knew something about contemporary rhetoric and constructing arguments. He recognized that persuasion could go much further than command in getting people to make choices and live lives rooted in gospel values. That much is evident from Philemon 8–9, "though I am bold enough in Christ to command you . . . yet I would rather appeal to you on the basis of love, and I, Paul, do this as an old man, and now also as a prisoner of Christ Jesus."

Questions for Review and Reflection

1. Explain why it is difficult to provide a chronology of Paul's missionary career when scholars have both his letters and Luke's Acts of the Apostles.
2. What are the historical references in Acts that can be linked to external data and provide key dates for constructing Paul's chronology?

3. What was a house church and why were house churches essential to Paul's ministry? How is a "house church" different from a church attended by Christians today?

4. What are the three types of rhetorical proofs? How many of each can you find in Paul's shortest letter, Philemon?

5. Why did Paul carry out his ministry in large urban settings? Why was he well suited for an urban mission to Gentiles?

6. What are the key parts of a Pauline letter? Explain why his letters are called occasional writings.

Opening More Windows

Alexander, L. C. A. "Chronology of Paul," in *Dictionary of Paul and His Letters*, ed. Gerald F. Hawthorne, Ralph P. Martin, Daniel G. Reid. Downers Grove, IL: InterVarsity Press, 1993, 115–23.

Aristotle. *Art of Rhetoric*. Eng. trans. J. H. Freese. Cambridge, MA: Harvard University Press, 1982.

Banks, Robert. *Paul's Idea of Community: The Early House Churches in Their Historical Setting*, rev. ed. Peabody, MA: Hendrickson, 1994.

Billings, Bradly. "From House Church to Tenement Church: Domestic Space and the Development of Early Urban Christianity—the Example of Ephesus." *Journal of Theological Studies* 62. 2 (2011): 541–69.

Blue, Bradley B. "Acts and the House Church," in *The Book of Acts in Its Graeco-Roman Setting*, ed. D. W. J. Gill and C. Gempf. Grand Rapids, MI: William B. Eerdmans, 1994, 119–22.

Branick, Vincent P. *The House Church in the Writings of Paul*. Wilmington, DE: Michael Glazier, 1989.

Quintilian, Marcus F. *Institutio Oratoria*. Eng. trans. H. E. Butler. Cambridge, MA: Harvard University Press, 1996.

Stowers, Stanley K. *Letter Writing in Greco-Roman Antiquity*. Philadelphia: Westminster Press, 1986.

Internet Resources

media.artgallery.yale.edu/duraeuropos/dura.html

This website provides information and images from Yale University's excavation of Dura-Europos in the 1920s and 1930s.

smarthistory.khanacademy.org/early-christian-Art-after-constantine.html

This link will take you to an essay titled, "Early Christian Art and Architecture after Constantine," where you can read further about the evolution from house churches to basilicas.

Chapter 3

The World
of Paul's Ministry

Overview

This chapter takes as its point of departure the realization that information about Paul's cultural context furthers one's understanding of him and his first converts and provides greater insight into his letters. After the brief introduction, this chapter examines the political, religious, philosophical, and social landscape of Paul's first-century-CE Greco-Roman world.

Paul's Reality

Paul and the people he talks about in his letters, whether named coworkers and friends or nameless detractors and others who rejected his message, all come from a shared past. That past, lived out in the large urban centers around the Mediterranean, was no less pluralistic and bustling with conflicting ideas and opinions than the present. There was no end of politicians, philosophers, and teachers of religion—some wise, others charlatans—vying to be heard. As today, people in Paul's time argued about the existence of God, life's purpose, how to live, and other questions of ultimate concern. The political and economic realities of their day also shaped their lives. For these reasons, in order to understand Paul, one needs to consider the multiple realities that formed the context in which he and his contemporaries lived and died.

The Political Landscape

Without a doubt, the reality that most impacted the life and times of Paul and his peers was Roman imperial rule. By the time Paul began his missionary career in the mid to late 30s ce, Rome had been ruling the Mediterranean world for almost sixty years. The empire emerged after decades of civil war brought about the collapse of the Roman republic.[1] In 42 bce future Roman emperor Octavian joined Marc Antony to defeat Brutus and Cassius and avenge the murder of Julius

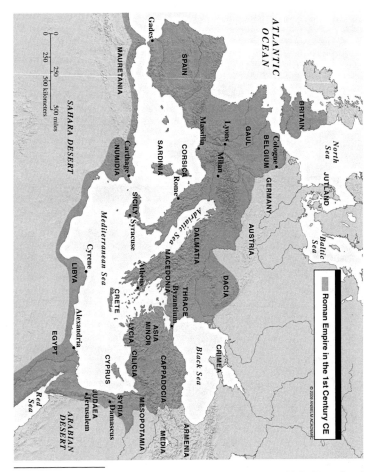

Roman Empire in the 1st Century CE

© 2009 ANSELM ACADEMIC

---

1. See, e.g., Géza Alföldy, *The Social History of Rome*, trans. T. D. Braund and F. Pollock (London: Croom Helm, 1985), esp. 65–85.

Caesar. At the Battle of Actium in 31 bce, Octavian, Julius Caesar's heir, defeated Antony and became the uncontested ruler of Rome.

Octavian, better known as Caesar Augustus, was shrewd. He concealed his political ambitions by insisting that he was not an emperor but only Rome's chief citizen or "princeps." In reality, he exercised absolute rule from 31 bce to 14 ce over a vast territorial empire of ethnically and culturally diverse subjugated peoples. Under Augustus and his successors, this empire grew into the greatest economic, military, and political power the world had ever known.

Some poets idealized this new period of peace and prosperity, known as the *Pax Romana* or "Peace of Rome," as the restoration of a lost "golden age."[2] The Roman people, tired of war, strife, and corruption, accepted Octavian's program of political, cultural, and religious reform and gave him various honors and titles, including Augustus (the revered one). To celebrate Augustus' victories over Gaul (France) and Hispania (Spain) and the establishment of universal peace, the Roman Senate commissioned the building of an altar to peace, *Ara Pacis* in Latin, which was dedicated in 9 bce.

© Scala / Art Resource, NY

The *Ara Pacis*, built alongside the Tiber River in Rome, remains one of the greatest monuments to the Augustan Age.

---

2. See Virgil, *Aeneid*, Bks. 1–6, trans. H. Rushton Fairclough (Cambridge, MA: Harvard University Press, 1916), Bk. 1:291–96 and Bk. 6:791–95.

Good and Bad News

Augustus celebrated the accomplishments of his reign in a first-person account entitled the *Res Gestae Divi Augusti* (The Deeds of the Divine Augustus).[3] It is clear from this and other accounts of Augustus' reign that he did many positive things, especially for the city and people of Rome. However, for the majority of the population spread across the Mediterranean, this was no new golden age. Rome resorted to violence to extend imperial rule and bring the so-called peace. Rome's propaganda did not deceive all of the subjugated, as evident from this remark: "to robbery, slaughter, plunder, they give the lying name of empire; they make a solitude and call it peace."[4] Nor did all conquered peoples quietly submit. Archeological remains of the cities the empire built atop the ashes of the cities and civilizations it destroyed serve as reminders of the massive power the empire brought against those who rejected the "divine" gifts of peace and freedom offered them through Rome's agency.[5]

After conquest, in collaboration with the local elites of the conquered cities, Rome imposed a social-political infrastructure that consolidated its power. Rome repopulated these newly constructed cities with Roman army veterans, slaves, and others taken captive from different parts of the empire. Meanwhile, it exiled former city inhabitants to other areas under Roman control. Though Rome enforced its will through violence, the eventual unification and acculturation that allowed Roman civilization to take hold depended to a very large extent on three other factors: the social system of patronage, the imperial use of rhetoric, and the spread of the imperial cult.

Patronage

The patronage system was an elaborate spiderweb of relations between the imperial family and the elite members of the major cities of the empire.[6] Local elites cultivated the personal favor of the

---

3. The English translation is available at *classics.mit.edu/Augustus/deeds.html*.

4. See Tacitus, *Agricola*, 30, available at *www.fordham.edu/halsall/ancient/tacitus-agricola.asp*.

5. A prime example is Jerusalem, which the Romans extensively destroyed in 70 ce and later obliterated in 135 ce. At that point, Hadrian built the new Roman city, Aelia Capitolina, over the ruins of Jerusalem.

6. On the patronage system, see, e.g., Andrew Lintott, *Imperium Romanum: Politics and Administration* (New York: Routledge, 1993), 168–74.

emperor, the supreme patron, upon whose benefaction their economic well-being, power, and status depended. In return, the local elites were expected to pledge themselves to advance Rome and its interests. For promoting Rome and erecting monuments and public works to its glory, they won honors and appointments to high office, as well as the esteem and envy of the local citizens. This exchange of favors was replicated at every level. Those of lower social status ingratiated themselves to the local elites and remained indebted to them. This was a hierarchically structured network of mutual obligations, with lesser subjects depending on local patrons and local patrons depending on Rome. Everyone was either directly or indirectly obligated to the emperor—the chief benefactor and father of this new global household. Roman philosopher Seneca's observation that the emperor had no need of guards because his benefaction was his greatest protection may be a bit exaggerated.[7] However, it underscores the dependence the patronage system created, whose significance cannot be overestimated. As one scholar observed, it was the basis of control and power that allowed a relatively small imperial administration to rule an entire empire.[8]

Rhetoric

As noted in the previous chapter, rhetoric was the "art of speaking well" for the purpose of persuasion. With the rise of democracies and democratic institutions in the fifth century bce in Syracuse and Athens, as well as the recognition that society was best ordered by reason, politicians needed to speak well in order to persuade the *dēmos,* or the people.[9] When the assembly, or *ekklēsia,*[10] of local

---

7. Seneca makes the comment in his essay *De Clementia* (On Mercy). See *Moral Essays,* vol. I, trans. J. W. Basore (Cambridge, MA: Harvard University Press, 1928), I.13.5.

8. See Ramsay MacMullen, *Corruption and the Decline of Rome* (New Haven, CT: Yale University Press, 1988), 121.

9. See George. A. Kennedy, *A New History of Classical Rhetoric* (Princeton, NJ: Princeton University Press, 1994), 3–10.

10. In the NT, the word *ekklēsia* is rendered "church." In its original, secular usage it referred to a political assembly of the *dēmos,* or people; see Gerhard Kittel (ed.), *Theological Dictionary of the New Testament* (Grand Rapids, MI: William B. Eerdmans, 1965), vol. 3, 513.

citizens met, it was expected that everyone would participate in political debates and decide what courses of action to adopt. Persuasive speech played a critical role in such deliberations. With the emergence of the empire, decisions were made at the imperial level and passed down through imperial appointees. This process eliminated the need for the local *ekklēsia*, as imperial decrees determined the course of people's lives.

Under the Romans, rhetoric served imperial propaganda. At public festivals and sporting events, trained speakers used the power of words to persuade audiences to believe that Rome was the agent of the divine plan of salvation and that as beneficiaries of the good Rome wrought, the people owed Rome and the emperor their praise, gratitude, and allegiance. As biblical scholar Walter Wink noted, empires depend on rhetoric to legitimate themselves and persuade people to believe "that they benefit from a system that is in fact harmful to them, that no other system is feasible, that God has placed the divine imprimatur on this system and no other."[11]

Imperial Cult and Theology

Along with patronage and rhetoric, the cult of the emperor and its accompanying imperial theology proved critical to the cohesion of the empire. What Augustus accomplished was referred to as *euangelion* (good news; gospel). Moreover, because he did what many had considered humanly impossible, his elevation to divine status was considered appropriate. Thus began the worship of Augustus, the *divi filius*, "son of the Divine One,"[12] as well as both the living and deceased members of the imperial family. The imperial cult took root at various times and places and in various forms throughout the empire. The Greek peoples of the eastern empire already practiced ruler worship beginning with Alexander the Great (d. 323 bce) and

---

11. See Walter Wink, *Engaging the Powers: Discernment and Resistance in a World of Domination* (Minneapolis, MN: Fortress Press, 1992), 93.

12. See Virgil, *Aeneid*, 6.789–794. The "divine one," referred to Julius Caesar, posthumously deified and granted the title *divus* (divine) *Iulius* by senate decree in 42 bce. See also Suetonius, *The Lives of the Caesars: The Deified Julius Caesar*, vol. I, trans. J. C. Rolfe (Cambridge, MA: Harvard University Press, 1914), Bk. 1, ch. 88.

had little problem accommodating worship of the Roman emperor. The cult was as much about politics as about religion. Through it, subjects expressed allegiance to both deified human rulers and to a deified cultural and political entity personified as the goddess *Roma*.[13]

Eventually, the worship of both Roma (the culture) and Augustus (the person) composed a sort of official form of the imperial cult.[14] It was practiced in almost every major city of the empire. As Josephus reports, Herod the Great made sure that Palestine also had cities, temples, and public games dedicated to the emperor:

Dea Roma, Piazza del Popolo, Rome. Statues representing the Tiber and Aniene Rivers flank *Roma* standing above a she-wolf feeding Rome's legendary founders, Romulus and Remus. The cult of the goddess *Roma*, who personified Rome's power, was a means, especially for those in the Greek East, to recognize and celebrate that power.

> there was not any place of his [Herod's] kingdom fit for the purpose that was permitted to be without something that was for Caesar's honor; and when he had filled his own country with temples, he poured out the like plentiful marks of his esteem into his province, and built many cities which he called Caesarea.[15]

---

13. On the origin and significance of "Roma" see Ronald Mellor, "The Goddess Roma," in *Religion*, 17.2 (*Aufstieg und Niedergang der römischen Welt* II); ed. Wolfgang Haase (Berlin: Walter de Gruyter, 1981), 952–1030.

14. Ibid., 981.

15. See Josephus *Jewish Wars* I.21.4 and further I.21.8 and 1.1.2.7.

By the time Paul began evangelizing, the architecture of the imperial cult had transformed the Mediterranean landscape.[16] Many cities were focused around large, newly erected temples, and altars to Augustus were centrally located. Every city the first Christian evangelizers visited had coins bearing images of the emperor and *Roma*. Most cities added new festivals to their liturgical calendar to celebrate the emperor's birthday, deeds, decrees, victories, and titles. The imperial cult existed alongside the variety of local cults and functioned as an important tool to unify disparate peoples and link them to the emperor.

The imperial cult had its own salvation story, which was rooted in two key theological convictions: (1) the emperor was divinely appointed and (2) Rome, under Augustus, was the divinely chosen instrument through which to realize the divine plan of universal salvation. The story was told through the media of the day: coins, inscriptions, literature, statues, and monuments. A stone inscription dating from ca. 9 bce, found at the city of Priene on the west coast of Turkey, provides insight into the emperor's role in this salvation story. The two extant fragments of this inscription relate to a proposal by a government official of Asia Minor to honor Caesar. One fragment calls for a change to the calendar so that the New Year coincides with Augustus' birthday (Sept. 23). It reads,

> the birthday of the most divine Caesar . . . is the day we might justly set on par with the beginning of everything, in that he restored order when everything was disintegrating . . . and gave a new look to the whole world, a world which would have met destruction had Caesar not been born as a common blessing to all. For that reason, one might justly take this to be the beginning of life and living and the end of regret at one's birth.[17]

---

16. See Simon R. F. Price, *Rituals and Power: The Roman Imperial Cult in Asia Minor* (Cambridge, MA: Cambridge University Press, 1998), 136–69.

17. This translation is provided by David C. Braund, *Augustus to Nero: A Sourcebook on Roman History, 31 bc–ad 68* (Totowa, NJ: Barnes & Noble, 1985), 122A, 56–57.

The second part of the inscription declares,

> Since the providence that has divinely ordered our exis-
> tence . . . has brought to life the most perfect good in
> Augustus, whom she filled with virtues for the benefit of man-
> kind, bestowing him upon us and our descendants as Savior,
> he who put an end to war and brought peace, Caesar who
> by his epiphany exceeds the hopes of all previous good
> news not only outdoing benefits of the past but allowing
> for no hope of any greater benefaction in the future; and
> since the birthday of this god first brought the world this
> good news . . .[18]

What is said of Augustus and what he has done will also be
said of Jesus. Augustus is the source of life and savior of the world,
responsible for its restoration and redemption. His deeds and benefaction have exceeded all that humans could have or will ever hope
for. This is the "good news," and it began with Augustus' epiphany,
or appearance, on Earth. Of Augustus, Virgil wrote, "it is a god who
wrought for us this peace, and a god he shall ever be to me."[19] In
short, the imperial salvation story proclaimed Augustus Lord, Savior,
son of god, and a god himself. His imperial rule brought to fruition
the divine plan of salvation, evident in the peace and abundance that
all were said to enjoy.

In addition to Augustus, Paul's life and work spanned the reigns
of four other emperors who composed the Julio-Claudian dynasty:[20]
Tiberius (14–37 ce), Caligula (37–41 ce), Claudius (41–54 ce), and
finally Nero (54–68 ce), under whom both Paul and Peter were
executed. Initially, Rome had no official policy toward the Jesus
movement, which was still identified with Judaism. The gospels and

---

18. Ibid., 122B, 57–58.

19. Virgil, *Eclogues,* trans. H. R. Fairclough (Cambridge, MA: Harvard University
Press, 1916), 1:6.

20. Augustus' four immediate successors were, like himself, descended from the
Julian family or from another patrician family, the Claudians, through his wife Livia;
hence the designation the Julio-Claudian dynasty. For more on the Julio-Claudian
emperors see *An Online Encyclopedia of Roman Rulers and Their Families* at *www.
roman-emperors.org/impindex.htm.*

Acts present the Jews as pulling the Romans (see, e.g., John 18:31; Acts 17:1–9, 24:1–9) into the persecution of Jesus and the first believers.[21] While there is no evidence that Rome targeted the Jesus movement for persecution in the first decades of its existence, Roman attitudes toward Christians were hardly benign. They disdained Christians as "notoriously depraved"[22] and disparaged Christianity as an oriental superstition that threatened the fabric of society.[23] The irony is that despite these negative views, it was precisely the empire's social and political infrastructure that allowed Christianity to spread throughout the Roman world.

The Religious Landscape

Paul directed his evangelizing work to "Gentiles." Jews used this term to designate people who were not ethnically and religiously Jewish. In Paul's day, Gentiles, alternately referred to as pagans, composed approximately 90 percent of the Roman Empire's population.

Pagans are commonly misperceived as people who practiced no religion. This misconception is often accompanied by the naive idea that when Christianity finally did arrive, pagans had no difficulty embracing its beliefs and practices since, as religious tabulae rasae (blank slates), they held no previous beliefs or practices. However, Paul's letters indicate that pagans did not come to Christianity out of a religious void. Rather, they were converts who "turned to God from idols" (1 Thess 1:9; also Gal 4:8) and from all the practices and beliefs that accompanied their worship. Acts shows Paul and his companions reckoning with pagan religious ideas and practices. The "extremely religious" pagans Paul addressed in Athens merely scoffed at his ideas (cf. Acts 17:22–23), but pagans in Ephesus rioted when they perceived Paul's preaching as a threat to the religious status quo (Acts 19:23–40). Clearly, pagans were not waiting for someone like

---

21. On the imperial government and developing policy toward Christians, see David S. Potter, "Persecution of the Early Church" in *The Anchor Bible Dictionary*, ed. David N. Freedman (New York: Doubleday, 1992), vol. 5, 231.

22. P. Cornelius Tacitus, *Annals. Books* 13–16, trans. J. Jackson (Cambridge, MA: Harvard University Press, 1937), Bk. 15, ch. 47.

23. Suetonius, *Lives of the Caesars*, vol. II, Bk. 6, ch. 16; also Bk. 5, ch. 25.

Paul to bring them religion. Religion already permeated their daily lives. Thus some general insights about pagan religion and religious practices prove critical to understanding Paul and the religious environment he navigated.

Polytheism

The first-century-ce Greco-Roman world was polytheistic. The Romans, like the Greeks whose gods they adopted and identified with their own, believed in the existence of many gods and goddesses as well as lesser spiritual entities, or gods, known as *daimonia* (demons). As a rendering for *daimonia,* "demons" should not be taken with the contemporary connotation of evil spirits. The *daimonia,* as stated, were benign spiritual entities or guardian spirits. Paul acknowledges this polytheistic environment at 1 Corinthians 8:5–6 where he states, "Indeed, even though there may be so-called gods in heaven or on earth—as in fact there are many gods and many lords—yet for us there is one God." At 1 Corinthians 10:20, Paul warns against eating food sacrificed by pagans because it is sacrificed to "demons and not to God" and eating it unites one to demons, instead of to God.

©istockphoto.com / foto-rolf

From prehistoric times, humans attributed natural phenomena they could not explain to some powerful spirit that they then personified. For example, agricultural fertility was thought to be the work of a powerful spirit, which the Canaanites personified as the god Baal, the Greeks as the goddess Demeter, and the Romans as

Iustitia, the Roman goddess of justice, is still widely used in Western culture as symbol of justice. Statues and depictions of her with scales, sword, and blindfold symbolizing the impartiality of justice abound in US courts of law and on state seals.

the goddess Ceres. Every inexplicable natural phenomenon from birth to death was attributed to some personified spiritual force; hence the multiplicity of deities. While pagans might have a preference for a particular god, this did not prevent them from valuing and worshipping other gods. By the first century ce, pagans also deified virtues, believing that noble qualities such as honor and justice also existed through the agency of a god. Finally, as previously noted, by Paul's day the deification and worship of the emperor was a political tool intended to seal allegiance to Rome.

Public Religion: State and Local

Cicero defined pagan religion as the *cultus deorum* or "cult of the gods."[24] *Cultus*, derived from the Latin verb *colere*, can mean to "till" or "cultivate."[25] *Cult* refers to the combination of observances, rituals, and practices pagans performed to cultivate the favor of the gods. Humans did this because they depended on the gods' goodwill to supply their daily needs and protect them from harm. Sacrificial offerings, whether of animals or food, were the most important part of the cult. Their purpose was to propitiate or placate the gods. Although today many equate the practice of religion with morality, the practice of Roman religion was not about ethics, doctrines, or beliefs. Instead, it was about performing the cult to honor the immortal gods and keep the state and its constituents in their favor. Thus the cult also expressed one's patriotism. The truly pious or religious person was the one who performed this duty.

By Paul's day, there were four groups, or *collegia*, of priests in charge of the complex state cult. In addition to offering prayers and sacrifices, they oversaw the liturgical calendar, marriage laws, the administration of sacred temples, and a host of other activities related to the state cult. Most priests also held a political office, which allowed the reinforcement of political ideology through religion and religious ritual. The emperor was the chief priest—in Latin, the

---

24. Cicero, *On the Nature of the Gods*, trans. H. Rackham (Cambridge, MA: Harvard University Press, 1933), 2.8.

25. See "*cōlo, cōlere*" in Charles Short and Charlton Lewis, *A Latin Dictionary* (New York: Oxford University Press, 1984).

Pontifex Maximus—literally, the "greatest bridge-builder." Applied in a religious sense, the term refers to the emperor's role as the bridge between humans and the divine. The emperor was a member and also the head of each of the four *collegia* of priests responsible for different aspects of the cult.[26]

Throughout the empire, the social and civic life of each city revolved around the local cults of the traditional patron deities associated with the city. Each local city council invoked the patronage of the deities to guide its deliberations, and almost every social and civic activity, including sporting events, had a religious dimension. Money to build temples and maintain the cult came from the city treasury or wealthy patrons. The city calendar was marked by the observance of religious festivals. Locally appointed priests offered prayers and sacrifices to honor the gods and ensured that religious law was observed. Rather than opposing local cults, Rome allowed them to flourish and found ways to associate them with the imperial cult.

Domestic Religion

While pagan religion was practiced for the most part in public space, it was not limited to the public sphere. Households honored the traditional family gods on whom generations of their ancestors had relied.[27] Each home had altars and small shrines for the *penates*, i.e., the gods who looked after a family's provisions, and the *lares*, i.e., the spirits of deceased family members. Representations of the *penates* and *lares* were kept in the house and were part of everyday religious devotion. People placed small statuettes symbolizing the household gods on the table at mealtimes and set aside a portion of food for them. If a family moved, their household gods moved with them. In addition to *penates* and *lares*, family members venerated another household spirit called "the genius," best understood as an object's or person's vital essence or generative power. The household genius was naturally associated with the *paterfamilias*, or head of the household.

---

26. The Roman priesthood is concisely discussed by Burkhard Gladigow, "Roman Religion," in *The Anchor Bible Dictionary*, ed. David N. Freedman (New York: Doubleday, 1992), vol. 5, 809–10.

27. Ibid., 810, for a concise explanation of domestic religion.

Mystery Religions

Another important feature of the Greco-Roman religious environment in Paul's day was the mystery religions.[28] As supplements to their practice of public and domestic religion, many pagans also joined one of the mystery religions. The mysteries were essentially religious cults that originated in Greece, Asia, and Egypt and eventually spread throughout the empire. Their name derives from the series of secret initiation rites by which one gradually became a full member.[29] All mystery cults were voluntary associations. Some appealed more to women than men, and vice versa. These cults met the spiritual needs of many in the first century ce, and they swept across the empire before Christian evangelizers had even set foot outside Palestine. The mystery cults of Dionysus, Demeter, Isis, and Cybele were among the most popular. There was hardly a place Paul visited where one or more mystery cults had not taken root. Rome's official posture toward these cults was a mixture of caution and tolerance.

Each cult had its own sacred myth, often involving the tribulations of a god who undergoes a violent death (e.g., Osiris, beloved of Isis, and Attis, beloved of Cybele) but for whom death and corruptibility were not final. By participation in the cult, initiates shared in both the tragedy and victory of the god. They also hoped to obtain salvation from present and future misfortunes and fears, especially those associated with death and the afterlife. Unlike outsiders, initiates were united in their shared secret knowledge of and identification with the deity. They were also united to the deity and each other through the sharing of sacred meals. Perhaps the greatest benefit of the mysteries came from the spiritual solidarity among the initiates, who came together to transcend daily woes and find deeper meaning and fulfillment in their lives.

---

28. For a concise introduction to the mystery religions, see Walter Burkert, *Ancient Mystery Cults* (Cambridge, MA: Harvard University Press, 1987).

29. The only extant first person account of initiation into a cult is found in Apuleius, *The Golden Ass Being the Metamorphoses of Lucius Apuleius,* rev. ed. by S. Gaselee, (London/ New York: Heinemann/Macmillan Co., 1915), Bk. XI, esp. §. 22–26. A free digital version of this edition is available at *ia600307.us.archive.org/8/items/goldenass beingme00apuliala/goldenassbeingme00apuliala.pdf.*

© Erich Lessing / Art Resource, NY

Fresco from Herculaneum ca. 50–79 CE, National Archeological Museum, Naples, depicting priests performing the rites of the goddess Isis. As with all mystery religions, Isis was worshipped in secret rites whose details remain largely unknown.

In addition to mystery cults, the East exported a number of other practices that appealed to the peoples of the empire who felt their lives were in the hands of the "fates"—the inescapable forces controlling the destiny of humans. These people welcomed the knowledge they could gain about the present and future through astrology and divination. They were also attracted by the power of magic, through which they believed they could manipulate the supernatural forces controlling their lives.

Much of what constituted religion in the first century Greco-Roman world may appear to have little in common with today's practice of religion. Nonetheless, it is important to recognize that whether preaching to pagans in the eastern or western empire, Paul preached to people whose everyday public and private lives were permeated by religion and religious experiences. However, the exclusive allegiance to one God that both Judaism and Christianity demanded would have been a challenge to pagans. Paul's letters make clear that even after conversion, many pagans kept their ideas about many gods and spirits (see, e.g., Gal 4:8–11).

The Philosophical Landscape

In addition to its traditional focus on physics, metaphysics, epistemology, and logic, philosophy had also taken on a more practical focus by the first century ce. This focus attracted many to it, if not as a substitute, then certainly as a possible supplement to conventional public religion. The latter focused on pleasing the gods, while philosophy focused on improving peoples' lives. Philosophers concerned themselves with questions about what a good and meaningful life was and what life strategy best led to self-fulfillment and happiness (Grk. *eudaimonia*), the goal of human life. Philosophy was thus concerned with ethics, and much of Greco-Roman philosophy took the form of moral instruction and exhortation.[30] To their disciples, philosophers functioned as intellectual and spiritual mentors— quasi-religious teachers. They were similar to today's "life coaches" who aim to help individuals achieve their goals, be their best selves, and live happy, integrated, and fulfilled lives. But beyond generally agreeing on happiness and self-fulfillment as life's most important goals, philosophers often prescribed different paths to achieve them. Individuals had to choose to become a disciple of a particular philosopher and adhere to that philosopher's recommended way of life. This choice required careful consideration, since philosophers could advocate radically different life paths. For example, whether or not to marry was a much-debated topic among first-century-ce philosophers.[31] One philosophical school believed marriage was to be avoided because it detracted from the pursuit of self-fulfillment

---

30. On the broadening of philosophy to include ethics, see Abraham J. Malherbe, *Moral Exhortation, A Greco-Roman Sourcebook* (Philadelphia: Westminster Press, 1989), 11–16.

31. Primary sources illustrating opposing views held by philosophers on marriage are examined in Will Deming, *Paul on Marriage and Celibacy: The Hellenistic Background of 1 Corinthians 7* (Cambridge, MA: Cambridge University Press, 1995), esp. 50–106.

and happiness, while another considered marriage part of the cosmic order and necessary for the survival of society. In 1 Corinthians 7, Paul also weighs in on the topic of marriage. Because both religious preachers and philosophers voiced their views on a number of the same issues, one can see how Paul might be mistaken for just another philosopher and his first followers mistaken for members of just another philosophical school.[32] It is also easy to see how philosophy resembled Judaism and Christianity, with its concern for virtuous and upright living and its critique of pagan religion for its superstitious practices and indifference to moral living. Thus to many, philosophy appeared to be a religion whose focus on helping people achieve happiness held great appeal.

Among the philosophical schools of Paul's day, three proved especially popular: the Cynics, Stoics, and Epicureans.[33] Cynicism started in the fourth century bce and is associated less with a school of thought than with a way of life.[34] According to the Cynics, the only life worth living, the truly virtuous life, was the one lived "according to nature." This meant a life unconstrained by social, political, and religious conventions and values, which the Cynics considered nothing more than arbitrary human constructs cluttering and encumbering one's life. Thus Cynics advocated rejection of society's rules and values. They lived countercultural, radically individualistic lives and practiced *askesis* (Eng. asceticism)—rugged self-discipline. They renounced possessions and all human comforts, which they considered obstacles to true freedom and happiness, and offered their lives as examples of true virtuous living. They were also known for their bold speech (Grk. *parrēsia*), attacking social conventions as well as the unenlightened people who promoted and practiced them.

---

32. As Malherbe noted, the similarities between Christian and philosophical moral teaching were eventually cited by Christianity's detractors as evidence that Christianity was merely derivative (see *Moral Exhortation*, 11–12).

33. Additional information about each group can be found at *The Internet Encyclopedia of Philosophy*, a peer-reviewed electronic source providing entries on each group, at *www.iep.utm.edu*. An important primary source from the third century ce is Diogenes Laertius, *Lives of Eminent Philosophers*, 2 vols., trans. R. D. Hicks (Cambridge, MA: Harvard University Press, 1925).

34. The characteristic ascetic manner of life and bold speech are on display in the life of the Cynic, Diogenes of Sinope, as recounted by Diog. Laertius, *Lives*, vol. 2, Bk. 6.

As with many countercultural movements, the Cynics had both supporters and detractors, who denounced them for their antisocial behavior. Whether the Cynics influenced Paul is not certain. However, especially where he describes his self-discipline and renunciation of comforts, status, and anything else that would deter him from his single-minded pursuit of Christ (see, e.g., 1 Cor 4:8–13; 9:26–27; Phil 3:7–10), one may detect Cynic strains.

Stoicism, a philosophical school originating in the 300s bce, got its name from the school's place of meeting: the *stoa*, a roofed, colonnaded walkway or portico that was usually attached to the side of a building. By the first century ce, Stoicism was exclusively focused on moral philosophy and was one of the most influential schools of the day. A few of Paul's contemporaries were important stoic teachers, such as the Roman statesman Seneca, Musonius Rufus, and Epictetus.[35]

Stoics believed the whole physical universe was ordered and coherent because everything in it was structured, penetrated, and sustained by the same rational principle. They called this principle "nature," but they also referred to it as "god" or the "soul" or "mind" of the world.[36] Stoics integrated their physics with ethics and believed that because humans participated in this cosmic order, their moral purpose was to live according to nature. This was the truly virtuous life through which to attain happiness. The Stoics divided humans into two groups: the wise and truly free who understood this purpose, and the foolish and still enslaved who did not. The latter were incapable of distinguishing things not under their control from things that were, and things that mattered from things of no importance. For example, rather than accepting the death of a loved one as something dictated by divine will and necessity, fools let themselves

---

35. The moral teaching of each of these Stoics is still extant. See, e.g., Seneca, *Moral Essays*, 3 vols., trans. J. W. Basore (Cambridge, MA: Harvard University Press, 1928, 1932, 1935); idem., *Moral Epistles*, 3 vols., trans. R. M. Gummere (Cambridge, MA: Harvard University Press, 1917, 1920, 1925); Epictetus, *Discourses*, 2 vols., trans. W. A. Oldfather (Cambridge, MA: Harvard University Press, 1925, 1928); Amand Jagu, *Musonius Rufus Entretiens et Fragments: Introduction, Traduction, et Commentaire* (Hildesheim, Germany/New York: G. Olms, 1979).

36. Zeno, the stoic, identified this universal structuring principle as Zeus. See Diog. Laertius, *Lives*, Bk. 7.88 and 136.

be overcome by emotions (Grk. *pathos*, pl. *pathē*). For the Stoics, a truly wise person was "*a-pathos*" (Eng. apathetic), which meant not controlled by emotions or subject to the desires and things not in accord with nature. The ideal Stoic remained unperturbed despite life's ups and downs and accepted that some things in life could not be controlled or changed.[37] The truly wise person could distinguish between things that mattered and things that did not, such as fame, beauty, sickness, health, and wealth. These had no affect on a wise person's happiness because true freedom and happiness derived not from external factors but from one's inner attitude toward them. Stoics, like Cynics, believed that a virtuous life was a life according to nature. They were also radically individualistic in their pursuit of wisdom and perfection. However, Stoics did not reject the social order, which they saw as both necessary and consistent with the cosmic order.

Epicureanism was a philosophical school based on the teachings of its founder Epicurus, ca. 300 bce. For Epicurus, the point of philosophy was to help people free themselves from intense anxiety, especially the dread of death, and to attain peace of mind, or tranquility (Grk. *ataraxia*).[38] He taught that the clash of atoms—that is, physical, not supernatural forces—caused every event. Nothing was fixed or predetermined. According to Epicurus, the acknowledgment of life's randomness was itself a source of tranquility.

Epicurus and his school are usually identified with the pursuit of pleasure, considered "the alpha and omega of a blessed life," the "first and kindred good."[39] By the pursuit of pleasure, (Grk. *hēdonē;* Eng. hedonism), Epicurus was not advocating a life of wanton, self-indulgent behavior, although some did misconstrue him and his followers as promoting licentiousness. Rather, what the Epicureans intended by the pursuit of pleasure was actually the pursuit of tranquility, a life free of physical and psychological pain and stress. Epicurus preached that to attain this tranquility, one needed to practice the virtues, especially prudence; accept the inevitable in

---

37. See Epictetus, *Discourses*, Bk. 3, ch. 18.

38. See Diog. Laertius, *Lives*, vol. 2, Bk. 10. 81–82, 124–26.

39. Diog. Laertius, *Lives*, Bk. 10, 128–29.

life, especially death, which was nothing more than extinction; and recognize that the gods do not punish humans according to their deeds, but live in eternal bliss and are quite disinterested in human affairs.[40] Epicurus' strategy for a happy life attracted many with its assertion that one could flourish by relieving oneself of unnecessary fear and anxiety and its stress on the supreme importance of having a community of friends.

Though Epicureanism and Stoicism were distinct philosophical schools, they both promoted a rational, modest, and reflective manner of life as the pathway to happiness. They were the two most influential schools of philosophy in Paul's day. Their importance is perhaps reflected in Acts 17:18, where Luke singles out the Stoics and Epicureans for special mention among Paul's audience in the Areopagus. Whether they were actually among the audience that day in Athens remains uncertain. However, it is clear from his letters that Paul was conversant with their ideas. He may have been contending with their influence when he affirmed the resurrection and the afterlife (1 Cor 15; 1 Thess 4:13–18), redefined true wisdom (1 Cor 1:18–2:16), confronted radically individualistic behavior that destroyed the community (1 Cor 5:1–6:20), and preached union with and imitation of Christ as the greatest good to pursue in life (Phil 3:8–11). It is possible, even likely, that some of Paul's converts had been adherents of one or more of the philosophical schools and carried into the Christian community the ideas and patterns of behavior of a philosophical school.

The Social Landscape

Since imperial society was complex and diversified, this chapter provides general comments about only a few aspects of it. In Paul's day, a person's quality of life depended in large measure on gender and class status. In contemporary American society, people can transcend a particular socioeconomic status through education, hard work, or even by chance, such as by winning the lottery. Although first-century-ce Greco-Roman society offered some social mobility,

---

40. Ibid., Bk. 10, 123–35.

it was not widespread. Imperial society, like most ancient societies, was stratified and stable. People were born into one of the strata or categories into which society was divided, and most remained in that category.

The strata of Roman imperial society were carefully delineated and legally established. At the imperial level were the senatorial and equestrian orders. Some prosperous plebeians and soldiers also might move up rank to the equestrian order or even the senate. There were also local municipal aristocracies, known as the Decurion class. A Decurion was a member of the local city council who was expected to pay for that privilege by financing public works and entertainment and even providing food when production failed.[41]

By far, most of the population in the imperial period belonged to the lower class, a combination of urban poor and peasants who cultivated their ancestral lands. Of the lower-class population, the most fundamental change of status was from slave to freed-person.

Slaves

Slavery was an important institution of Roman imperial society.[42] Slaves were forced to do the work and the will of their owners. "Slave" constituted a legal category. The classification did not depend on race, ethnicity, education, or economic status. In fact, some slaves were highly educated, independently wealthy, and held important managerial positions. Many functioned at the imperial and municipal level, serving as the ancient equivalent of today's civil servants. Most people were enslaved as a result of war. Taken captive, they were sold as property. Others were debt-slaves—that is, people who defaulted on payments and had no choice but to turn themselves or their children over to their landlords and lenders. By Paul's day, anyone born of a slave woman was a slave.

---

41. These strata of Roman society are discussed by Everett Ferguson, *Backgrounds of Early Christianity*, 3rd ed. (Grand Rapids, MI: William. B. Eerdmans, 2003), 55–57.

42. This discussion of slavery follows S. Scott Bartchy, "Slavery—New Testament," in *The Anchor Bible Dictionary*, ed. David N. Freedman (New York: Doubleday, 1995), vol. 6, 65–73. On the ancient institution of slavery see further, Dale B. Martin, *Slavery as Salvation: The Metaphor of Slavery in Pauline Christianity* (New Haven, CT: Yale University Press, 1990), esp. 1–49.

How a slave was treated depended on his or her owner. Household slaves were subject to the authority of the head of the household. This patriarch or *paterfamilias* held *potestas*, or power, that was absolute over all the enslaved members of his household. As property, slaves could be used and abused, both physically and sexually. Fortunately, there was a way out of slavery. Slaves who had saved wages and had served well could be manumitted or set free by buying their way out of slavery. Sometimes owners manumitted slaves who could no longer physically perform their duties. Manumission on these grounds was not always welcome, as the slave could be freed into abject poverty with no place to go. Manumitted slaves never became "free"—a condition acquired at birth—but were known as "freed-persons," who held a peculiar niche in society. Though superior to a slave, the freed-person usually remained obligated to the former owner. A number of freed-women actually married their former owners and acquired high status.[43]

Women

Chapter 9 will discuss the role and status of women more fully. Here, a few general points are made with the understanding that women in the imperial period came from a variety of ethnicities and places across the Mediterranean, and their experiences were not homogenous. In the imperial period, the family served as the basic unit of society. It remained a hierarchically arranged institution with the male, *paterfamilias*, exercising *patria potestas* (paternal power) over his wife, children, and anyone else in his household. By and large, women's sphere was the home, where they were expected to manage the household and raise the children. However, women could and did acquire wealth and social position. They made money by trading goods and were involved in all kinds of occupations and commerce.[44] Their wealth enabled them to act as patrons and benefactors, roles through which they exercised power and influence. Women also became involved in religious matters, whether participating in or

43. See Sarah Pomeroy, *Goddesses, Whores, Wives and Slaves: Women in Classical Antiquity* (New York: Schocken Books, 1975), 195–96.

44. Ibid., 200.

taking on leading roles in cults, especially those for female deities. Not everyone approved of women's social mobility, their education, or their engagement in public affairs.[45] Among other things, too much education for a woman was thought to lead to sexual licentiousness and insubordination, which would bring dishonor to herself and above all, to her husband.

Group Belonging and Personal Identity

In the first-century-ce Mediterranean world, individuals did not think of personal identity apart from the identity of the group or groups to which they belonged. Today, people try to understand themselves in their uniqueness. In Paul's day, individuals saw themselves as connected to other persons or embedded in groups and derived their self-understanding in view of their social networks.[46] Individuals were rooted in different social groups by birth, marriage, geography, voluntary membership in craft associations, politics, or religion.

Honor and Shame

The pursuit of honor and avoidance of shame was a peculiar preoccupation of classical culture that continued into the first-century-ce Mediterranean society, especially among the elite. People thought of honor as the value of a person in his or her own eyes, as well as that person's value in the eyes of his or her social network.[47] Honor could either be ascribed or acquired. Ascribed honor is bestowed on a person at birth or as a result of receiving some role or rank. Individuals could also acquire honor in the eyes of others by excelling in physical strength, virtue, oratorical skills, martial arts, or other competitive situations. This competitive spirit fostered boasting, jealousy, and divisiveness as people vied to outdo each other to gain esteem and status for themselves.

---

45. See Craig Keener, "Women's Education and Public Speech in Antiquity," *Journal of the Evangelical Theological Society* 50.4 (2007): 747–59.

46. See Bruce Malina, *The New Testament World: Insights from Cultural Anthropology* (Louisville, KY: John Knox Press, 1981), 53–60.

47. Ibid., 27.

A person's success had implications for his social network, as every person was embedded in a group. Whatever honor came to one personally also accrued to one's family. Likewise, if one acted shamefully, he or she brought dishonor to the social network. Whenever a person interacted in public, the honor of that person's whole family or clan was on the line.[48] Thus individuals were expected to behave in ways that brought honor and to avoid behavior that brought dishonor on themselves and their social networks. Those behaviors depended on the values and virtues upheld by one's social networks. Behaviors were also gendered. Although males could expect to garner praise on account of their courage and boldness, too much forthrightness from females, who were expected to be submissive and docile, could bring condemnation. Further, within society as a whole, what constituted behavior worthy of praise or blame for Greco-Roman pagans may have been very different from what Jews and Christians valued and avoided.

Paul considered group belonging of fundamental importance to the survival of the first Christian communities. He devoted much of his effort to resocializing believers into their new family in Christ. In the process, Paul sought to eliminate the competitive spirit that characterized secular society by stressing the unity and equality of all believers in Christ (see 1 Cor 12:12–20; Gal 3:28). Moreover, he sought to inculcate Christian community values and behavior consonant with those values. He advocated whatever actions reinforced group solidarity and discouraged behavior that harmed the community or brought shame on the body of believers in Christ.

Summary

This examination of first-century-ce Greco-Roman society, while far from exhaustive, highlights some of the most important aspects of the cultural context in which Paul ministered and composed his

---

48. A concise discussion of honor and shame and its significance for the study of the NT is provided by Halvor Moxnes, "Honor and Shame," in *Social Sciences and New Testament Interpretation*, ed. Richard L. Rohrbaugh (Peabody, MA: Hendrickson, 2004), 19–40, especially 19–28.

letters. Paul did not believe in a multiplicity of deities or necessarily share the convictions of the philosophers about what constituted the greatest good a human should pursue. Nor did Paul, the Jew, succumb to imperial propaganda or participate in the imperial cult. However, Paul understood the various religious, social, philosophical, and political currents because he lived in this first-century-ce Greco-Roman society and shared this cultural context. He was familiar with the polytheistic worldview of the pagans, the human yearning for true happiness and self-fulfillment, the insatiable quest for honor, and the pretensions of Rome. At times, Paul's gospel ran completely counter to the religious, philosophical, social, and political currents of his day. At other times, Paul exploited what he knew for his own purposes by creating new social networks, redefining wisdom, and helping humans to see union with Christ as the greatest good one could pursue. Acquiring information about Paul's cultural context allows for a better understanding of him and greater insight into his letters.

Questions for Review and Reflection

1. Explain how patronage, rhetoric, and the imperial cult contributed to solidifying Roman imperial rule in the Mediterranean world.

2. What are four aspects of Paul's social, political, and religious world featured in this chapter that interested you and why?

3. What did each of the principal schools of philosophy discussed in this chapter propose as life's greatest good and the surest guarantee of happiness? What did Paul propose?

4. If you were a citizen of ancient Corinth in the first century ce, which philosophical school would have been most attractive to you and why?

5. Where in American culture can you find examples of groups that still operate with strong concern for honor, shame, and group identity?

6. Describe two ways that Roman imperial society is similar to and different from US society today.

Opening More Windows

Burkert, Walter. *Ancient Mystery Cults.* Cambridge, MA: Harvard University Press, 1987.

de Silva, David A. *Honor, Patronage, Kinship and Purity: Unlocking New Testament Culture.* Downers Grove, IL: InterVarsity Press, 2000.

Fay, Ron C. "Greco-Roman Concepts of Deity," in *Paul's World*, ed. S. E. Porter. Leiden, The Netherlands: Brill, 2008, 51–79.

Galinsky, Karl. *Augustan Culture.* Princeton, NJ: Princeton University Press, 1996.

Hornblower, Simon, and Tony Spawforth, eds. *The Oxford Companion to Classical Civilization.* New York: Oxford University Press, 2004.

_____, eds. *Who's Who in the Classical World.* New York: Oxford University Press, print 2003, online 2003.

Malherbe, Abraham J. *Moral Exhortation, A Greco-Roman Sourcebook.* Philadelphia: Westminster John Knox Press, 1989.

Meeks, Wayne. *The Moral World of the First Christians.* Philadelphia: Westminster John Knox Press, 1986, especially 40–64, on the Greco-Roman philosophical schools.

Meyer, Marvin W., ed. *The Ancient Mysteries: A Sourcebook of Sacred Texts.* Philadelphia: University of Pennsylvania Press, 1999.

Peachin, Michael, ed. *The Oxford Handbook of Social Relations in the Roman World.* New York: Oxford University Press, 2011.

Warrior, Valerie M. *Roman Religion.* New York: Cambridge University Press, 2006.

Wright, N. T. *Paul and the Faithfulness of God: Parts I & II.* Minneapolis, MN: Fortress Press, 2013, especially the first five chapters on "Paul and His World," 3–347.

Internet Resources

"Ostia Antica Chapter 5: Religions of the Roman World," YouTube video, 9:26, produced by the American Institute for Roman

Culture in collaboration with Northeastern University, *www. youtube.com/watch?v=cedaiFk-LFI.*

This video presents Roman religious practice using evidence from daily life at the ancient Roman port city of Ostia.

"The Roman Empire in the First Century, Episode 1: Order from Chaos." 2001: PBS Video, 54:16, *www.youtube.com/ watch?v=FOTjDpDay30.*

This video presents the rise and reign of Caesar Augustus.

Chapter 4

Paul's Good News
What God Has Done in Christ

Overview

This chapter begins with an explanation of apocalyptic eschatology, the conceptual framework Paul used to make sense of Christ's death and Resurrection. The focus then turns to Christ's role in God's redemptive historical plan for the world. This is followed by a consideration of the language Paul used to express the effects of God's saving work in Christ and its implications. The final section of this chapter considers how Paul's contemporaries may have responded to his "good news" of "Christ-crucified."

Recommended Reading

Daniel 7:1–12:13	Romans 5:1–11
Leviticus 4–7; 16–17	1 Corinthians 1:18–2:16
Romans 1:16–32	2 Corinthians 5:1–15
Romans 3:21–26	1 Thessalonians 4:13–5:11

Paul's Apocalyptic Worldview

Though Paul directed his evangelizing efforts and letters to Gentiles, his thought remained firmly rooted in Jewish ideas and tradition. Among other things, Paul shared with many first-century Jews an "apocalyptic eschatology." The phrase denotes a particular outlook on the world and human history, accompanied by a certain set of expectations. Stated succinctly, apocalyptic eschatology was rooted in the hope that God would intervene to overthrow the present evil age, after which a new age under God's sovereignty would be inaugurated. A consideration of this outlook is crucial to understanding how Paul interpreted the Christ-event (i.e., Christ's life, death, and Resurrection), within the scope of history as he understood it. However, this requires some explanation of the terms *eschatology* and *apocalyptic*.

The Greek word *eschaton* means "last" or "end." In biblical studies, broadly speaking, eschatology concerns the end-time, or future of Israel. In the prophetic literature, where eschatology becomes prominent, the end-time ("last days" or "end of the world") did not refer to the dissolution of the physical universe. Rather, the prophets anticipated the end of the present historical era, or age, which would culminate in divine judgment. After judgment, God would usher in a new age.[1] The prophets envisioned this age as a new earthly paradise characterized by longevity, well-being, harmony, cessation of war, and other idyllic conditions (see, e.g., Isa 65:16–25; Hos 2:18). An ideal messiah king from the line of David would rule over this new kingdom and uphold justice and righteousness (Isa 11:1–9, 9:7). Thus far from being a transcendent, other worldly reality, the new age would take place here and now in this world where Israel lived, via normal historical processes: "The present cosmos, created as 'good' by Yahweh but temporarily marred by injustice, infirmity, war and sin, and in general by evil, will be reclaimed and redeemed by God."[2] Thus the "end of the world" was not about its destruction but its transformation.

Anchored in the conviction of God's absolute sovereignty, prophetic eschatology was largely optimistic. The prophets believed that God was in charge of and active in this world and that all

---

1. It was expected that the dawn of the new age would be preceded by divine judgment and punishment of the unrighteous (see, e.g., Isa 24:1; Jer 25:33) and salvation for the just (see, e.g., Isa 25:9; Jer 39:17) who would live in the "new age" and enjoy the idyllic conditions.

2. Bill T. Arnold, "Old Testament Eschatology and the Rise of Apocalypticism," in *The Oxford Handbook of Eschatology*, ed. Jerry L. Walls (New York: Oxford University Press, 2008), 23–39, here 24.

history moved toward a fixed end (*eschaton*) according to God's plan. For the prophets then, history was never just history but always *salvation history*, because, in and through it, God was working out his salvific plan for the world. Within this redemptive-historical schema, the people of Israel had a privileged place and unique role to play in God's plan for the world. But the people of Israel failed, ignoring prophetic warnings to repent or face God's judgment. As a result, they suffered the loss of their land and were exiled to Babylon. After the Persians defeated the Babylonians, the exiles were permitted to go back to Judah, beginning ca. 539 bce, but their return was fraught with physical hardships (see, e.g., Hag 1:6–11) and ideological differences with those who had remained in the land (see, e.g., Ezra 4:1–4). Despite the challenges, postexilic prophets continued to express a positive eschatological vision of a renewed and transformed world under an ideal ruler (see, e.g., Zech 8:1–14, 11:15–16, 14:6–9; Isa 25:6–10). This hope remained alive even though after returning to Judea, the Jews lived under the rule of successive foreign occupiers. As previously noted, the Jews did attain a brief period of relative independence from 164 bce to 63 bce resulting from the Maccabean Revolt. This attainment intensified their apocalyptic hopes that God's kingdom would soon come, and all foreign rulers would be vanquished.

The adjective *apocalyptic* and noun *apocalypse* both derive from the Greek verb *apocalyptein*, which means to reveal or disclose. Biblical scholars refer to a text disclosing divine plans as an "apocalypse," a genre of writing with distinct literary features. Apocalypses contained divine revelation on a variety of topics, but apocalyptic literature focused primarily on the end-time, specifically how, and how far into the future, the end-time events would occur when God would intervene to save his faithful from hostile forces.[3] These plans were a secret, known only to God, until revealed, usually via dreams and visions, to a special individual who makes them known to others. The Bible contains two apocalypses,

---

3. On apocalyptic thought and literature, see Paul D. Hanson, "Apocalypse and Apocalypticism," in *The Anchor Bible Dictionary*, ed. David N. Freedman (New York: Doubleday, 1992), vol. 1, 280–81; John J. Collins, "Early Jewish Apocalypticism," *Anchor Bible Dictionary*, vol. 1, 282–87.

the book of Daniel[4] in the Hebrew Bible and Revelation in the New Testament, which record the divine revelations given to Daniel and John, respectively.[5]

Apocalyptic thought seems to have arisen in the latter half of the third century bce. By then the Jews had been under Greek rule for almost one hundred years, following more than two hundred years of subjectivity to the Persians and before them, the Babylonians. As evident from the literature associated with it, apocalyptic thought reflects both the despair and hope of the Jewish people: despair over the present course of human history and their current plight, and hope in the power of God and his promised Messiah to redeem and liberate them. While the origins of "apocalyptic eschatology" cannot be known with certainty, many maintain that it grew gradually out of prophetic eschatology.[6] As biblical scholar Paul Hanson notes, "Common to both is the belief that, in accordance with the divine plan, the adverse conditions of the present world would end in judgment of the wicked and vindication of the righteous, thereby ushering in a new era of prosperity and peace."[7] In contrast to prophetic eschatology, apocalyptic eschatology was characterized by a sharp dualism: on one side were God's faithful ones; on the other, the evil ones who opposed God's will and oppressed his people. This dualism is apparent in the language used by the Qumran covenanters, who referred to themselves as the justice-seeking "sons of light"(see, e.g., 1QS III.13: 1QM I:1,8) in contrast to the "sons of darkness" and "deceit" (see, e.g., 1QM I.10–17; 1QS III.13:

---

4. Chapters 1–6 relate stories of Daniel's faithfulness on account of which the Lord rescues him from death. The apocalypse proper extends from 7:1 to 12:13 where the hidden revelation is given.

5. Between the second century bce and the second century ce, many other apocalypses were written that were not included in the Bible. There is no agreed-upon list of noncanonical Jewish apocalypses, but the following are generally regarded as apocalypses: *1 Enoch, Apocalypse of Zephaniah, Apocalypse of Abraham, 2 Enoch, 4 Ezra* 3–14, and *2* and *3 Baruch*. Examples of noncanonical Christian apocalypses are *Apocalypse of Paul; Apocalypse of Peter; First* and *Second Apocalypse of James;* and *Apocalypse of Blessed John.*

6. On the origins of apocalyptic eschatology, see John J. Collins, "Apocalyptic Eschatology in the Ancient World," in *The Oxford Handbook of Eschatology,* ed. Jerry L. Walls (New York: Oxford University Press, 2008), 40–55.

7. Hanson, "Apocalypse and Apocalypticism," 280.

21–22). Apocalyptic eschatology also introduced a cosmic perspective in which the unrighteous foreign rulers were depicted as tools of evil cosmic powers. Belial, the leader of the forces of darkness, assisted these rulers (see, e.g., 1QM XVI.11; Testament of Levi 19:1; Testament of Naphtali 2:6, 3:1; 1QMXV:15–17). Thus within the processes of human history, a battle between good and evil was playing out that was cosmic in scope. Since the world was so evil, and the evil so insuperable, apocalyptic-minded Jews believed nothing short of a divine cosmic intervention could save them. They believed God stood poised to act and would judge and destroy those oppressing his faithful ones. In this catastrophic clash between good and evil, God would unleash his wrath against the evildoers and the cosmic powers operating through them. When the destruction was complete, the crossover from the present evil age to the new age would begin. God's kingdom or rule would be established, signaling the inauguration of the new age. The righteous, vindicated by God's saving intervention, would finally live in peace under God's sovereignty. For the faithful who had suffered persecution and death, a blessed eternity awaited (see Dan 12:2). First-century-ce Jews, including Jesus, lived with a sense of expectancy that the reign of God was close at hand. In fact, Jesus began his public ministry proclaiming, "the time is fulfilled and the Kingdom of God has come near." (Mark 1:15; cf. Matt 4:15). Pious Jews everywhere believed that at any moment, God would intervene to deliver them from the present age and inaugurate the new age.

Paul not only shared this "two-age" view of history, he also was convinced that the time of judgment had already arrived, as evidenced at Romans 1:18, where he declares "the wrath of God is revealed from heaven against all ungodliness." Elsewhere, he refers to himself and other believers as the generation "on whom the end of the ages have come" (1 Cor 10:11)—the ones already living in the new age of eschatological redemption and fulfillment (cf. 2 Cor 5:17, 6:2). But how did Paul get the idea that the crossover from the old to the new age had taken place? When and how had God dramatically intervened to destroy the evil rulers of this age and the cosmic forces controlling them? Weren't Paul and his contemporaries still living under Roman rule, under the power of forces hostile to God and his people?

Two Aeon Schema Envisioned in Jewish Apocalyptic

The Present Aeon or Age	The New Aeon or Age to Come
Characteristics • Irredeemably evil • Ruled by evil powers • Injustice, sin, and death reign • Corruptibility	Characteristics • New age is good • God rules through an earthly king • God dwells in the world through his Spirit • Incorruptibility and new life

Essentially, Paul took the ideas and two-age schema of apocalyptic eschatology and read them through the lens of Jesus Christ, convinced that the transition from the present evil age to the new age hinged on Christ's death and Resurrection. Because in apocalyptic thought the arrival of the new age was associated with both the overcoming of powers hostile to God and the resurrection of the dead, Christ's death and Resurrection convinced Paul that the new age had begun.[8] Thus he insisted that Christ's death and Resurrection was the long-awaited eschatological (end-time) salvation event through which God had acted decisively in history, ending one historical age and inaugurating the new age of renewed existence that Jewish tradition associated with the end-time. Paul was convinced believers were living at a crucial juncture point—the very time the crossover of the ages had begun! The world in its present form was passing away (1 Cor 7:31, 10:11); the new order was beginning (2 Cor 5:17). Paul also insisted that God had devised his program of redemptive historical salvation in Christ before the ages, but kept it "secret and hidden" (1 Cor 2:7, 4:1). Now it had been revealed to Paul, who was charged with making known the divine mystery of salvation. According to Paul, only those who have received the gift of God's Spirit can fathom this mystery (1 Cor 2:7–14).

---

8. On the apocalyptic framework for Paul's understanding of Christ's death and Resurrection, see J. Christiaan Beker, *The Triumph of God: The Essence of Paul's Thought*, trans. Loren T. Stuckenbruck (Minneapolis, MN: Fortress Press, 1990), 65–87.

Paul introduced at least two notable variations on the two-age category of Jewish apocalyptic. First, Paul traces the "present evil age" to Adam, through whom sin and death were introduced into the world (see Rom 5:12–21), a point considered in more detail in chapter 5. Second, he envisions the new age as already *inaugurated* by Christ's death and Resurrection but still awaiting its *complete fulfillment* in the future, when Christ returns. For Paul, two things await completion at the second coming. These are first, the final destruction of every hostile power, climaxing with the obliteration of death, which has been in process since Christ's death and Resurrection (1 Cor 15:24–27); and second, the establishment of God's reign in its fullness, when believers will be filled with God's power and presence, and God will be "all in all" (1 Cor 15:28). As the following chart illustrates, in Paul's envisioning of the two ages of Jewish apocalyptic, the present evil age includes all history from the time of Adam. The new age is expanded to accommodate a future consummation of God's kingdom at Christ's second coming.

The Present Age	The New Age	
From Adam up to the time of Christ	*Inaugurated* with the death and Resurrection of Christ	*Fulfilled* when Christ returns
Characteristics • Satan • Sin • Death	Characteristics • Christ • Reconciliation • New resurrected life in Christ	Characteristics • God's invisible rule is complete and permanent
	Believers live between the inauguration of the new age, which is *now*,	and its completion, which is still in the *future*

Since the new age had "already" begun, but was "not yet" here in all its fullness, believers were in a period of waiting (1 Thess 1:10; Phil 3:20). They were living between two times: the time of the beginning of this new age and the time of Christ's *parousia*, literally "arrival," when he would return from heaven. Paul's Jewish contemporaries expected the return of Elijah, so the idea that someone who had left Earth could return was familiar to them.[9] But the Judaism of Paul's day had no precedent for the expectation that a crucified and vindicated Messiah would return to Earth.[10] This idea was unique to Christians, who expected and prayed for the Lord's quick return (1 Cor 16:22).[11] Paul expected to be alive for the second coming, as 1 Thessalonians 4:15 makes clear: "For this we declare to you by the word of the Lord that we who are alive, who are left until the coming of the Lord will by no means precede those who have died."[12] He apparently taught his first converts that they also would be alive, which probably explains why the death of some believers in Thessalonica, before Christ's return, created a pastoral crisis to which Paul responded at 1 Thessalonians 4:13–17.

Paul conceived of the "in-between" time as a brief, yet very critical period (see, e.g., 1 Cor 7:29). There was no time for backsliding (Rom 6:12–13). He expected believers to live with a heightened sense of expectation of Christ's imminent return (Rom 13:11b–12a; further 1 Thess 1:10, 5:5–10; Phil 4:20) when he would come to judge humans (1 Cor 4:4–5). Whether Paul actually expected Christ to literally descend and reign over a world renewed and transformed through his death and Resurrection (see Rom 8:18–27) is not certain. In other passages, such as Philippians 1:12–26 and 2 Corinthians 5:1–10, Paul describes renewed existence not as a collective experience here on Earth, but as an individual phenomenon to be experienced in an otherworldly, transcendent place.

In brief, Paul took over the categories of Jewish apocalyptic and reread them through the lens of Christ, insisting God's long-awaited

---

9. According to tradition, Elijah, a ninth-century-bce prophet, was taken up into heaven on a fiery chariot as his disciple Elisha watched (see 2 Kgs 2:1–12). The prophet Malachi foretold Elijah's return (see Mal 4:5).

10. On this point, see James D. G. Dunn, *The Theology of Paul the Apostle* (Grand Rapids, MI: William B. Eerdmans, 1998), 294–98.

11. The Aramaic phrase, *maranâthâ*, which occurs just once in the NT at 1 Corinthians 16:22, is translated in both the NRSV and NAB, rev. ed., as "Our Lord, come!" It is understood as a prayer for the early return of Christ that was probably used in the early Christian liturgy.

12. During the imprisonment in which he wrote Philippians, a letter composed after 1 Thessalonians, Paul may have entertained the possibility that he would die before the Lord's second coming, (see Phil 2:17).

intervention had already taken place in the Christ's death and Resurrection. The destruction of the old age and defeat of the powers had begun, as had the inauguration of the new age. Believers now lived in faithful anticipation of its consummation.

What God Has Done in Christ

As much as Paul's teaching about salvation revolves around the Christ-event, he never understood or presented Christ as a self-anointed savior who decided to take up humanity's cause on his own initiative and sacrifice himself on the cross in order to save the world. Paul completely shared the Jewish theocentric view of history. He believed God alone was in charge of history, through which God unfolds his salvific plan for the world. Paul asserts that this redemptive historical plan climaxed and was ultimately accomplished through the death and Resurrection of Jesus. However, it was God who sent his Son (Gal 4:4; Rom 8:3), and God who raised Jesus from the dead and who will raise us (Rom 4:24, 8:11; 1 Cor 6:14, 15:15). It was God whose righteousness was revealed in the gospel (Rom 1:17), and God who destined humanity to obtain salvation through Christ, who died for our trespasses and was raised for our justification (Rom 4: 25; 1 Thess 5:10). For Paul, the initiative is God's. He always keeps a theocentric focus: what God has done in Christ. That emphasis shapes Paul's understanding of Christ's death in God's plan.

Christ's Role in God's Plan to Save

Two words, "Christ crucified" (1 Cor 1:23), sum up the content of the gospel that Paul said he was sent to preach. Three words, "for our sins" (1 Cor 15:3), sum up the purpose of Christ's death. In dying on the cross, Christ did something for humans. He atoned for their transgressions, which estranged them from God. With his usual stress on God's initiative, Paul says at Romans 3:24–25 that redemption is "in Christ Jesus whom God put forward as a sacrifice of atonement by his blood . . ."

Sacrifice played an integral part in biblical religion. Leviticus 1–7 contains detailed instructions about the various types of sacrifices, their distinct purposes, and how to perform them. Those

Fragment of a marble relief ca. 15–16 CE, Louvre Museum, Paris. Animal sacrifice was a ritual element common to all ancient religions. This panel from a Roman sarcophagus depicts the sacrifice of a pig, sheep, and bull to the god Mars.

through which humans atoned or expiated their sins ranked among the most important. This usually required the slaughter and offering of an animal whose blood was smeared on the altar (see, e.g., Lev 5:9). Leviticus does not explain exactly how sacrificing an animal atoned for human transgression, but it had something to do with shedding blood. According to Leviticus 17:10, God prohibited eating blood. The reason given was that "the life of the flesh is in the blood; and I have given it to you for making atonement for your lives on the altar; for as life, it is the blood that makes atonement" (17:11). Thus the blood of a sacrificed animal, poured out on the altar, constituted an offering of life that apparently did two things. It conserved the life of the human sinner, who presumably merited death, and it atoned for, or erased, human transgressions, which interrupted right relations with God. This sacrificial framework assumed that atonement for human sin could be achieved vicariously. That is, an animal, incapable of sin, could substitute for a human, whose sins would be atoned for through the shedding of the animal's blood rather than the sinner's own. Animal sacrifice was not the only means to achieve vicarious atonement. Fourth Maccabees mentions that the blood of Jewish martyrs was considered an atoning sacrifice benefiting the whole Jewish people. [13]

---

13. "And through the blood of those devout ones and their death as an atoning sacrifice, divine Providence preserved Israel that previously had been mistreated" (4 Macc 17:22).

Paul obviously borrowed categories from the Jewish cult to explain Christ's role in God's salvific plan. He insists that Christ's blood atones for sins (Rom 3:24–25) and is the source of the believer's justification (Rom 5:9). He also emphasizes the vicarious nature of Christ's death: "for our sins" (1 Cor 15:3); "for our trespasses" (Rom 4:25); "for all" (2 Cor 5:14); "for our sake he made him to be sin who knew no sin, so that in him we might become the righteousness of God" (2 Cor 5:21).

Paul's Language to Express What God Has Done in Christ

Paul uses about ten different images to describe what happens to believers as a result of what God has done in Christ.[14] For example, he speaks about believers as freed, sanctified, transformed, redeemed, a new creation. Each image affords a slightly different insight about the benefits believers now enjoy because of God's act in Christ.[15]

The English term *reconcile* translates the compound Greek verb *katallassein* (*kata* + *allassein*), which literally means to "make otherwise" in the sense of changing a condition. When used with reference to social relations, it implies a change from hostility and anger to peace and friendship. In using this verb, Paul presents what God has done in Christ as the restoring of peace and right relations between God and all humans and all humans with each other (see Rom 5:10 [2x]; 2 Cor 5:18–19). Thus when Paul says believers have "peace" with God (Rom 5:1) and have received "reconciliation" (*katallagē*, Rom 5:11), he is effectively saying the same thing. Since Paul continuously speaks about God's reconciling activity in Christ in relation to humans, one could understandably interpret reconciliation in strictly

---

14. Joseph Fitzmyer provides a concise but informative discussion of Paul's ten images, cf. *Paul and His Theology: A Brief Sketch* (Saddle River, NJ: Prentice Hall, 1989), 59–71.

15. Information about Paul's terminology is based on entries in Gerhard Kittel and Gerhard Friedrich (eds.), *Theological Dictionary of the New Testament*, 10 vols., trans. G. W. Bromiley (Grand Rapids, MI: William B. Eerdmans, 1964–76). This multivolume resource covers terms Paul used and their origin. Also useful is Verlyn Verbrugge (ed.), *New International Dictionary of New Testament Theology*, abridged ed. (Grand Rapids, MI: Zondervan, 2003).

anthropomorphic terms. However, Paul does not limit God's reconciling activity to humans. Rather, he sees it as embracing the whole
world (2 Cor 5:19), which along with its human inhabitants awaits
complete liberation (Rom 8:18–25). In the meantime, Paul's mission
consists of calling men and women to be reconciled to God. This
"ministry of reconciliation" is not Paul's initiative, but God's, who has
entrusted it to Paul (2 Cor 5:18).

Paul tells believers that as a result of the Christ-event, they
have "redemption." Behind the word *redemption* is the Greek noun
apolytrōsis and the related act of buying, *agorazein*. Paul may have
picked up the imagery of redemption and buying from a common
social practice in his day involving the emancipation of slaves.[16]
Either the slave, or someone acting on the slave's behalf, would hand
over money in exchange for freedom from bondage. When Paul uses
the language of redemption, he conveys the image of God redeeming
humans through the death of Jesus, understood as the price paid to
purchase the release of humans from enslavement to sin and death.
Paul makes this explicit at 1 Corinthians 6:19–20 and 7:23, where he
reminds believers, "You were bought with a price." In Paul's thought,
being bought back *from* the slavery of sin and death by God has a
corollary: reenslavement to God in Christ, which leads to eternal
life (Rom 6:22, 7:20–23). The image of the believer as freed (*eleu-
theros*) relates to the image of redemption. However, this is not a
freedom to live licentiously and become enslaved again to sin (Gal
5:1, 13). Rather, believers enjoy this freedom in order to live for
God in Christ.

The imagery of redemption from slavery and Paul's conceptualization of true freedom as a reenslavement to God likely have
little appeal for contemporary audiences. However, Paul's readers
would have been familiar with transactions involving the emancipation of slaves. This imagery gave Paul one more avenue to express
the saving significance of Christ's death in a way comprehensible to
his first converts.

Of all the images Paul employs to describe the effects of the
Christ-event, he uses the justification of believers most frequently.

---

16. But Paul may also be drawing on texts from the Hebrew Bible concerning the
buying and emancipation of slaves, as well as other texts featuring God as redeemer
(*gōʾēl*). See comments by Fitzmyer, *Paul and His Theology*, 66–67.

This image has also generated the most debate.[17] Behind the notion of justification lies a group of words all built on the same Greek root: the noun *dikaiosynē*, which means "righteousness"; the adjective *dikaios*, which means "righteous"; and the verb *dikaioun*, which means "to righteous" or "to right something." Since "to righteous" does not exist in English, *dikaioun* is usually translated "to justify," "to rectify," or "to make righteous." Paul borrows the justification language from the courtroom context. When a person standing before a tribunal was acquitted of a crime, the person was pronounced righteous (*dikaios*). By applying this image to the Christ-event, Paul effectively communicates that humans are acquitted and found righteous in the sight of God on account of Christ, who by his blood, "became for us . . . righteousness." (1 Cor 1:30). Benefiting from God's justifying activity in Christ, which Paul says comes about by the gift of God's freely given grace, requires faith (Rom 3:24–25), for through faith in Christ[18] a person is justified (see Gal 2:15–16; Phil 3:9).

Paul's Imagery and Its Implications

Paul's conceptualization of Christ's death as an atonement sacrifice for sin and the language he uses to describe what God has accomplished through this sacrifice create a redemptive historical scenario familiar to most Christians. In it, humans are sinners meriting the death penalty. They are enslaved to sin and live as enemies of God. God, on the other hand, is loving and compassionate. Rather than

---

17. One aspect of the debate, which goes back to the sixteenth century, concerns whether the process of justification causes an internal transformation of the sinner (Catholic position) or whether the sinner remains a sinner while at the same time being declared righteous on account of his/her faith in Christ (Protestant position). On the state of the debate, in its many aspects, see David E. Aune (ed.), *Rereading Paul Together: Protestant and Catholic Perspectives on Justification* (Grand Rapids, MI: Baker Academic, 2006).

18. The Greek phrase *pistis Christou* can be translated either as a subjective genitive, "the faith OF Christ," or as an objective genitive, "faith IN Christ." Scholars debate whether Paul intended to say that salvation results from humans' faith or from Christ's own faithfulness to God's salvific plan. James D. G. Dunn, who leans toward the objective rendering, provides a concise analysis of Paul's use of the phrase; see *The Theology of Paul the Apostle* (Grand Rapids, MI: William B. Eerdmans, 1998), 379–84. On the drawbacks of both interpretations, see Matthew C. Easter, "The *Pistis Christou* Debate: Main Arguments and Responses in Summary," *Currents in Biblical Research* 9.1 (2010): 33–47.

condemning humans to the death they deserve, God puts forth Christ as a sacrifice to die in place of humans and pour out his blood on their behalf (Rom 3:5; 2 Cor 5:21). God does not wait for humans to repent or seek forgiveness. Instead, as proof of his love, he saves and reconciles humans to himself while they are still weak, ungodly sinners (Rom 5:6–8). As a result, humans are spared the death penalty. They are acquitted of wrongdoing on account of Christ's act of righteousness, which was his death (Rom 5:18). Right relations with God, interrupted by their transgressions, are now restored.

As noted, this scenario echoes courtroom procedures (crime, judgment, condemnation to death, or acquittal) and relies on forensic, or judicial, language to portray Christ's role in God's salvific plan. However, many New Testament scholars argue that this complex of ideas, which focus on death as sacrifice and depend on juridical categories such as acquittal and justification, does not reflect Paul's true understanding of Christ's death. According to New Testament scholar E. P. Sanders, a prominent advocate of this view, "There can be no doubt as to where the heart of Paul's theology lies. He is not primarily concerned with juristic categories, although he works with them."[19] Sanders goes on to insist that the real heart of Paul's theology lies in his insight that Christ's death was a "dying to sin" in which believers "participate" through baptism. Dying *with* Christ in baptism frees believers from sin's grip, which remained inescapable while they lived. Having died to sin, they emerge from baptism to new life under Christ's Lordship. In this scenario, Christ does not die as a substitute for humans. Rather, humans die *with* Christ, which brings about their transfer from the realm of sin and death to the realm of Christ. Scholars point to Paul's insights about the participatory significance of Christ's death (e.g., Rom 6:3–11, 7:4, 8:1), where dying *with* Christ to sin, life *in* Christ, and belonging to Christ figure prominently.[20] Curiously, these key texts where Paul's concern focuses

---

19. E. P. Sanders, *Paul and Palestinian Judaism* (London: SCM, 1977), 502. Sanders' statement is preceded by a lengthy discussion of Pauline soteriology, which begins on p. 431.

20. Other passages cited to show that Paul's focus was really "participation" in Christ are Galatians 2:20, 2 Corinthians 5:17, and Philippians 3:10. Sanders considers Romans 8:3, 2 Corinthians 5:21, and Galatians 3:16, texts he refers to as the "foundation stones of the substitution theory," to be primarily participationist (cf. *Paul and Palestinian Judaism*, 466).

on "participation" in Christ's dying and life appear also in Romans. They follow the texts cited above from Romans 3, 4, and 5, which illustrate Paul's sacrificial understanding of Christ's death.

Scholars who insist that Paul's central understanding of Christ's death revolves around its "participatory" character offer two arguments. First, they argue that where Paul uses sacrificial language, he is simply repeating tradition. This seems certain at 1 Corinthians 15:3, where he specifies, "For I handed on . . . what I in turn had received: that Christ died for our sins . . ." Sometimes odd phrasing not typical of Paul (see 1 Thess 1:9–10) might suggest he cites tradition. It may even be the case that Paul repeats a primitive Christian creedal statement when he says, "We believe that Jesus died and rose again" (1 Thess 4:14). However, apart from Paul's explicit say-so, there is no certain way to confirm when he is citing tradition. Even if Paul does simply repeat tradition every time he refers to the sacrificial character of Christ's death, the implicit assumption that tradition does not contain what Paul finds most significant about Christ's death is questionable.

The second argument holds that apart from Romans and Galatians, Paul does not develop his sacrificial/juridical understanding of Christ's death in his other letters. However, he does develop his "participatory" focus, as shown by the recurring emphasis on being *in* Christ and union *with* Christ found throughout his letters.[21] While true, this fact does not necessarily mean that unless Paul develops a theme in every letter, he deemed it less important. Given the "occasional" character of Paul's letters, it may be that the situations Paul addressed in Romans and Galatians required his emphasis on the juridical effects of Christ's sacrificial death, whereas the situations eliciting his other letters did not. In the end, what can be known for certain is this: Jesus was crucified and died. Already in primitive Christianity, that bare historical fact took on theological significance when Christ's death was interpreted as being "for our sins" (1 Cor 15:3). In his own letters, even in the same letter, Paul speaks of the function and significance of Christ's death in two different ways. Perhaps in Paul's mind, neither the juridical nor the participatory category alone could express the full significance of Christ's death in God's salvific plan.[22]

---

21. See Sanders, *Paul and Palestinian Judaism*, 503.

22. See further, Peter Stuhlmacher, *Revisiting Paul's Doctrine of Justification* (Downers Grove, IL: InterVarsity Press, 2001), esp. 55–60.

The Reception of the Good News: Jews, Gentiles, and Christ Crucified

Although much is known about Paul's thought and the language he chose to convey it, information about audience reaction to his gospel is harder to determine. There is no independent account of what the first hearers of Paul's gospel thought or to what degree they accepted and lived by it. What can be known is limited to information retrieved from Paul's letters, which essentially consists of Paul's description of how people or types of people responded to the gospel.

Even if Paul expressed his understanding of what God had done in Christ using images familiar to his contemporaries, his gospel must have sounded bizarre to those who first heard it. How was "Christ-crucified" good news, and what exactly was in it for hustling city people trying to scratch out a living, whether as shopkeepers, bakers, or tavernkeepers? Paul's gospel certainly did not stack up well against the imperial gospel of power and victory. Yet Paul insisted that the gospel he preached *is* power: "the power of God for salvation to everyone who has faith, to the Jew first and also to the Greek" (Rom 1:16). It is the power of God, Paul explains, because through Christ-crucified, God's justifying activity—that is, his righteousness—is revealed (Rom 1:17). In 1 Corinthians, which he wrote a few years earlier than Romans, Paul also refers to Christ-crucified as God's power to save and provides insight about how his contemporaries may have reacted to his "good news."

First Corinthians addressed a community deeply divided on a number of religious issues. As Paul saw it, the Corinthians had been blessed with spiritual gifts and insight (1 Cor 1:5), but they failed to see that because the Christ-event inaugurated a new age they needed to live entirely different lives based on new values rooted in Christ-crucified. For this reason, Paul tackles the crisis at Corinth by focusing their attention on the cross in the first chapter of the letter.

Beginning at 1 Corinthians 1:18, Paul reframes the notion of power in the revelation of Christ crucified. He insists that the "word of the cross," here a synonym for the gospel, is *the power of God*. Thus in the starkest terms possible, Paul asserts that the message of

© Album / Art Resource, NY

Thermopolium of Asellina, Pompeii, a tavern selling hot food and drinks. The food and drinks were stored in terra cotta containers that sat in openings in the bar. The rear-wall fresco depicts the household's Genius, flanked by the *lares*. Asellina's tavern had an upper floor with rooms that may have been used as a brothel.

the crucified messiah is inseparable from the activity of God, who manifests his power through the cross. In fact, the cross is all about God's power and wisdom, which turns human wisdom and ideas about power upside down. According to Paul (v. 19), the divine over-throw of human wisdom was part of God's plan to save humanity. As evidence Paul cites Isaiah 29:14, where God says, "I will destroy the wisdom of the wise and the discernment of the discerning I will thwart."[23] In its original context, the Isaiah saying was directed to the Israelites who showed arrogance and indifference toward God,

23. Other translations of 1 Corinthians 1:19 include "I will destroy the wisdom of the wise; the intelligence of the intelligent I will frustrate" (NIV); "I will destroy the wisdom of the wise and the learning of the learned I will set aside" (NAB rev. ed.)

presuming to have a superior wisdom by which to live. Paul interprets this passage eschatologically and claims that God's plan to nullify human wisdom was happening now in the cross, in the Crucified One. It results in division—some will understand and be saved, some will not—because in the cross, God self-reveals where no one, not even Paul before God disclosed it to him, expected to find God's self-revelation. Paul says even the sharpest thinkers of his day are incapable of seeing in Christ-crucified God's power to save (v. 20) because they think like humans. According to human standards and values, crucifixion—a punishment reserved for common criminals—does not add up to any kind of wisdom or power, let alone divine wisdom and power. It adds up to weakness and shame.

Paul presents reactions to the message of the cross via the two groups of people he knows best, Jews and Greeks. Jews wanted *signs* (1:22; see also Luke 11:15–20; Mark 8:11–13; Matt 12:38–39). They were accustomed to a God who did incredible signs and wonders. That was how God had displayed his power and saved them in the past. It seemed scandalous to even suggest that the God who parted the sea, fed his people with manna in the desert, and brought them back from Babylonian captivity would demonstrate his power in weakness and especially in a crucified man whom every Jew would consider cursed by God (Deut 21:23; Gal 3:13–14).

Greeks, on the other hand, sought wisdom (1:22). As noted in chapter 3, pagans turned to philosophy to learn practical insights and strategies to achieve power, success, honor, and self-fulfillment. In Greco-Roman society, those attributes were the markers of the truly wise, spiritual, self-fulfilled person. For highly competitive, status-seeking pagans, the cross signified everything counter to what they sought. To say Christ crucified *is* either power or wisdom seemed sheer foolishness to them.

Jews and Greeks differed about manifestations of divine wisdom and power, but they agreed that it was not in the cross and the inversion of values it symbolized: power in weakness, wisdom in absurdity, glory in humility, self-emptying rather than self-fulfillment. Yet Paul insisted that authentic Christian living meant living out this paradox springing from the recognition that in Christ-crucified, one encounters the supreme wisdom and power of God. Without God's grace, no one can understand this—not because humans lack intelligence, but because human intelligence apart from grace is incapable of knowing God (1:21, 2:11–12). Paul illustrates this point at Romans 1:19–25. He observes that although humans are capable of knowing God through the created order, they always misconstrue God and wind up creating gods in their own image. As Paul sees it, human intelligence always leads to idolatry—to the creation of God in one's own image (Rom 1:22–23).[24] Just as a flat map of the round world distorts one's sense of geography, Paul insists that human intelligence distorts human understanding of God and God's ways. Humans have a flat view of a round God, so to speak. They perceive God's wisdom as absurdity and absurdity as wisdom and God's power as weakness and weakness as power.

In deciding "to know nothing . . . except Jesus Christ, and him crucified" (1 Cor 2:2), Paul acknowledges that his perception, his way of knowing God, underwent a radical change. He could now see in Christ-crucified not only God's wisdom and power but also God's reconciling love (Rom 5:6–11). Eventually, he even came to boast in Christ-crucified (Gal 6:14). Not everyone experienced the epistemic shift—the changed way of knowing God—that Paul was graced to experience. Jews in a number of cities are featured as especially resistant to Paul's "good news" (cf., e.g., Acts 17:1–9, 18:12–17) and more than a few pagans resisted as well (Acts 19:23–27, 17:16–34).[25] Paul's own letters indicate some wavering even among baptized believers, whether Jew and Gentile. In Philippi and Galatia, some believers doubted whether faith alone in Christ-crucified was enough for salvation. Paul's rivals, who contradicted his preaching about how God saves, often triggered these doubts. Throughout the letter to the Galatians, Paul argues forcefully to keep believers focused on God's offer of salvation in and through Christ (see also Phil 3:2–16).

---

24. The author of 2 Clement also linked flawed understanding and idolatry: "Our minds were blinded, and we worshipped stones and wood and gold and silver and brass, the works of men," see Michael W. Holmes (ed.), *The Apostolic Fathers: Greek Texts and English Translation*, rev. ed. (Grand Rapids, MI: Baker Book, 1999), 1:6.

25. Sociologist Rodney Stark estimates that by 60 ce, there were just fewer than 2,000 Christians throughout the empire; see, *The Rise of Christianity* (San Francisco: Harper Collins, 1997), 4–12, esp. Table 1.1, p. 7.

Others rejected the inverted value system and other-centered behavior associated with the cross. They continued to fight for honor and status; boasted in human leaders, which fueled rivalries; and acted out of selfish ambition and conceit (see, e.g., 1 Cor 1:10–17, 4:6–21; Phil 2:1–5). Decades after Paul's death, the competitive, divisive situation worsened in Corinth, as attested in a letter of Clement of Rome, who wrote to admonish the Corinthians for their behavior.[26] Like Paul, some men and women were also radically transformed by the gospel. Paul partnered with them in the ministry of the gospel and commended them to others (see, e.g., Phil 2:19–24; 1 Cor 4:17; 2 Cor 8:23; Rom 16:3). However, the radically transformed who shared Paul's profound understanding of the gospel seem to have been the minority. The famous historian and classicist Ramsay MacMullan observed, "Christianity presented ideas that demanded a choice, not tolerance; and while some lay easily within the bounds of the acceptable, others were a lot harder to swallow."[27] Paul's good news that in Christ-crucified one encounters God's offer of salvation obviously fell among the latter.

Summary

Like other Jewish monotheists, Paul firmly believed that God controlled history and worked through historical processes to unfold his redemptive plan for the world. Paul also came to believe what many would reject as absurd and scandalous; that is, in the Christ-event, God had acted definitively in history to redeem the world. By using Jewish apocalyptic as his conceptual framework, Paul integrated the Christ-event into God's historical redemptive plan for the world. Paul did not view the Christ-event as just one more development or stage in God's plan to save and restore the world, but as its climax and fulfillment. Through language and imagery borrowed from both religious and secular spheres, Paul expressed his understanding of Christ's role in God's plan and its many effects. With his stress on Jesus Christ-crucified, the power and

---

26. See 1 Clement 47:1–3, available also at *www.ccel.org/ccel/schaff/anf01.pdf.*

27. Ramsay MacMullan, *Christianizing the Roman Empire* A.D. *100–400* (New Haven, CT: Yale University Press, 1984), 17.

wisdom of God, Paul introduced language into early Christianity that eventually became the hallmark of the later Christian tradition. According to German theologian Hans Kung, in his insistent proclamation of "Jesus Christ, and him crucified" (1 Cor 2:2), as the ground, norm, and content of his gospel, Paul succeeded more clearly than anyone in expressing the ultimate distinctive feature of Christianity.[28] Paul used various concepts and images to make this message as intelligible as possible. He did this not primarily as a matter of theological exposition, but as a basis for praxis. For Paul, belief in Christ was meaningless apart from patterning one's life after his (see Rom 15:1–3; 1 Cor 11:1).

Questions for Review and Reflection

1. Describe "prophetic eschatology" and "apocalyptic eschatology." How are they different?

2. How does Paul frame the Christ-event within the context of Jewish apocalyptic thought? What variations did Paul introduce into the two-age schema of Jewish apocalyptic?

3. What is meant by a Jewish theocentric view of history? How does Paul maintain this same focus?

4. How does Paul use the following images to explain God's action in the Christ-event to his listeners: reconciliation, redemption, justification, and righteousness?

5. How does the juridical understanding of Christ's death differ from the participationist understanding?

6. Why was Paul's gospel of a crucified messiah unappealing to Jews and Greeks of his day? Why might it still be unappealing to people today?

Opening More Windows

Beker, J. Christiaan. *Paul's Apocalyptic Gospel: The Coming Triumph of God.* Philadelphia: Fortress Press, 1982.

---

28. Hans Küng, *On Being a Christian* (Garden City, NY: Doubleday, 1976), 409–10.

_____. *Paul the Apostle*. Philadelphia: Fortress Press, 1980.

Finlan, Stephen. *Options on Atonement in Christian Thought*. Collegeville, MN: Liturgical Press, 2007.

_____. *Problems with Atonement: The Origins of, and Controversy about, the Atonement Doctrine*. Collegeville, MN: Liturgical Press, 2005.

Madigan, Kevin J., and Jon D. Levinson. *Resurrection: The Power of God for Christians and Jews*. New Haven, CT: Yale University, 2008.

Penna, Romano. *Paul the Apostle: Jews and Greeks Alike*, vol. 1, trans. Thomas P. Wahl. Collegeville, MN: Liturgical Press, 1996.

_____. *Paul the Apostle. Wisdom and Folly of the Cross*, vol. 2, trans. Thomas P. Wahl. Collegeville, MN: Liturgical Press, 1996.

Chapter 5

Why and From What Did Humans Need to Be Saved?

Overview

In Romans 1–3, Paul argues that all humans are under the power of Sin and are saved, whether Jew or Gentile, the same way: in Christ. The chapter considers Paul's explanation of how humans found themselves in this enslaved state. This involves examining the figure of Adam, Paul's anthropology, and key terms associated with Adamic existence. According to Paul, Christ, the new Adam, rescued humans from Sin and death. Next, the chapter examines Paul's discussion of how that happens and what it means to be humanity in Christ. The final section raises questions about Paul's insistence on the necessity of faith and whether he saw any continuing role for the Mosaic Law for humanity in Christ.

Recommended Reading

Genesis 2–3   Galatians 1–6

Romans 1–8, 10

Saving the World from Sin

Paul's insistence that in Christ God saved the world presupposes that the world and its inhabitants needed saving. In Romans 5:6–10, Paul says that at the time God reconciled humanity, all humans were "weak," "ungodly," "sinners": in a word, they were "enemies" of God. According to Paul, humanity was in this state of alienation from God because before Christ all humans, both Jews and Gentiles, lived "under the power of Sin"[1] (Rom 3:9). Immediately following that assertion, Paul strings together various scriptural passages, mostly from the Psalms, that express what it means for humans to live under the power of Sin: no one was in right relationship with God or other humans; no one was capable of doing good; human existence was filled with violence and treachery, devoid of God (see Rom 3:10–18). Paul knew of individuals, whether legendary ancestors such as Noah and Abraham or men and women of his own day, who were just and

Paul's Bible: The Septuagint

Scripture, for Paul, meant the writings of the Jewish people. Sometime between third century BCE and second century CE, Jewish scholars translated the Jewish scriptures into Greek. This translation, called the "Septuagint" from the Latin *Septuaginta*, which means "seventy," is also designated by the Roman numeral LXX. The Septuagint contains the Greek versions of the thirty-nine canonical books of the Hebrew Bible. In addition, the Septuagint contains seven other books in Greek not included in the Hebrew canon. They are Judith, Tobit, Baruch, Sirach (or Ecclesiasticus), Wisdom of Solomon, and 1 and 2 Maccabees. Jews do not accept these books as inspired and refer to them as apocryphal. Over time, the forty-six-book Septuagint came to be known as the Christian Old Testament. It is widely recognized that when Paul references the scriptures, he cites the LXX. For Paul, the Septuagint was not an "Old Testament"—there was as yet no "New Testament"—but simply the collection of sacred writings translated into Greek, the first language of diaspora Jews like himself.

---

1. The spelling of *sin* with a capital *S* is intentional. It is meant to distinguish Sin, a cosmic power, from sin, specific human acts opposed to God's will. The distinction will be discussed later in this chapter.

upright. Therefore, Paul's description of humanity here aligns with his understanding of redemptive history and the watershed position he accords to the Christ-event in this history: slavery to Sin and alienation from God characterized life *before* the Christ-event, "*but now*" a new era has emerged, characterized by reconciliation and grace.[2] How humans got themselves in this sorry state has to do with their constitution, which makes them slaves to Sin. As a result, they are subject to death. Paul traces these two realities back to Adam. Thus Paul's understanding of how humans are constituted—his anthropology—directly relates to his understanding of Adam's pivotal role in salvation history.

It All Goes Back to Adam

In Israel's scriptures, it is a theological axiom that humans—along with the rest of the created order—are good, a fact affirmed by God multiple times in Genesis 1. Despite being created good, humans were far from perfect, as attested in the many biblical accounts of human transgression. However, nowhere do the Hebrew Scriptures suggest that the human condition is existence "under the power of sin." To be sure, humans sin and through sin disrupt their relationship with God, but as noted in chapter 4, they have ways to expiate their sins and renew their relationship with God. Thus although the Hebrew scriptures testify to the pervasiveness of sinful acts and the sinner's need for God's mercy, they do not characterize human existence as hopeless bondage to Sin from which helpless humans cannot escape. What they do teach is that sin originated with humans, as seen in the familiar story recounted at Genesis 2–3. Often referred to as "The Fall," the story recounts the disobedience of a man and woman. This is not a factual historical account involving actual persons named Adam and Eve, but rather an etiology—a story explaining the origins of some known phenomena whose exact beginnings remain obscure. The etiologies found in the Bible are non-historical, non-scientific explanations of how something came to exist in the world. Genesis 2–3 responds to the question: how did

---

2. Paul frequently contrasts believers' former life before Christ with their new life Christ (see e.g. Rom 3:21, 6:19, 6:21-22, 7:5-6; 1 Cor 6:11; Gal 4:8-9).

Sin come into a world created good? It answers that an archetypal man, (Heb. '*Adam*) and an archetypal woman, Eve (Heb. *Hawwah*), were seduced by something outside themselves—a manipulative power in the form of a serpent—to disobey God. As envisioned in the story, this act of disobedience resulted in alienation from God and a life of hardship, pain, and death. The account presents death not as something humans experience naturally because of aging or illness, but rather as a consequence of Adam and Eve's having transgressed God's law.

After Genesis 2–3, the figure of Adam and story of this primordial act of disobedience and its consequences all but disappear from the Hebrew Scriptures. This changes in the postbiblical era of the Hellenistic and Roman periods, which sees a resurgence of interest in the origin of Sin and death. However, the deuterocanonical and noncanonical literature[3] produced during this span of time does not necessarily trace Sin, evil, and death to Adam. Instead, it offers various explanations, such as rebellious, fallen angels (see *1 Enoch* 6–11); the demonic offspring of these fallen angels (*Jubilees* 10:1–14); Belial, or Satan, a dark figure who incites humans to sin (see, e.g., *Testament of Levi* 19:1; *Testament of Naphtali* 2:6; 3:1; *Martyrdom of Isaiah* 2:4); and the devil's envy, through which death entered the world (Wis 2:24). Moreover, in this same period, a current emerges within Judaism that exalts Adam. While especially notable in the literature from Qumran, it also appears elsewhere.[4] In Sirach, for example, the author concluded his six-chapter review and praise of illustrious biblical figures stating, "But above every other created being was Adam" (Sir 49:16). While Adam enjoyed good press in late pre-Christian Jewish tradition, the same cannot be said of Eve, who is featured as

---

3. Between the third century bce and second century ce, a vast body of literature was produced that was not included in the Jewish canon of scripture but that provides important insight into Jewish life and thought in this period. This literature, sometimes referred to as "intertestamental literature" is collected in James Charlesworth, ed. *The Old Testament Pseudepigrapha*, 2 vols. (Garden City, NY: Doubleday & Co., 1983, 1985); for the Dead Sea Scrolls see Florentino García Martínez and Eibert J. C. Tigchelaar, eds. *The Dead Sea Scrolls: Study Edition*, 2 vols. (Leiden, The Netherlands: Brill; Grand Rapids, MN: William. B. Eerdmans, 2000).

4. For example, a Qumran text, "The Rule of the Community," states that to those whom God purifies and chooses for an everlasting covenant "will belong all the glory of Adam" (1 QS 4:22–23).

the sole originator of sin, evil, and death: "From a woman sin had its beginning and because of her, we all die" (Sir 25:24). In a work referred to as the *Apocalypse of Moses*,[5] Eve assumes responsibility for Adam's misery saying, "Adam, . . . give me half of thy trouble and I will endure it; for it is on my account that this hath happened to thee, on my account thou art beset with toils and troubles" (*Apoc. Mos.* 9:2). For his part, Adam lays blame exclusively on Eve: "Eve, what hast thou wrought in us? Thou hast brought upon us great wrath which is

Adam and Eve, fresco, Catacombs of Marcellinus and Peter, Rome, Italy, fourth century CE.

© Album / Art Resource, NY

death, [lording it over all our race]" (*Apoc. Mos.* 14:2). Again, death is not a biological inevitability, but results from an act of disobedience that these two texts associate exclusively with Eve.

Though on one occasion Paul mentions her seduction by the serpent (2 Cor 11:3), he does not develop the tradition concerning Eve. Instead, he focuses on Adam. As Pauline scholar James Dunn points out, during and after Paul's lifetime, some Jews began to focus attention on Adam's disobedience—his agency in bringing Sin and death into the world—and thus his responsibility for the human condition.[6] *4 Ezra* and *2 Baruch*, two texts written ca. 90 CE that reflect the Jewish theological thought emerging in Paul's lifetime, link humanity's plight to Adam. The author of *4 Ezra* asks, "O Adam, what have you done! For though it was you who sinned, the fall was not yours alone, but ours also who are your descendants" (*4 Ezra* 7:118). In *2 Baruch* a

---

5. The full text of the Apocalypse of Moses cited here is available at *www.ccel. org/c/charles/otpseudepig/apcmose.htm.*

6. James D. G. Dunn, *The Theology of Paul the Apostle* (Grand Rapids, MI: William B. Eerdmans, 1998), 86.

similar question is posed: "O Adam, what did you do to all who were born after you . . . ?" (*2 Bar.* 48:42). The author of this work also points the finger at Adam as the cause of brevity of life and the inevitability of death (*2 Bar.* 17:3).

Paul explicitly references Adam only three times in his undisputed letters: twice in 1 Corinthians 15, in his argument against those who denied the resurrection of the dead, and once in Romans 5. In 1 Corinthians 15:21–22, Paul ascribes death to Adam, in line with Jewish theological thought of his day: "For since death came through a human being, the resurrection of the dead came also through a human being. For as all die in Adam, so all will be made alive in Christ." In the dense passage at Rom 5:12–21—in which Paul contrasts the human condition attributable to Adam with that attributable to Christ—Paul goes a step further, tracing both death and Sin to Adam: "Therefore just as Sin came into the world through one man and death came through sin, and death spread to all because all have sinned . . ." (Rom 5:12). Although Paul does not finish his thought here—instead digressing to comment about the relationship between Sin and the law (Rom 5:13)—he does affirm two important points in verse 12. First, Adam, the source of death, has introduced Sin into the world and made it a factor of human existence. Second, Paul attributes the universality of death to the fact that all humans have sinned. For Paul, death provides the physical evidence that all have sinned, because death results from sin. While likely not a logical deduction for most people today, it was for Paul, whose thought was shaped by the etiological narrative in Genesis 2–3, as well as views prevalent in first-century-ce Judaism. However, notwithstanding his acknowledgment that humans sin and are complicit in their own death, Paul ultimately attributes the whole sinful condition of humanity to Adam. On account of him, human existence becomes entangled in the corruption of Sin and death (Rom 5:19). Paul underscores the singular responsibility of Adam for this condition by his repetitive use of "one" in Romans 5:12–19: sin came "through *one* man" (v. 12), "the *one* man's trespass" (v. 15 and 17, 18), the "*one* man's sin" (v. 16), "*one* man's disobedience" (v. 19). Paul omits any mention of Eve or the serpent, making this all about Adam, one archetypal figure, in contrast to Christ, another archetypal figure. Whether Paul considered Adam an actual historical figure remains unknown. However, Paul uses Adam to exemplify what it means to be human in contrast to Christ who embodies in his life, and makes possible through his death and Resurrection, another type of human existence.

The Human Person in Paul's Thought

In order to appreciate how Paul understood grace and redemption, one must first consider Paul's views on what it meant to be human. This requires an examination of two key anthropological terms Paul uses in his writings: *sōma*, which means "body," and *sarx*, whose literal meaning is "flesh."

The term *sōma* appears more than seventy times in Paul's letters, with about forty-five occurrences in 1 Corinthians. *Sōma* includes the notion of corporeality. Paul uses the term in that sense when he says he carries the marks of Christ on his body (Gal 6:17), or that husbands and wives have rights over each other's bodies when it comes to conjugal relations (1 Cor 7:4), or that Abraham considered his old body "good as dead" (Rom 4:19). In other places, Paul uses *sōma* as a comprehensive term for the self who, apart from bodily existence, cannot be present in the world. As all Pauline scholars point out, Paul understands the human person as an embodied self who does not simply *have* a body but rather *is* a body.[7] Only as an "embodied self" can one interact with the world and engage with others. In this regard, *sōma* is a relational concept.

First Corinthians 6:12–20, where Paul argues against casual sex with prostitutes, draws on this richer, relational significance of the word *sōma*. His argument rests on the fact that believers' bodies—that is, believers—belong to Christ (1 Cor 6:15). As Paul sees it, as "embodied persons," believers manifest the depth and character of their commitment to Christ in their bodies. Consequently, Paul argues, a believer's body cannot join to a prostitute's body without that act uniting his whole person to the prostitute. However, a believer is already united to Christ (1 Cor 6:15–17). Since illicit sex

---

7. See, e.g., Rudolf Bultmann, *The Theology of the New Testament,* vol 1., trans. K. Grobel (Waco, TX: Baylor University Press, 2007), 192–203, esp. 194.

would contravene the union with Christ, Paul says believers must "shun fornication!" (1 Cor 6:18). Therefore, although a reference to something physical, *sōma* moves beyond the merely physical to include the whole person. For Paul, *sōma* expresses the character of created humankind as *embodied existence*. This fact of embodiment makes possible one's participation in the world and makes humans socially interdependent. On the level of moral evaluation, Paul affirms that the *body* is good and can be transformed and raised again (cf. 1 Cor 6:13, 15:44).

Paul uses the term *sarx* sixty-two times. After *sōma*, it is the term he employs most frequently to refer to the constitution of the human person. Like *sōma*, it has a range of meanings.[8] In a neutral sense, it can refer to the "flesh" or material stuff of the body. Paul uses it that way when describing an illness he had as a "weakness of the flesh," the literal translation of the Greek phrase, *astheneian tēs sarkos*, found at Galatians 4:13, or when referring to the flesh as the place of circumcision (Rom 2:28). Paul also uses the term in a neutral sense to connote ethnicity or ancestry. For example, he references Abraham as a forefather, *kata sarka*, that is, "according to the flesh" (Rom 4:1); he describes Jesus as "descended from David according to the flesh" (see Rom 1:3); and he speaks of the Jewish people as his "kindred according to the flesh" (Rom 9:3). Sometimes Paul uses the phrase "according to the flesh" to refer to judgments made according to merely human standards (see, e.g., 1 Cor 1:26; 2 Cor 5:16). Most frequently, though, Paul uses "flesh" as a designation for humans in their weakness (Rom 6:19, 7:5). In this sense, "flesh" is not a substance but a *non-material place* or sphere that lets evil take over and so becomes a locus of activity hostile to God. When understood this way, living "according to the flesh" or being "in the flesh" means existence within this sphere of human weakness. The "flesh," then, is not sinful in and of itself. Rather, as the symbol of human weakness, the "flesh" signifies the human who cannot resist engaging in self-serving and other-destroying behavior. Typically, "according to the flesh" is

---

8. Other terms Paul uses less frequently to refer to the constitution of the human person are *nous* (mind) used thirteen times, *psychē* (soul) used eleven times, *kardia* (heart) used thirty-five times, *syneidēsis* (conscience) used fourteen times.

taken in a narrow sense as a reference to sexual activity. However, Paul makes it clear in Galatians 5:16–25 that living "according to the flesh" goes beyond sexual indulgence to include a variety of behaviors destructive of others and the fabric of community life. Paul uses the phrase "according to the flesh" as shorthand for describing weakened humanity, incapable of resisting evil desires, and thereby prone to a variety of sinful behaviors. Humanity living according to the flesh is humanity hostile and opposed to God.

According to Paul, this weakness characterizes the human condition and leaves humans impotent to work against the power of Sin, no matter how much they wish to resist its control. In a well-known passage from Romans, although he speaks in the first person, Paul voices the frustration of all humans who cannot escape the powerlessness of the human condition: "So I find it to be a law that when I want to do what is good, evil lies close at hand. For I delight in the law of God in my inmost self, but I see in my members another law at war with the law of my mind, making me captive to . . . sin . . ." (Rom 7:21–23). Thus when Sin gains access through the "flesh," the willing "I" cannot do the good and heads toward death. Unfortunately, as Paul argues in Romans 1:18–3:20, the human condition apart from Christ is one of subjection to Sin and judgment. He blames Adam for setting in motion the reign of Sin and death (Rom 5:14). The only escape from existence "according to the flesh" is to be in Christ, the new Adam, who makes it possible for humans to live "according to the spirit."

The Deadly Trio: Flesh, Sin, and Death

By establishing "the flesh" as a constitutive part of the human person, Paul could acknowledge and explain the human inclination toward evil while continuing to affirm with Jewish tradition that humans, who are corporeal (somatic), have been created good. For Paul, "the flesh" has no power at all. The problem is that it can be exploited. It can be manipulated by Sin, against which humans have no power. This explains why in Romans 7, just a few verses before those cited above, the willing "I" says, "I do not understand my own actions. For I do not do what I want but the very thing I hate . . . But in fact, it is no longer I who do it, but Sin that dwells within me" (Rom 7:15–17). The repetition of that sentiment at Romans 7:20—"it is no longer I who do it, but Sin that dwells within me"—reflects the self's utter frustration over its inability to escape Sin's grip.

First-century philosophers also recognized the conflict between intentions and deeds. However, they tended to be more optimistic than Paul. They believed that, at least sometimes, humans had the capacity to do the good they intended.[9] As most Pauline scholars agree, Paul's pessimism has more to do with his theological convictions than with actual human behavior, as elsewhere he recognizes that some people do the good (see Rom 2:6–11). In other words, the idea that all humans, weakened by the flesh, needed something beyond themselves to free them from Sin's grip serves as the corollary to Paul's conviction that in Christ God has saved *all* humans.

Paul used the term *Sin* (Grk. *hamartia*) sixty-four times in his writings. It appears forty-eight times in the letter to the Romans, with forty-one of these concentrated in Romans 5–8. These four chapters contain Paul's most extensive reflection on the nature of Sin, with two points being of special significance. First, with one exception at Romans 7:5, Paul always uses *hamartia* in the singular, Sin. This signals that Paul had something in mind other than individual human actions.[10] Second, Paul presents *hamartia* as a personified power or force. This reality was not originally part of creation, but "came into the world" (Rom 5:12) and became a pervasive influence in the human environment. It exercises dominion, making its reign evident in the fact of death (Rom 5:21, 6:12); it enslaves humans (Rom 6:16); it can dwell in a person and cause one to do what one hates (Rom 7:14). Sin can even pervert something ordered to the good, such as the law, so that it becomes disordered and causes death (Rom 7:13). It is Sin understood as this reality that underlies the use of the capital *S*. Adam bears responsibility for allowing this power to enter the world, and, because

---

9. The Stoic philosopher Epictetus, for example, believed that progress in virtue was possible and that the continuous acquisition of knowledge would lead one to avoid doing contradictory things, cf. *Epictetus Discourses*, Bks. 1–2, trans. W. A. Oldfather (Cambridge, MA: Harvard University Press, 1925), Bk. 2.26.

10. Paul employs other terms, such as *paraptōma* (trespass) and *parabasis* (transgression) to refer to individual acts (see, e.g., Rom 4:15, 5:15–20; Gal 3:19).

humans live in the world, they cannot avoid Sin's reach. Sin works constantly to manipulate the flesh, which remains susceptible to its pull. As a result, humans are inescapably enslaved to Sin's power. However, this does not completely relieve humans of responsibility for their behavior. Though Paul presents Sin as a despotic ruler and acknowledges that humans are not their own masters, he still recognizes individual complicity for sinful deeds and exhorts believers to stop submitting themselves so readily to Sin's power (Rom 6:13, 16). The vices listed at 1 Corinthians 6:9–10 and Galatians 5:19–21 offer examples of the sinful behavior for which individuals bear responsibility and through which Sin manifests its power in the world.

While Paul sometimes uses the term *death* (*thanatos*) in a neutral sense, the majority of its forty-two occurrences in his letters carry a purely negative connotation. Death is the fruit of sinful passions (Rom 7:5). Sin produces death, which is the due punishment for sins (Rom 7:13). Death is the destiny of all those who have lived "according to the flesh," or under Sin's power, because "the wages of Sin is death" (Rom 6:23). Paul considers death not only the ultimate but also the worst effect of Sin. Though God had destined humans for immortality, they cannot escape death any more than they can escape the "flesh," which remains enslaved to Sin. Every individual is trapped in this triad of flesh, Sin, and death. In brief, Paul sees humankind as weak, material, corruptible, and under the power of Sin. Humanity, in the likeness of Adam, has not only lost the possibility of sharing God's glory and eternal life, it is incapable of moving toward God and is oriented toward death.

Reoriented in Christ, The New Adam

The only escape from the Adam-determined existence that leads to death lies in participation in a new type of humanity determined by a new Adam, a new prototype of what it means to be human. In Romans 5:12–21, Paul presents Christ as this New Adam and contrasts the positive universal consequences wrought in Christ with the negative universal consequences the first Adam wrought. Before contrasting the two archetypal figures, Paul traces the history of salvation from Adam to the law and from the law to Christ (5:12–14).

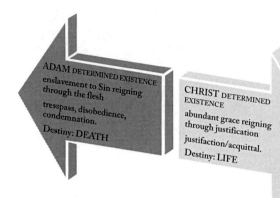

ADAM DETERMINED EXISTENCE
enslavement to Sin reigning through the flesh
tresspass, disobedience, condemnation.
Destiny: DEATH

CHRIST DETERMINED EXISTENCE
abundant grace reigning through justification
justifaction/acquittal.
Destiny: LIFE

From the time of Adam up to the law, the situation was bleak. Sin and death proliferated. Although God gave the law to Moses to stop the spread of sin and death and bring about obedience unto life, Paul insists it actually made matters worse: "Law came in with the result that trespass multiplied" (5:20a). His logic is this: the more laws to observe, the more laws to break, leading to the continuance of Sin's reign and death. This desperate situation changes with the advent of Christ. The repetition of the phrase "much more surely" at Romans 5:15 and 17 underscores that what Christ has effectuated for humanity surpasses the effects of Adam's sin. Because of Christ's death, grace now reigns and proves greater than the trespass, precisely because it can undo the power and effects of Sin. Whereas Sin brought condemnation and death to the many, grace brings justification and life (5:15–16). Finally, a force arrives that is more powerful than Sin and the law, which Sin has perverted to serve its own purposes. One person's act of obedience inaugurated the reign of grace, just as one person's act of disobedience brought about the reign of Sin. Humans no longer have to be conditioned by Adam, existing as fleshly creatures enslaved by Sin, alienated from God, and oriented to death. In Christ, humanity is reoriented to life, justified by Christ's death, reconciled to God, and ruled by grace. In Romans 6, Paul explains how one passes from the power and dominion of Sin to live under the dominion of grace. For the next two chapters, he explains what that means—dead to Sin, dead to the law, and impelled by a new force, the Spirit.

Dead to Sin

Throughout his letters, and especially in Romans, Paul uses rhetorical questions to advance his arguments. In his day, philosophers and teachers frequently used such questions as points of departure to teach students a lesson or further clarify a point.[11] Rhetorical questions give Paul's letters a conversational quality, suggesting a real give-and-take between himself and his readers. Paul begins Romans 6 by asking, "Should we continue in sin in order that grace may abound?" The question would seem to flow logically from Paul's assertion at the end of chapter 5 that where sin increased, grace increased all the more. Paul, however, considers this logic erroneous. In order to correct it, he poses another question: "How can we who died to Sin go on living in it?" (Rom 6:2). This second question allows Paul to consider how one dies to Sin.

Paul begins his explanation at 6:3–11 by considering the dynamics of baptism and its effects. Appreciating Paul's argument requires an understanding of the reasoning behind these verses. Paul believes that as long as a person is alive, Sin can reign through that person's flesh. Only a dead person is free of the power of Sin, hence incapable of sinning against God and incurring condemnation. But if one is dead, what good is the liberation from Sin? One cannot enjoy the freedom and choose to live for God. The question then becomes: how could one die to Sin but yet come back free from Sin's power to live for God? Paul's answer is baptism, which he understands as a dynamic process through which one dies through participation in Christ's death (see also 2 Cor 5:14). Therefore, with regard to Sin, a baptized person has actually died to its power. *Paul does not say Sin has been put to death.* The complete obliteration of Sin and death is still to come. For now, Sin remains active. Thus Paul reminds believers that after being liberated from Sin, they cannot let Sin continue to run their lives. They cannot resubmit themselves to its power. Rather, they must give themselves to God as people liberated through death and made alive to God (Rom 6:12–14). Through baptism, the liberation from Sin and

---

11. On rhetorical questions in the context of instruction, see Stanley K. Stowers, "The Diatribe," in *Anchor Bible Dictionary*, ed. David N. Freedman (Garden City, NY: Doubleday, 1992), vol. 2, 190–93.

death that God accomplished in the Christ-event becomes the new reality for believers. Their existence is no longer conditioned by participation in the life of the first Adam but in that of the new Adam, Christ. They are dead to Sin. If believers now subject themselves to the power of Sin and continue to transgress, it is not because they have no choice but to be and act like Adam. Humanity in Christ is humanity now freed to choose either an Adamlike existence oriented to death or a Christlike existence, alive to God now (6:11) and destined for eternal life (6:5).

Freed from the Law

At Romans 6:15, Paul poses another question containing a false inference that could be drawn from what he has just said in verses 1–14: "Should we sin because we are not under law but under grace?" Here Paul mentions the law for the first time since Romans 5:20, where he stated that the law only increased transgressions. It also marks the first time Paul speaks of believers as no longer "under the law." At Romans 7:5, Paul adds that believers are dead to the law. Since he had already said believers no longer remain under the dominion of Sin, and in fact are dead to Sin, one might be tempted to conclude that Paul equates Sin and the law. In fact, Paul realizes that some might misunderstand his words in just that way. At Romans 7:7, he explicitly denies equating the two. Paul does not view the law as evil, nor does he consider it a pervasive power such as Sin. However, he does see a connection between Sin and the law. Sin uses the law as a tool to "arouse sinful passions" (7:5) and to cause transgression, because it details prohibitions without empowering the person to avoid them (7:7). Without that empowerment, Sin takes over and compels the weak human to transgress the commandment. An analogy may help clarify this point. Stoplights not only direct traffic, they symbolize the law. If someone drives through a red light, he not only risks his life, he also breaks the law. Of itself, the red light cannot stop the person from breaking the law. It can only signal what is prohibited and stand as silent testimony that a transgression has occurred. Were there no red light, this behavior might still be considered reckless, but a driver would remain unaware of having committed a transgression deserving of condemnation and punishment.

Earlier in Romans, Paul stated, "through the law comes knowledge of sin" (3:20b) and "where there is no law, neither is there violation" (4:15b). In Romans 7:7–8, he essentially repeats his earlier comments, adding that where there is no law, "Sin lies dead" (7:8). It cannot do its work of inciting disobedience to God through compelling humans to transgress God's commandments. While Paul insists that the law is intrinsically good, just, and holy (7:12), the law has no power to make the "willing I" do the right thing (7:14–25) because Sin, which perverts the law's purpose, exploits it. Thus the law also belongs to the human condition of enslavement to Sin, which the first Adam determined. But the death and resurrection of the new Adam has freed believers from that existence, including freedom from the law and its condemnation (7:6).

Impelled by the Spirit

In Romans 8, Paul concludes the discussion of humanity in Christ that he began in chapter 5. These two chapters, which focus on God's gift in Christ, serve as literary bookends enclosing the arguments set out in chapters 6 and 7. Paul began Romans 5 with the solemn proclamation, "Therefore, since we are justified by faith, we have peace with God through our Lord Jesus Christ" (Rom 5:1). Now at 8:1, he solemnly proclaims that the condemnation attached to life ruled by Sin, which resulted from Adam's disobedience, is part of the old age and no longer applies to those in Christ: "There is therefore now no condemnation for those who are in Christ Jesus. For the law of the Spirit of life in Christ Jesus has set you free from the law of sin and death" (8:1–2). Each chapter's opening proclamation focuses on the results of what God has done in Christ: the restoration of right relations with God (ch. 5) and the freeing of those in Christ from enslavement to Sin and death (ch. 8). Paul says God brought about this emancipation by sending his own Son to do what the law, weakened by the flesh, could not do (8:3). By taking on human flesh, Jesus rescued humans from Sin's power by disabling it and empowering believers with the Spirit (8:9). Unlike the flesh, the Spirit is not beholden to Sin and does not leave those in Christ weak-kneed before Sin's power, as it does unbelievers who have not received this empowering presence (8:4).

Paul uses the word "spirit" (*pneuma*) nineteen times in this chapter to signify a way of life opposed to the "flesh" (*sarx*). Paul contrasts life "according to the Spirit" and life "according to the flesh" at Romans 8:5–8. He does not make the comparison in view of specific deeds or behaviors as one finds elsewhere, such as at Galatians 5:16–23. Instead, he contrasts two orientations, which Paul expresses in terms of "setting one's mind." Either one is oriented toward the things of the flesh—the temptations that leave humans vulnerable to the power of Sin—or toward the things of the Spirit. A "fleshly" existence is hostile to God and leads to death; a "pneumatic" existence is "life and peace."

Paul announces that believers have put that "fleshly" existence behind them: "But you are not in the flesh; you are in the Spirit since the Spirit of God dwells in you" (8:9). The power of the indwelling Spirit now orients believers' lives toward God and guarantees eternal life (8:11). Being gifted with the Spirit within means believers have become part of a new family, where, having received the gift of adoption, they are coheirs with Christ. Along with him, they experience God as "Abba! Father!" (8:15).

While believers enjoy this new redeemed existence in Christ, Paul reminds them that what has occurred is a "beginning." Believers already enjoy Spirit-empowered life and are being gradually transformed (2 Cor 3:18). However, complete freedom from bondage and decay remains a future reality, for which humans and the rest of creation long (8:19–25). When that final transformation of creation takes place, it will completely undo/reverse the consequences of the first Adam's rebellion. Creation will regain its original goodness. For the present, believers still suffer and share in the pains and hardships of the rest of creation. However, as Paul hastens to assure his audience, any suffering experienced now is small in comparison to the future glory awaiting those whom God has conformed to the image of His Son, the new Adam (8:28).

Paul wraps up his four-chapter discussion of the human condition in Christ in Romans 8:31–39, where he echoes Romans 5:1–11:

> Believers are part of a new humanity determined by Christ and stand in a new relationship to God. God, who demonstrated His love for humans by sending His Son, is not

against us, but for us. Thus whoever is united to Christ can never be separated from God's love poured out in him.

Saved by Faith in Christ, Not by the Law

In Romans 5–8, Paul explores what it means to be humanity in Christ—namely, humanity freed from Sin, flesh, the law and death—and set right again with God, or justified. Baptism "into Christ"—and specifically into his death, through which believers die to Sin—incorporates one into this new humanity. Before that incorporation, or certainly accompanying that act of incorporation, a person must have what Paul terms "faith." For many today, faith means belief in or acceptance of a series of propositions. As biblical scholar Joseph Fitzmyer observes, based on Romans 10:5–17, Paul understood faith as an experience that included hearing, acceptance, and commitment: hearing the good news of what God had done in Christ, accepting the gift of salvation offered through Christ, and then committing oneself to live under the Lordship of Christ.[12]

In both Romans and Galatians, written a few years before Romans, Paul sets up a striking opposition between faith and law. He repeatedly insists that no person is justified in God's sight by works of the law, but only by faith (see, e.g., Rom 3:20, 21, 28; 4:6). Paul devotes all of Romans 4 to the figure of Abraham, the premier illustration that righteousness comes through faith apart from the works of the law. In Galatians 2–4, the opposition between faith and works of the law is even more pronounced. Paul wrote the letter to combat the influence of rival apostles who had arrived in Galatia preaching a gospel requiring Gentile believers to observe the Jewish law, especially the requirement of circumcision. The intruders were apparently persuasive, and with good reason: God established the requirement of circumcision as recorded in Genesis 17, and to be a son of Abraham meant conformity to Abraham in terms of circumcision.

---

12. Joseph A. Fitzmyer, *Paul and His Theology: A Brief Sketch* (Saddle River, NJ: Prentice Hall, 1989), 84.

A few years before these preachers arrived in Galatia, Paul had taken up the fight over Gentile observance of the law. He argued against demanding observance before the "pillars," or leaders, of the church in Jerusalem: James, John, and Cephas, or Peter. In Paul's recounting of that meeting in Galatians 2:1–10, he says the leaders gave only one requirement to him and the Gentiles to whom he ministered: "remember the poor" (Gal 2:10). Paul considered the matter settled, but some in Jerusalem disapproved of his "law-free" evangelization and came to Galatia to set his converts straight. When he heard of the intruders and the content of their preaching, he composed the letter to the Galatians. In it, Paul insists that no one is justified by the law (Gal 3:16) and marshals a variety of arguments—such as the Galatians' own experience (3:1), the example of Abraham (3:6–19), and the enslavement of the law (4:21–31)—to support his point that the law cannot justify, and its observance can even cut one off from Christ (5:4).

In both Romans and Galatians, Paul adamantly rejects the idea that justification has anything to do with the law. He asserts that God justifies completely apart from the law. Why? What exactly was wrong with the law? In Romans, Paul insisted that the law was holy, and the commandment was holy, just, and good (7:12). Sin may have compromised and perverted it, but Sin had had the same effect on humans who were also created good. If God's reconciling activity in Christ rehabilitated humanity and the indwelling of the Spirit empowered humanity to do the good and live for God, why wasn't the law similarly rehabilitated? Why did Paul no longer see a role for the Mosaic Law God himself gave to his chosen people or for the customs and practices included in Jewish tradition for centuries?

When a book written more than 2,000 years after the fact poses questions such as these, they may seem academic and irrelevant. But they were far from academic or irrelevant to Paul or to those who disagreed with him in those early decades of the Jesus movement. In fact, Paul was so impassioned over this issue and so furious that intruders demanded his Gentile converts undergo circumcision, that he suggested they go "castrate themselves" (Gal 5:12)—and that comes after he had already cursed them in the first chapter of this letter at verse 9. Paul did not give measured responses in this letter. They were extreme and regarding the law, totally negative: if you want to justify yourself by the law, you are cut off from Christ (Gal 5:4); the law enslaves (4:21–31); if justification is by the law, Christ died for nothing (2:21). To say otherwise would have compromised Paul's whole ministry. This was no small thing for a man who claimed a direct divine origin for his gospel, unmediated by any human being (Gal 1:11–17).

Summary

While the next chapter will explore the questions posed in the preceding section in greater depth, this chapter raised a number of salient points concerning Paul's depiction of humanity in Christ. First, the reign of Sin and death, to which humans were subjected before Christ, resulted from one act of disobedience with universal consequences. It allowed Sin to enter the human sphere, where it gained a foothold in the "flesh" and the "law" and exploited both in order to turn humans from God. God did not intend death for humans, but through Adam it became an inescapable aspect of the human condition. Second, Christ's one act of obedience also had universal effects. It created the condition for the possibility of a new type of humanity, conformed to Christ and subject to the reign of grace. Third, baptism incorporates one into this new humanity in Christ, for in baptism believers die to Sin and their former pattern of life ruled by Sin. Believers are no longer "fleshly" but "pneumatic," having been indwelt by the Spirit, which empowers them to walk in the newness of life. Fourth, humanity in Christ has a new destiny. Whereas humanity enslaved to Sin was headed for death, humanity in Christ is destined for future resurrection and life eternal. Fifth, the possibility of a new justified and reconciled existence is a gift that God brings about apart from the law through the Christ-event. Believers receive it in faith, itself a gift from God, which enables a person to apprehend the mystery of God's salvation in Christ.

Paul's depiction of humanity, as well as his presentation of humanity gone wrong before Christ and then restored and reoriented to God after the Christ-event, is based on a number of factors. They include a mythic understanding of the origin of evil, an apocalyptic view of history, a personal revelation of Christ, and beliefs about how mystical participation in Christ's death frees believers from Sin's grip and pneumatically empowers them. For contemporary readers who do not inhabit Paul's symbolic world and base their understanding of human origins, death, and human nature on the life and social sciences, Paul's thought may seem unintelligible or even absurd. Therefore, when reading Paul, it is important to keep in mind and appreciate his symbolic world. Within that world, his thought was coherent and credible.

Questions for Review and Reflection

1. How much realism do you find in Paul's assessment of the human condition? Are humans really as Paul describes them?
2. In Paul's thinking, how does baptism create the possibility of escaping Sin's power?
3. In what way is the law a tool of Sin, according to Paul?
4. How is humanity determined by Adam different from humanity determined by the New Adam, Christ?
5. What is the relationship between faith and the Spirit of God for believers in Christ Jesus?
6. Paul attributed the human tendency to evil to an extraneous force called Sin. How do today's behavioral scientists and sociologists, or anyone who maintains the essential goodness of humans, account for the human tendency toward evil?

Opening More Windows

Byrne, Brendan. *Romans*. Sacra Pagina, vol. 6. Collegeville, MN: Liturgical Press, 2007.

Gundry, Robert H. *Sōma in Biblical Theology: With Emphasis on Pauline Anthropology*. Grand Rapids, MI: Zondervan Books, 1987.

Johnson, Luke Timothy. *Reading Romans: A Literary and Theological Commentary*. Macon, GA: Smyth & Helwys, 2001.

Murphy-O'Connor, Jerome. *Becoming Human Together: The Pastoral Anthropology of St. Paul*. Wilmington, DE: Michael Glazier, Inc., 1984.

Penna, Romano. *Paul the Apostle: Wisdom and the Folly of the Cross*, vol. 2. Trans. Thomas P. Wahl. Collegeville, MN: Liturgical Press, 1996. (Esp. ch. 18, "Sin and Redemption. A Synthesis.")

Schnelle, Udo. *The Human Condition: Anthropology in the Teachings of Jesus, Paul and John.* Trans. O. C. Dean. Minneapolis, MN: Fortress Press, 1996.

Scroggs, Robin. *The Last Adam: A Study in Pauline Anthropology.* Oxford: Blackwell, 1966.

Chapter 6

What Was Wrong with the Law?

Overview

This chapter addresses the questions previously raised concerning the relationship between faith and the law in Paul's thought. The chapter has two main parts enclosed within its introduction and summary. Part one considers the traditional view on Paul's opposition to law. This view, now referred to as the "old perspective on Paul" and associated with Martin Luther, prevailed until the 1960s. Part two will focus on the main findings of a current in Pauline studies known as the "New Perspective on Paul," whose advocates have challenged Luther's reading of Paul.

Recommended Reading

Exodus 19:16–23:19	Romans 3:19–8:12
Deuteronomy 28:1–30:20	Philippians 3:1–11
Galatians 1–6	James 2:14–26

Opposition between Faith and Law in Paul

At the end of the previous chapter, it was observed that while Paul referred to the law as good and holy (Rom 7:12), he nonetheless adamantly rejected the idea that justification had anything to do with keeping the law. That observation was made in view of a number of passages from Paul's letters to the Galatians and Romans, such as the following:

- Gal 2:16 "yet we know that a person is justified not by the works of the law but through faith in Jesus Christ. And we have come to believe in Christ Jesus, so that we might be justified by faith in Christ, and not by doing the works of the law, because no one will be justified by the works of the law."
- Gal 2:21 "for if justification comes through the law, then Christ died for nothing."
- Gal 3:10 "For all who rely on the works of the law are under a curse."
- Gal 3:11 "Now it is evident that no one is justified before God by the law."
- Gal 3:19 "Why then the law? It was added because of transgressions . . ."
- Gal 3:23 "Now before faith came we were imprisoned and guarded under the law until faith would be revealed."
- Gal 5:2, 4 ". . . if you let yourselves be circumcised, Christ will be of no benefit to you. (4) "You who want to be justified by the law have cut yourselves off from Christ; you have fallen away from grace."
- Rom 3:20 "For no human being will be justified in his sight by deeds prescribed by the law, for through the law comes the knowledge of sin."
- Rom 3:28 "For we hold a person is justified by faith apart from works prescribed by the law."
- Rom 7:6 "But now we are discharged from the law, dead to that which held us captive . . ."
- Rom 10:4 "Christ is the end of the law so that there may be righteousness for everyone who believes."

A thoughtful reader of these passages might conclude that Paul thought and preached that the law and the gospel, as well as faith and works, were opposed to each other. This leads to questions: Why does he consider these realities antithetical? What did Paul find wrong with the law? Hadn't God given it to the people of Israel on Sinai, through Moses (cf. Exod 19:16–30:18)? Weren't they commanded to obey these laws, neither adding nor eliminating any precept, so they would have life and blessing (see Deut 4:1–2; 28:1–14)? One could also ask what, if anything, does this antithesis reflect about Paul's attitude toward his ancestral religion and his fellow Jews who refused the gospel and adhered exclusively to the law? In contemporary Pauline studies, no aspect of Paul's thought is as discussed and disputed as his views of the Jewish law.

Until the 1960s, scholars had a rather standard answer to why Paul opposed the law. It was part of an approach to this issue usually referred to as the "old perspective" on Paul and the law. Since the 1960s, the field of Pauline studies has witnessed the emergence of a new current of thought that has challenged the old or traditional perspective on Paul. Not everyone accepts every view of the proponents of this new perspective, but many agree that new perspective scholarship has introduced important insights that have contributed to a more accurate understanding of Paul's posture toward the Jews and the Jewish law.

The Old Perspective on Paul's View of the Law

The old or traditional perspective on Paul and his views on the law can be summarized as follows: Paul was a Jew who tried to earn his salvation by doing the works of the law. However, he was always frustrated and discouraged because no matter how hard he tried, he could never quite do them perfectly (Rom 7:7–25). In consequence, he was filled with anxiety, afraid he would not attain salvation. Then one day, Paul had an encounter with the Risen Lord. As a result, Paul converted from Judaism, a legalistic religion of works-righteousness,[1] to Christianity, which he perceived to be a superior religion of grace. Once Paul understood that salvation was a grace that comes only through faith in Christ, he repudiated his ancestral religion and criticized the law as inefficacious. He held that Jews who believed they

---

1. "Works-righteousness" is shorthand for the belief that one could become acceptable to God and merit one's own righteousness, or salvation, through strict observance of the law and faithful performance of its precepts.

could merit God's favor or earn salvation by doing good works were wrong and demonstrated an arrogant and misguided belief in their own capacity.

This traditional interpretation of Paul's postconversion view of the law, with its negative portrayal of Judaism as a legalistic religion and of Jews as arrogant people who presumed they could merit salvation through their own efforts, is usually associated with the sixteenth-century-ce Protestant reformer Martin Luther. Luther grounded both his protest against the Roman Catholic Church and his understanding of God's salvific plan in his interpretation of Paul. For Luther, Paul's teaching on justification presented a clear opposition between faith and works of the law.[2] He interpreted the Pauline texts cited at the beginning of this chapter as unequivocally pointing to the complete inadequacy of the law. Thus Luther concluded that humans were justified not through their meritorious deeds but solely by faith (*sola fide*) in Christ.[3] In Luther's view, "works-righteousness" was rooted in a mistaken reliance on human effort and a refusal to acknowledge that God's righteousness comes through Christ to those who have faith. Luther understood Paul as leaving no place for law and human effort in the work of justification, which was completely God's doing in Christ-crucified. As Luther saw it, faith in Christ allowed the Christian to transcend the law, whose only purpose was to show humans sin, terrify and humble them, and drive them to Christ.[4] In brief, Luther was convinced that justification by faith was Paul's central teaching and the principal doctrine of Christianity.

A succession of scholars reinforced Luther's negative portrayal of Judaism via Paul. These scholars characterized Paul's theology as antithetical to Judaism and Paul as hostile to his fellow Jews. The influential twentieth-century New Testament scholar Rudolf

---

2. All references to the works of Martin Luther are from Jaroslav Pelikan and Helmut Lehman (eds.), *Luther's Works* (American Edition, 55 Volumes; St. Louis: Concordia, Fortress and Muhlenberg, 1955–86); here *Works* 26:208, 272. Luther believed that James 2:14–26, which argues for the necessity of works, challenged his position, and so to overcome this obstacle, he disparaged James as "an epistle of straw," or an epistle of no theological weight in comparison to Paul's letters (cf. *Works,* 35: 362 and 397).

3. Ibid., 26:4–6.

4. Ibid., 26:156–57, 26:106.

Bultmann provided one of the most scathing portraits of Judaism, a religion that he believed both Jesus and Paul completely repudiated.[5] The old perspective posted a complete disjuncture between Judaism and Christianity.

Already in the late 1800s and early 1900s, a few Jewish and Christian scholars argued that Luther's reading of Paul seriously distorted both Paul and Judaism.[6] However, the negative understanding of Judaism and hostility toward Jews remained largely intact until the 1960s, when scholars began to have a more informed understanding of second temple Judaism (ca. 500 bce–70 ce) and greater insight into the occasional nature of Paul's letters. These new insights, as well as ethical concerns about the way Paul's writings had been used to endorse two millennia of Christian anti-Judaism and supersessionism, catalyzed a new investigation of Paul's letters.

Supersessionism

Christians have cited many of Paul's statements throughout his letters, especially those in Romans 9–10, to support "supersessionism." This term refers to the belief that the Church supersedes, or replaces, Israel or fulfills Israel's role in God's redemptive historical plan. Throughout the first two Christian millennia, art and architecture have mirrored Christianity's belief in its superiority over Judaism. One recurring image depicts "Ecclesia" (church) and "Synagoga" (Judaism) as two women. Ecclesia is always joyful and confident, while Synagoga is usually blindfolded, downcast, and rejected. The sculptures from the Strasbourg Cathedral in France depict the "church" casting a triumphant eye on the forlorn figure representing Judaism.

---

5. Rudolf Bultmann, *Primitive Christianity in Its Contemporary Setting*, trans. R. H. Fuller (London: Collins, 1956/Fontana 1960), especially chapter 6.

6. See, e.g., George Foot Moore, "Christian Writers on Judaism," *Harvard Theological Review* 14.3 (1921): 197–254; Claude G. Montefiore, "Rabbinic Judaism and the Epistles of Paul," *Jewish Quarterly Review* 13 (1900–01): 161–217.

The statues of crowned and triumphant Ecclesia holding a chalice and blind-folded and forlorn Synagoga holding a broken rod and a copy of the Torah, south transept portal of the Cathédrale de Nôtre Dame, Strasbourg, France.

This new investigation aims to establish a more accurate under-standing of Paul's views about the Jews and the law and remove the wedge that traditional Christian interpretation drove between Paul and his ancestral religion. Scholars engaged in this work belong to a current within Pauline studies referred to as the "New Perspective on Paul."

The New Perspective on Paul's View of the Law

The insights of Lutheran bishop and New Testament scholar Krister Stendahl provided a key impetus in the development of the new per-spective on Paul. In a seminal article published in 1963,[7] Stendahl argued persuasively that Luther read Paul's letters through the lens

---

7. Krister Stendahl, "The Apostle Paul and the Introspective Conscience of the West," *Harvard Theological Review* 56.3 (1963): 199–213; reprinted in *Paul among Jews and Gentiles* (London: SCM Press, 1976), 78–96.

of his personal experience, which differed greatly from Paul's own. This resulted in a skewed understanding of the letters. As evident from his own writings, Luther was plagued by anxiety and a guilt-ridden conscience:

> When I was a monk, I made a great effort to live according to the requirements of the Mosaic rule . . . Nevertheless, my conscience could never achieve certainty but was always in doubt and said, "You have not done this correctly. You were not contrite enough. You omitted this in your confessions." Therefore the longer I tried to heal my uncertain, weak and troubled conscience with human traditions, the more uncertain, weak and troubled I continually made it.[8]

On the contrary, as Stendahl observed, Paul had a robust conscience as attested at 2 Corinthians 1:12a, 1 Corinthians 9:27, 2 Corinthians 5:10, and especially Philippians 3:4b–6, where Paul states,

> If anyone else has reason to be confident in the flesh, I have more: circumcised on the eighth day, a member of the people of Israel, of the tribe of Benjamin, a Hebrew of Hebrews; as to the law a Pharisee; as to zeal a persecutor of the church; as to righteousness under the law, blameless.

In addition, taking seriously the occasional nature of Paul's letters, Stendahl observed that Paul's teaching that justification is by faith developed in response to his missionary outreach to Gentiles and the ensuing questions about how to integrate Gentiles into the church. Thus Paul's teaching that justification is by faith was not a polemical doctrine aimed against Jews or their alleged bankrupt legalistic religion of works-righteousness. Nor was it meant to respond to the concerns of an anxiety-ridden sixteenth-century monk named Luther who feared he might not earn salvation because of the insufficiency of his works.

Rather, Paul's teaching set forth the terms through which Gentiles would be admitted into the community of God's elect to share fully in God's promises alongside Jewish believers. Stendahl's

---

8. See Pelikan and Lehman, *Luther's Works*, 27:13; cf. 26:387–88; 404–406.

Martin Luther

Martin Luther

© istockphoto.com / GeorgiosArt

Martin Luther read Paul's teaching on justification as if it were speaking directly to his anguished conscience and interior struggles over his own sinfulness. He also construed Paul's statements about works of the law in terms of his own discontent with sixteenth-century Catholicism. By reading Paul's statements about the law through the lens of the Catholic merit system he opposed, Luther concluded Paul opposed the Judaism of his day on the same grounds that he opposed the late medieval Catholicism of his day. Luther's characterization of the Judaism Paul allegedly rejected dominated Christian views of Judaism well into the twentieth century, when scholars began to argue the "Lutheran Paul" and Luther's Judaism bore little resemblance to historical Paul and first-century Palestinian Judaism.

insights, which seriously undermined the traditional reading of Paul, received further support from the groundbreaking study of New Testament scholar E. P. Sanders.

In *Paul and Palestinian Judaism*, Sanders compared the "pattern of religion" evident in Paul's writings with the "pattern of religion" reflected in Jewish intertestamental literature produced between ca. 200 bce and 200 ce.[9] By a "pattern of religion" Sanders meant the way a religion understands how one "gets in," or becomes a member of the community of God's people, and how one "stays in," or maintains membership in this community of the saved.[10]

---

9. E. P. Sanders, *Paul and Palestinian Judaism: A Comparison of Patterns of Religion* (London: SCM Press Ltd., 1977). Sanders aimed to distill and compare the essence of both Judaism and Pauline Christianity.

10. Ibid., 17–18.

In the first two-thirds of his book, Sanders investigated the Jewish evidence. After an extensive examination of Rabbinic sources, the Dead Sea Scrolls, and a selection of Apocryphal and Pseudepigraphal literature, Sanders concluded that Palestinian Judaism exhibited a "pattern of religion" best described by the phrase *covenantal nomism*. The phrase suggests a link between covenant and law (Grk. *nomos*). According to Sanders this pattern of religion is structured around the following notions:

1. God has graciously chosen Israel.
2. God has given Israel the commandments.
3. Along with the giving of the commandments is the demand that they be obeyed.
4. The law implies God's promise to maintain his elect ones.
5. God rewards faithful obedience and punishes transgression.
6. The law provides for means of atonement.
7. Atonement allows for the maintenance of the covenant relationship between God and Israel.
8. All those elected by God's grace and maintained in the covenant by obedience to the law, by the atonement the law makes possible, and by God's mercy will be saved.[11]

Significantly, both the first and last points characterize election and salvation as functions of God's graciousness and mercy and not the result of human achievement or merit. These eight points summarize the whole notion of covenantal nomism which holds that "one's place in God's plan is established on the basis of covenant and that the covenant requires as the proper response of man obedience to its commandments."[12] Despite the number of commandments, Judaism perceived the law as a blessing.

Contrary to the typical caricature of pre–70 ce Palestinian Judaism as a legalistic system of works-righteousness, Sanders showed that the Judaism emerging from its own presentation in the literature

---

11. The eight points are extracted from Sanders' summary of the pattern of "covenantal nomism," see *Paul and Palestinian Judaism*, 180.

12. Ibid., 75.

was a religion of grace. Regarding "getting in" to the covenanted people, Jews always understood this was by God's gracious initiative, not human achievement. Moreover, Jews never saw obedience to God's commandments as a means of "getting in," but as a requirement for "staying in" the covenant. As Sanders points out, "By consistently maintaining the framework of covenantal nomism the minutiae of the law were observed on the basis of the larger principles of religion and because of commitment to God, and humility before the God who chose and would ultimately redeem Israel."[13]

Sanders' study about the nature of first-century-ce Palestinian Judaism effectively dismantled the traditional, legalistic caricature of Judaism. However, if Sanders is correct that a) the Judaism of Paul's day was a religion of grace; b) Jews understood their election as God's covenanted people as pure grace and the law as God's greatest gift to them; and c) Paul's Jewish contemporaries could not have been against faith and grace because both were essential components of the pattern of their own religion, then this question remains: What exactly was the nature of the controversy in which Paul seems to be embroiled in his letters, especially Galatians and Romans? If Paul was not protesting a works-righteousness approach to salvation, then how does one interpret the statements listed at the beginning of this chapter? It becomes more difficult to answer this question if the "legalistic Judaism" Paul had supposedly opposed never actually existed.

Sanders' investigation of Paul's pattern of religion, the focus of the final third of his study, shaped his answer. In contrast to the covenantal nomism of Judaism, Sanders argued that Paul's pattern of religion is "Participationist Eschatology."[14] This pattern of religion entails the following notions:

1. God sent Christ to save all.
2. One participates in salvation by becoming one with Christ, dying with him to sin and sharing the promise of resurrection.
3. The transformation that begins in Baptism will be complete when the Lord returns.

---

13. Ibid., 427.
14. Ibid., 543.

4. Meanwhile, one who is "in Christ" is freed from the power of sin and,

5. therefore, must live and act as one in Christ.

6. Since Christ died to save all, all humans must have been under the power of sin, "in the flesh" as opposed to "in the spirit."

In contrast to Palestinian Judaism, where entrance into the covenanted people of God is through election, Sanders claims that Paul sees entrance into the people of God through participation "in Christ." To be justified, as Sanders believes Paul intends the term, means to be admitted to the community that lives under the Lordship of Jesus Christ. Thus justification is not about the acquittal of one's sins, but about membership in the people of God through Christ.[15]

So what was Paul's objection to the law? The traditional perspective held that Paul saw himself and all others in a hopeless predicament, under the power of Sin, from which the law provided no escape. Thus they believed that Paul envisioned salvation in Christ as the solution to this plight. Sanders claimed that Paul's thinking developed in precisely the opposite direction. Paul's view of the human plight *was a result* of his view of salvation. Because Paul believed Christ saved all, all humans needed saving. Starting with Christ as the "solution" to the human predicament, Paul depicted the human predicament to correspond to Christ's saving work. As Sanders stated, "There is no need to think that Paul felt the need for a universal savior to deal with universal human sinfulness, prior to his conviction that Christ was such a universal savior."[16]

Sanders perceived Paul's solution-to-plight thought pattern at Galatians 2:21 where he states, "if righteousness could come through the law, then Christ died for nothing." Because Paul clearly believes that Christ did not die in vain, but rather to save the whole world and bring it under his Lordship, it follows that the whole world is saved through Christ. Thus for Paul, salvation through faith in Christ excludes all other means of salvation, including the law. If Sanders is correct, even though Paul begins with the plight of

---

15. Both the participatory and juridical understandings of justification were considered in chapter 4.

16. Sanders, *Paul and Palestinian Judaism*, 443.

sinful humans under divine indictment at Romans 1:18 and moves forward to the solution—God's act in Christ—beginning in 3:21, Paul's actual thought process did not begin with anthropological considerations. Instead, it began with the theological conviction that God was saving all humanity in Christ.[17] According to Sanders, this core belief stands at the center of Paul's thought and preaching. Paul develops his views of the human plight and the inadequacy of the law around it.

Then what does Paul see as wrong with the law? In Sanders' view, Paul rejected the law for two reasons:[18] (1) because of his exclusivist Christological soteriology, that is, his belief that salvation comes only in Christ and cannot be attained in any other way;[19] (2) because the law excludes the Gentiles, whereas the new reality of God's saving work in Christ allows Gentiles access to this salvation apart from the Jewish law. Sanders summed up his understanding of Paul's posture toward the law and Judaism in the now infamous phrase: "This is what Paul finds wrong with Judaism: it is not Christianity."[20] For Sanders, Paul's objection to Judaism had nothing to do with "legalism" but with its refusal to recognize what God was doing in Christ for both Jews and Gentiles apart from the law.

Sanders' study has provided the foundation for all subsequent new perspective scholarship. Among the many who have built on and refined Sanders' insights, James D. G. Dunn, who coined the phrase "The New Perspective on Paul," stands out. Dunn, a foremost Pauline scholar, praised Sanders for his groundbreaking work on Palestinian Judaism but lamented that Sanders' interpretation left Paul appearing contradictory. In Dunn's view, Sanders simply replaced the traditional Paul, fighting against Jewish legalism and for faith alone, with a Paul who arbitrarily seems to turns his face against Judaism simply because it is not Christianity. Moreover, Dunn criticized Sanders for characterizing Paul as making a radical break with the law, Judaism, and the Jewish people when sections of his letters—for example,

---

17. Ibid., 444.

18. Ibid., 497. Sanders reaffirmed these views in a second study entitled *Paul, the Law and the Jewish People* (Philadelphia: Fortress Press, 1983).

19. *Sanders, Paul and Palestinian Judaism*, 550.

20. Ibid., 552.

Romans 3:1, 3:31, 7:12, 9:1–11:36, and 1 Corinthians 7:19—show he is not against the law, Jews, or Judaism.

Dunn critiqued Sanders and presented his own views on Paul and the law in a 1982 publication. He has continued to espouse the position set forth in that article in subsequent writings.[21] In Dunn's view, Paul did not attack the law, but rather the exclusivist attitude accompanying covenantal nomism, which was so completely associated with a sense of national identity that the law became identical with ethnic Israel. The law marked Israel as a privileged ethnic group that enjoyed God's gracious activity—in contrast to the Gentiles, who were "not God's people." According to Dunn, Paul rejected the law not on account of legalism but because of its social function, which was to discriminate between Jews and non-Jews and reinforce Jewish nationalism.

In support of his argument, Dunn notes that Paul never uses the expression "works of the law" as a reference to all *good works*, as if Paul opposed good works to faith. Rather, Dunn argues, in view of literary evidence from a variety of Jewish sources from the intertestamental period, that these "works of the law" functioned as identity markers, distinguishing Jews from all others.[22] He highlights two in particular: circumcision and food laws.[23] These texts suggest to Dunn that when Jewish identity came into question in moments of persecution and national crisis, circumcision and food laws reinforced Jewish identity and indicated whether one was a faithful Jew and member of the covenanted people. These particular works/commandments set Jews apart as God's special people. Hence they served, to use Dunn's expression, as the "badges" of Judaism[24]—the signs of membership in this exclusive ethnic group. According to Dunn, Paul objected to the

---

21. Dunn's 1982 Manson Lecture entitled, "The New Perspective on Paul," was published in the *Bulletin of the John Rylands Library* 65.2 (1983): 95–122. It was later included in J. D. G. Dunn, *Jesus, Paul and the Law: Studies in Mark and Galatians* (London: SPCK, 1990), 183–214. See also J. D. G. Dunn, *The Theology of Paul the Apostle* (Grand Rapids, MI: William B. Eerdmans, 1998), 334–389.

22. For example, 1 Maccabees 1:60–63; *Jubilees* 22:16; *Letter of Aristeas*, 139–142; Philo, *On the Life of Moses*, 1.278 and 4QMMT entitled *Miqsat Ma'aseh ha-Torah*, (Some of the Works of the Law).

23. Dunn, "New Perspective," 101.

24. Ibid., 102.

use of these badges to reinforce ethnic distinctions. Thus his critique of the law had nothing to do with arrogant Jews who thought they could merit salvation through works. Rather, Paul opposed the arrogant nationalism associated with these badges.

Dunn illustrates his point via Paul's letter to the Galatians. In Dunn's view, Paul opposed the Jewish-Christian missionaries who came to Galatia after him because they used these "works of the law" as ethnic badges to discriminate against uncircumcised Gentile believers and those who did not follow Jewish food laws. Dunn claims that at Galatians 2:15–16, Galatians 3:10–14, and throughout Romans, Paul opposes this socially discriminatory use of the law. Dunn's argument strengthens Stendahl's thesis that Paul focused on how Gentile believers attained full membership in the covenant community. For Dunn, Paul does not disparage the law in itself. Paul is neither against doing good works nor arguing that the law and faith are mutually exclusive. Rather, he is contending against Jewish Christians who have come to Galatia and are pushing Jewish practices on Gentiles. In his letter to the Galatians, Paul argues *against* the necessity of doing certain works to demonstrate one's membership and *for* faith in Christ as the sole requirement for being counted among the saved. Faith puts everyone, whether Jew or Gentile, on equal footing and eliminates the social/ethnic distinctions that circumcision and the observance of food laws represent. As Dunn observed, "What Jesus has done by his death and resurrection, in Paul's understanding, is to free the grace of God in justifying from its nationalistically restrictive clamps."[25] Covenant promises are not limited to ethnic Jews and extended only to those Gentiles who show the badges of Judaism. Rather, as Paul illustrated through the Genesis 15 account of God's covenant with Abraham (see Rom 4:1–25; Gal 3:6–9), one's right-standing with God and covenant membership have always been based on faith.

Dunn's reading of Paul as a man engaged in what is essentially social-cultural critique has some advantages. First, it keeps Paul in continuity with his ancestral religion, which he never rejected—and certainly not on the grounds that Judaism was not Christianity. If Dunn is correct, then Paul was actually taking aim at the arrogant

---

25. Ibid., 107.

ethnic particularism that derived from the doing of certain works. Second, Dunn's reading absolves Paul of the charge of inconsistency. It shows that he does not oppose obedience to the law, which is good and holy (Rom 7:12), but only *certain works* of the law.[26] By understanding Paul's critique of the law as focused on a few limited practices that fostered discrimination, Dunn avoided positing the disjuncture between Paul and the law that Sanders' work advanced. Dunn's explanation of what Paul intended when he contrasted faith in Christ to works of the law has won many adherents. It keeps Paul positive about the Jews, his ancestral religion, and the law in general. Moreover, rather than featuring Paul as a repudiator of any group, it presents him as a model of "inclusion" based on faith. Most contemporary readers find this inclusive Paul much more appealing. However, some have objected that Dunn's reading depends on and reinforces a xenophobic portrait of the Jews, which in the end is no less negative than the legalistic portrait.[27]

Sanders and Dunn are two of the more prominent advocates of the new perspective scholarship, which has continued to evolve in a number of different directions. While some issues remain unresolved, new theses and studies—some even from Jewish scholars who have offered a Jewish reading of a Jewish Paul[28]—continually enrich the debate over Paul's posture toward the law and the Jewish people. Indeed, many positive contributions to an understanding of Paul have issued from new perspective scholarship.

In the first place, new perspective scholarship provides a long overdue critique of Luther's misreading of Paul through his personal predicament and its accompanying distorted representation of first-century Judaism.

Second, as a result of new perspective scholarship, scholars now recognize that Paul did not intend his teaching on justification by

---

26. Ibid., 108.

27. See, e.g., Pamela Eisenbaum, *Paul Was Not a Christian: The Original Message of a Misunderstood Apostle* (New York: Harper Collins Publishers, 2009), esp. 99–115 and also 215, 221. See further, Neil Elliott, "An American 'Myth of Innocence' and Contemporary Pauline Studies," *Biblical Interpretation* 13.3 (2005): 239–49, esp. 245–47.

28. For a concise overview of Jewish scholarship see Michael F. Bird and Preston M. Sprinkle, "Jewish Interpretation of Paul in the Last Thirty Years," *Currents in Biblical Research* 6.3 (2008): 355–376.

faith as an attack on Judaism. As the founder and pastor of largely Gentile communities, Paul had a practical pastoral problem: on what basis could Gentiles, who had never had the law, share equally with Jews in God's promise of salvation to Abraham? Thus one can more accurately understand Paul's teaching of justification by faith by reading it within the specific context of his attempts to defend the rights of Gentiles and establish their admission requirements into the community called into being in Christ.

Third, new perspective scholarship reminds readers that Paul makes harsh statements about law-observance and circumcision only in letters where Gentiles' admission requirements and their status relative to Jews within the new community in Christ are in dispute. In these letters, Paul addresses fellow Jewish-Christian missionaries who want to impose Jewish practices on Gentile converts. He is not against Judaism or the law, but rather against requiring Gentiles to adopt practices that were never meant for them and traditionally identify ethnic Jews.

Fourth, new perspective scholarship has reestablished continuity between Paul and his ancestral religion. Although Paul's convictions changed with regard to Messiah Jesus, Paul did not convert from Judaism to a distinct new religion, Christianity. Nor did Paul's embrace of Christ necessarily entail a wholesale rejection of Torah. Paul remained a Jew his whole life. As indicated in chapter 1, many expressions of Judaism existed in first-century ce. Jews such as Paul who came to believe in Jesus constituted one more Jewish sect within Judaism.

Fifth, the new perspective's insistence on the occasional nature of Paul's letters means they can no longer be read as unbiased representations of Judaism or used uncritically as sources to construct an accurate portrayal of Jewish thought and practice. As new perspective advocates point out, Paul was a Jew who had come to believe that the promises of God are actualized in Christ. He filtered his presentation of the law as inefficacious through what he believed God has accomplished for all, without distinction, through Christ's death and Resurrection.

These important insights afforded by new perspective scholarship allow a more profitable and accurate reading of Paul's views on Judaism, Jews, and the law. However, some aspects of the new perspective have raised concerns. Among these are two that relate to Sanders' work, which is the foundation of new perspective scholarship.

The first regards the accuracy of Sanders' depiction of first-century Judaism as completely devoid of legalistic tendencies or any notion of works-righteousness. Rabbinic scholar Jacob Neusner has argued that Sanders' categorization of all of Judaism under the term *covenantal nomism* defies the evidence.[29] He points to various texts found in intertestamental literature that emphasize a works-righteousness approach to salvation.[30] For example, in *2 Baruch* one reads that living according to the law and doing its works leads to eternal life:

> Miracles, however, will appear at their own time to those who are saved because of their works, and for whom the law is now a hope, and intelligence, expectation and wisdom a trust. For they shall see that world which is now invisible to them and they will see a time which is now hidden to them. And time will no longer make them older.
>
> For they will live in the heights of that world and they will be like the angels and be equal to the stars. And they will be changed into any shape which they wished, from beauty to loveliness and from light to the splendor of glory. (51:7–10)[31]

In a similar vein, *4 Ezra* states "those who have shown scorn and have not kept the way of the Most High, and who have despised his Law" will suffer various torments, while those who have "laboriously served the Most High, and withstood danger every hour, that they might keep the Law of the Lawgiver perfectly" will have eternal life (cf. *4 Ezra* 7:79–87).[32] One finds similar views about

---

29. Jacob Neusner, *Judaic Law from Jesus to the Mishnah: A Systematic Reply to Professor E. P. Sanders* (Atlanta: Scholars Press, 1993).

30. For example, Tobit 13–14, *Psalms of Solomon* 13–14; 4 Ezra 2:15–32, 7:21–22, 75–87, 88–100; and *2 Baruch* 17:4, 51:1–9, 84:1–11.

31. From A. J. F. Klijn's translation of *2 Baruch* in James H. Charlesworth (ed.), *The Old Testament Pseudepigrapha*, vol. 1 (Garden City, NY: Doubleday & Co., Inc., 1983).

32. From Bruce M. Metzger's translation of *4 Ezra* in James H. Charlesworth (ed.), *The Old Testament Pseudepigrapha*, vol. 1.

the necessity of keeping the law in various texts from Qumran (for example, 1QPHab 8:1–3; 4QPs 8:4–5; 1QS 4:6–8). Additionally, the evidence referenced at the beginning of this chapter from Deuteronomy 4:1–2 and 28:1–14 presents the keeping of the commandments as a matter of life and death. Given this textual evidence of Jewish belief that salvation was merited through doing the works of the law, the possibility must at least be entertained that in Romans and Galatians Paul was criticizing such a works-righteousness approach, or at least a "synergistic" approach, to salvation.[33] This evidence does not overturn Sanders' view of Palestinian Judaism as a religion of grace or Dunn's observations regarding the discriminatory nature of some "works of the law" that Paul may have had in view. Neither does it compel a return to Luther's distorted view of Jews and Judaism. However, it does require acknowledging the existence of a group, or groups, of Jews who kept the precepts of the law in order to merit salvation and who may have seen their efforts not as a denial of God's grace but as attempts to cooperate with it.

A second concern relates to the degree to which the new perspective disregards the theological and soteriological weight of Paul's teaching on justification by faith. New perspective scholarship insists that Paul intended justification by faith to signify only the condition for the admission of the Gentiles and their transfer to the Lordship of Christ. No one denies that justification entails a transfer from the realm of Sin to the realm of grace under the Lordship of Christ, which is actualized in baptism. However, Paul's teaching seems to include more than that. For Paul, because of what God has done in Christ through his expiatory death, all persons are justified. Regardless of class, ethnicity, or gender, they become members of the people of God in Christ through faith. As discussed in chapter 5, Paul saw humans as incapable of resisting the flesh, which Sin exploited to keep them under its reign and alienated from God. Sin even perverted the law, which became its accomplice by enticing humans to sin. Hence the incapacity of the law to rescue humans from the bondage of Sin and death necessitated the coming of Christ, who

---

33. A "synergistic" approach allows for the working together (synergy) of God's grace and meritorious deeds. Some argue that what Paul opposed with his grace-only gospel was this synergistic approach. See Charles Talbot, "Paul, Judaism and the Revisionists," *Catholic Biblical Quarterly* 63.1 (2001): 1–22.

accomplished what the law could not do. Sanders, in order to keep the law in a positive light, maintains that there was nothing wrong with it. God simply substituted a new righteousness rooted in Christ for one rooted in the law. However, as New Testament scholar Brendan Byrne observed, "In Paul's theology God did not simply substitute a new way of salvation in place of the Law. There is an intrinsic connection between the ineffectiveness of the Law and the death of Christ."[34] Paul makes this clear in Romans where he states,

> For God has done what the law, weakened by the flesh could not do: by sending his own Son in the likeness of sinful flesh, and to deal with sin, he condemned sin in the flesh, so that the just requirement of the law might be fulfilled. (Rom 8:3–4)

Even Paul, a Jew by birth, admitted that he did not have a righteousness of his own that comes from the law, but a righteousness that comes through faith in Christ (Phil 3:9; see further Gal 2:15–16) who died "for all" (cf. Gal 2:19–20 and 2 Cor 5:14–15). Especially in Galatians 2:19–20, the atoning, substitutionary purpose of Christ's death to save humans from Sin is present along with the participatory purpose.

Once one admits the theological and salvific import of Paul's teaching on justification by faith, the Lutheran understanding of Paul, especially when detached from Luther's distorted caricature of Judaism, cannot be so easily dismissed. Luther appears to have correctly grasped Paul's profound insights about human weakness and enslavement to Sin apart from God's saving act in Christ, which rescues humans from the power of Sin and death. Recognizing the soteriological dimension of Paul's teaching on justification by faith does not negate that this teaching also had a practical application to Paul's pastoral problem involving the admission of Gentiles. But to limit one's understanding of this teaching to the practical without attention to its theological import seems the exegetical equivalent of "throwing out the baby with the bath water." The parallels

---

34. Brendan Byrne, *Sons of God, Seed of Abraham: A Study of the Idea of the Sonship of God of All Christians in Paul Against the Jewish Background* (Rome: Pontifical Biblical Institute Press, 1979), 231.

Luther drew between his personal situation and Paul's and between first-century Judaism and medieval Roman Catholicism may have been misguided, but Luther's insights into Paul's theology need not be completely jettisoned on that account.

The two concerns raised regarding new perspective scholarship are legitimate. Nonetheless, as Luther's insights need not be completely dismissed despite distortions, neither can one dismiss insights advanced by new perspective scholarship because its portrait of first-century Judaism may be too uniform or because it has undervalued Paul's soteriology. Those concerns notwithstanding, new perspective scholarship has made an immeasurable contribution to an understanding of Paul and first-century Judaism. It is no longer possible to caricature first-century Judaism along the lines of Luther or to interpret Paul as hostile to the Jews or his ancestral religion, which he never repudiated. In fact, new perspective scholarship has refocused attention on Paul's continuous concern for fellow Jews who have not come to faith in Christ (Rom 9:1–5). Paul underscores their priority in the divine economy of salvation and presents Gentile salvation as inextricably linked to that of ethnic Israel (Rom 11:17–25). Moreover, he expresses absolute certainty that God, who acted inclusively with regard to the Gentiles, will not fail to include and save ethnic Israel, his elect and beloved people (see Rom 11:26–29). Finally, and most significantly, new perspective scholarship has taught the importance of learning to read Paul's struggles with the law through lenses cleansed of later interpreters, who turned Paul into the enemy of his own people and his words into a seedbed of anti-Judaism.[35]

Summary

Why did Paul oppose faith to law? What did he find objectionable about works of the law? This chapter considered the answers to these questions found in two diverse interpretive perspectives: the

---

35. Marcion (first to second century ce) seems to have been the first to misconstrue Paul for his own anti-Jewish purposes, cf. Joseph Tyson, "Anti-Judaism in Marcion and His Opponents," *Studies in Christian-Jewish Relations* 1.1 (2005). This is a peer-reviewed e-journal published by the Center for Christian-Jewish Learning at Boston College. The essay is available at *ejournals.bc.edu/ojs/index.php/scjr/article/view/1359*.

old perspective, or traditional Lutheran interpretation, and the new perspective, as represented by two of its most prominent advocates, E. P. Sanders and J. D. G. Dunn. In the last forty years, as a result of new perspective scholarship, both traditionalists and new perspective advocates now agree on a number of points. Most accept that first-century Judaism was not the legalistic religion depicted by Luther. Most agree Paul's letters are not theological treatises but occasional letters that need to be interpreted with awareness of the situation he addresses. Most welcome the stress on continuity between Paul and Judaism, especially given the heightened concern over anti-Semitism after the horror of the Holocaust. However, disagreement continues between and within these interpretive traditions about whether and to what degree Luther got Paul right; about what justification effectuates—transfer to the Lordship of Christ only (new perspective) or the acquittal of sin (old perspective) or both; about whether by "works of the law" Paul intended to exclude all human effort (old perspective) or only those works that reinforced ethnic identity and arrogant nationalism (new perspective). This is an ongoing debate. Although most scholars agree that Paul's image needed to be divorced from Luther's portrayal of him and Judaism detached from Luther's pernicious construction of it, they are still far from consensus about what exactly Paul opposed and why.

Questions for Review and Reflection

1. How did Luther recontextualize Paul in view of the theological categories and social context of his own day?

2. How does the new perspective on Paul elevate our awareness of the need to pay attention to both the social context of Paul's letters and their occasional nature?

3. What are the contributions and weaknesses of the new perspective on Paul?

4. Do you see or experience evidence of Christian supersessionism today in church and society? Explain.

5. How has new perspective scholarship contributed to making Paul's letters a site of dialogue instead of polemic with Jews and Judaism?

Opening More Windows

Boyarin, Daniel. *A Radical Jew: Paul and the Politics of Identity.* Berkeley: University of California Press, 1994. (Free digital access to this book is available at *publishing.cdlib.org/ucpressebooks.*)

Boys, Mary C. *Has God Only One Blessing? Judaism as a Source of Christian Self-Understanding.* Mahwah, NJ: Paulist Press, 2000.

Connelly, John. *From Enemy to Brother: The Revolution in Catholic Teaching on the Jews, 1933–1965.* Cambridge, MA: Harvard University Press, 2012.

Gager, John G. *Reinventing Paul.* Oxford: Oxford University Press, 2000.

Gathercole, Simon J. "What Did Paul Really Mean? 'New Perspective' Scholars Argue That We Need, Well, a New Perspective on Justification by Faith." *Christianity Today* 51.8 (2007): 22–28.

Heen, Erik M. "A Lutheran Response to the New Perspective on Paul." *Lutheran Quarterly* 24 (2010): 263–91.

Pascuzzi, Maria. "The Church without Israel? No Way!" *The Living Light* 40.3 (2004): 6–17. Also available at *nccbuscc.org/education/catechetics/spring2004.pdf.*

Ruether, Rosemary. *Faith and Fratricide: The Theological Roots of Anti-Semitism.* Eugene, OR: Wipf & Stock, 1996.

_____. "The Holocaust: Theological and Ethical Reflections," *The Twentieth Century: A Theological Overview*, ed. Gregory Baum. Maryknoll, NY: Orbis Books, 1999, 76–90.

Segal, Alan. *Paul the Convert: The Apostolate and Apostasy of Saul the Pharisee.* New Haven, CT: Yale University Press, 1990.

_____. *Rebecca's Children: Judaism and Christianity in the Roman World.* Cambridge, MA: Harvard University Press, 1986.

Stendahl, Krister. *Paul among Jews and Gentiles.* Philadelphia: Fortress Press, 1976.

Stuhlmacher, Peter, and Donald A. Haegner. *A Challenge to the New Perspective: Revisiting Paul's Doctrine of Justification.* Downers Grove, IL: InterVarsity Press, 2001.

Westerholm, Stephen. *Perspectives Old and New on Paul: The "Lutheran" Paul and His Critics.* Grand Rapids, MI: William B. Eerdmans, 2004.

Wright, N. T. *What Saint Paul Really Said.* Grand Rapids, MI: William B. Eerdmans, 1997.

Internet Resources

"A Sacred Obligation: Rethinking Christian Faith in Relation to Judaism and the Jewish People." Christian Scholars Group on Christian-Jewish Relations, *www.ccjr.us/dialogika-resources/documents-and-statements/ecumenical-christian/568-csg-02sep1.*

Chapter 7

Called into Fellowship with Christ: The Church

Overview

This chapter begins with an examination of Paul's understanding of the church's origin and its hallmarks. Then it considers the social composition of the Pauline churches in light of recent social historical studies. Paul's theological exposition of baptism and the social and ethical consequences of incorporation into the body of believers in Christ are explored next. The final focus of this chapter is the two key images Paul uses to describe the church and the significance of each.

Recommended Reading

1 Corinthians 1:1–14:40   Galatians 5:1–26

Romans 6:1–14, 9–11   Wisdom of Solomon 14:12–31

The Church: One and Holy

"Church" is the word used in the New Testament to translate the Greek *ekklēsia*, a term that signifies an assembly of people.[1] When Paul arrived in a city, there was no "church." Instead, there were many

---

1. In secular usage, *ekklēsia* originally referred to a political assembly of the *demos*, or people. See Gerhard Kittel (ed.), *Theological Dictionary of the New Testament* (Grand Rapids, MI: William B. Eerdmans, 1965), vol. 3, esp. 513.

ekklēsiai, or discrete associations of people, each structured around its own set of interests. As generally recognized, these local assemblies provided organizational models for Paul and his first converts as they began to coalesce into small communities, meeting in homes as did many other *ekklēsiai.*[2] However, as Paul insisted, the Christian assembly, or church, was distinct from every other human assembly in two unique ways. First, it came about not by human but by divine initiative. The church's existence coincided with the inauguration of the new eschatological age of redemption that God brought about through the Christ-event. Thus the church is part of the mystery of God's redemptive plan, a new community for the new age. It is God, Paul says, who calls people into the *koinōnia,* or fellowship, of his son Jesus Christ (1 Cor 1:9). The call comes to women and men through the preaching of the gospel to which one must respond in faith (Rom 10:17). No one simply chooses to join as if the *ekklēsia* were just another association. This is the *ekklēsia tou theou,* "of God," a possessive qualification that reinforces the church's divine origin (see, e.g., 1 Cor 1:2; 2 Cor 1:1; Gal 1:6, 13).[3] Second, the assembly of God's people does not revolve around the usual common denominators and interests that bring people together, such as occupation, language, gender, ethnicity, or politics. Rather, the singular reason why the Christian assembly exists is to be in union with Jesus Christ, the source and cause of the union of all those in him with each other. It cannot be overemphasized that for Paul, sharing in Christ's *koinōnia* or fellowship always means sharing in the life of Christ *with others.* It means belonging to a community centered on Christ, in which normal aggregating factors do not matter. In essence, the church is a network of human relationships deriving from and revolving around Christ. Because the union of believers in

---

2. A comparison of Paul's churches with other social groups and associations in the cities where they coexisted is provided by Wayne A. Meeks, *The First Urban Christians: The Social World of the Apostle Paul* (New Haven, CT: Yale University Press, 1983), 74–84. See further, Richard S. Ascough, *What Are They Saying about the Formation of the Pauline Churches?* (Mahwah, NJ: Paulist Press, 1998).

3. *Ekklēsia* is used many times in the LXX to translate the Hebrew word *qahal,* which means assembly, congregation, or convocation. In the Jewish Scriptures, those called, assembled, and identified as God's people constituted the *qahal* or "assembly" of God. This Jewish usage provides the principle background for Paul's reference to the assembly of Christ believers as the *ekklēsia tou theou.*

The church is a web of human relations, all deriving from and revolving around Christ.

Christ and with each other was willed by God, unity is an essential aspect of the church's nature.

Today it is common to hear people steadfastly proclaim their personal commitment to Christ, while simultaneously and just as adamantly declaring their dissociation from the church. This would have been foreign and no doubt troubling to Paul, for whom being "in" or "with" Christ never signified a private spiritual existence. For Paul, Christian identity was always intrinsically linked to ecclesial identity.

In addition to unity, those in Christ are called to "holiness." Also willed by God, holiness is, in Paul's view, the church's other essential characteristic (see 1 Thess 4:3). This is the same call and demand made of ancient Israel, and it was based on God's own holy character: "You shall be holy to me; for I the Lord am holy, and I have separated you from the other peoples to be mine" (Lev 20:26). However, for Paul and all Christ-believers, the vocation to holiness also is rooted in what God has done in Christ, through whose death they are redeemed and sanctified (see 1 Cor 1:30, 6:11).

In his letters, Paul frequently reminds community members of both their status as God's "holy ones" (*hagioi*) and their vocation:

they are "called to be holy (*klētoi hagioi*)."[4] In the Hebrew Bible, sanctification did not signify interior moral transformation, nor did holiness necessarily relate to a person's individual moral character or personal piety. Holiness was the status attributed to those things set apart from common use and dedicated to God. Nothing was holy in itself, but anything—whether a place, a thing, or a person—could become holy by its being set apart for God. This kind of holiness, usually referred to as ritual or cultic holiness, was not lost through individual moral failing, or sin, but by coming into contact with something considered ritually impure, such as a corpse or a type of food or utensil.[5] As evident from his letters, Paul clearly separates "holiness" from its cultic context and associates it with a pattern of moral behavior that will distinguish God's holy ones, or saints, from those who are not part of the assembly of believers united in Christ (see, e.g., 1 Thess 4:1–8; Phil 2:12–15; 1 Cor 6:1–11). In pursuing their vocation to holiness, Christ-believers did not need to retreat to a distant place (see 1 Cor 5:9–11). Rather, they needed to put distance between themselves and nonbelievers by their manner of life, both individually and corporately.

Paul's understanding of the church as the new eschatological community of God, whose essence was manifested in its unity and holiness, helps explain why he responded with urgency when either was threatened. In fact, most of Paul's disputes with his communities were about unity and holiness. Chapter 6 considered Paul's views on the law concerning how Jews and Gentiles would form one community of faith. Since insistence on law-observance threatened to create a two-tiered community, or worse, a community divided into separate ethnic constituencies, Paul argued in his letter to the Galatians that law-observance had to be set aside. In Philippians, Paul had to exhort believers to agree (2:1–2) and even designated a local community member to mediate a dispute and restore unity between two influential women in the community, Evodia and Syntyche (4:2–3). In Galatians, Paul reminds believers

---

4. See, e.g., Romans 1:7, 15:25, 16:2; 1 Corinthians 1:2, 14:33; 2 Corinthians 1:1, 9:1, 13:1; Philippians 1:1, 4:21–22; 1 Thessalonians 3:13, 5:23; Philemon 5, 7.

5. The Israelite conception of holiness and ritual purity and impurity is discussed in detail in David P. Wright, "Unclean and Clean," in *The Anchor Bible Dictionary*, ed. David N. Freedman (New York: Doubleday, 1996), vol. 6, 728–42.

that living by the Spirit leaves no room for rivalry, factions, or competitiveness (5:16–26). Throughout 1 Corinthians, Paul aims to reconcile a divided community and restore unity.[6] He first confronts community members who have aligned themselves behind preferred leaders—some declaring allegiance to Paul, others to Apollos, others Cephas, and still others to Christ (1:12). Paul offers the example of himself and Apollos to illustrate how God's ministers should work as collaborators, not rivals (3:1–22). Community members should view their ministers that way rather than splintering off into rival factions behind favorites.

In the same letter, Paul deals with disagreements over what one eats (1 Cor 8–10)—an apparent source of division within the community at Rome as well (Rom 14:1–3, 14–21)—and what spiritual gifts demonstrate greater spiritual maturity (1 Cor 12–14). Apparently some Corinthian believers boasted of their elite status because of their superior "knowledge" and "spiritual gifts." Paul tackles both issues in order to reconcile the community and restore unity. Perhaps nowhere were the divisions more apparent than at the Eucharistic table—the precise place where the community's unity, symbolized and sustained by sharing the one bread and one cup, was to be most evident (1 Cor 10:16–17). Yet the same elite arrived and ate and drank their fill in complete disregard for the poorer members of the community (1 Cor 11:17–22). Here again, Paul admonishes those who threaten the unity of the community. Without that unity, the church in Corinth—or any other place—is not church.

Paul exhibits equal urgency in the face of threats to the community's holiness—evident especially in 1 Corinthians, where he deals with different types of sexual immorality (5:1–13 and 6:12–20) and the prospect of community members lapsing back to idolatry (10:1–22). This type of behavior could not be tolerated; therefore, Paul commands the Corinthians to abstain from fornication (6:18) and the worship of idols (10:14) and to remove from their midst anyone who persists in compromising the community's holiness through sexual immorality (Cor 5:13).

---

6. Margaret Mitchell's comprehensive study of 1 Corinthians shows Paul involved in a sustained effort to restore unity in Corinth. See *Paul and the Rhetoric of Reconciliation: An Exegetical Investigation of the Language and Composition of 1 Corinthians* (Tübingen, Germany: Mohr Siebeck, 1991).

Paul's concern that the community's holiness be manifested in the avoidance of idolatry and sexual immorality was consistent with Jewish belief that Israel's holiness was manifested in behavior that differentiated it from pagans. Because from the Jewish perspective, sexual immorality and idolatry were the hallmark vices of pagans (see Wis 14:12–14, 21–27), these were to be avoided, and Christ-believers were not exempt. However, although Paul saw no place for sexual immorality among those called to union and holiness in Christ, he never used sexual morality as the exclusive measure of Christian holiness. As Pauline scholar Michael Gorman observes, a Christian was also expected to manifest holiness in Christlikeness.[7] For Paul, Christlikeness meant a way of life characterized by self-emptying love for the sake of others (see esp. Phil 2:5–8; 2 Cor 8:8–10; Gal 5:13–14), while any disregard for the holiness and unity of the community meant putting its continued existence as God's church in Christ at risk.

Those Called: A Social Profile

Paul's mission shifted the development of early Christianity away from a predominantly rural movement in Jewish Palestine to a largely Gentile and urban movement throughout the Mediterranean. As previously indicated, the mixed populations to whom Paul preached lived in a hierarchically structured society with processes in place that reinforced widespread social and economic inequality.[8] The working poor were exploited, with little opportunity to transcend their situation. They were the majority of the population, called the *humiliores,* or the humble masses, in contrast to *honestiores,* the small elite segment of the population.[9] In the past, scholars assumed most of the people of the Pauline churches were poor and uneducated. They based their assumption on a reading of 1 Corinthians

---

7. Michael J. Gorman, "You Shall Be Cruciform for I Am Cruciform," in *Holiness and Ecclesiology in the New Testament,* ed. Kent E. Brower and Andy Johnson (Grand Rapids, MI: William B. Eerdmans, 2007), 148–66.

8. See Peter Garnsey and Richard Saller, *The Roman Empire: Economy, Society, and Culture* (Berkeley: University of California Press, 1987), 107–25.

9. Ibid, 116; on social mobility, see esp. 123–25.

1:26–29 as a prima facie description of the social level of Paul's first converts. Paul states,

> Consider your own call brothers and sisters: not many of you were wise by human standards, not many were powerful, not many were of noble birth. But God chose what is foolish in the world to shame the wise. God chose what is weak in the world to shame the strong; God chose what is low and despised in the world, things that are not, to reduce to nothing things that are, so that no one might boast in the presence of God.

In addition to Paul's comments, the remarks of Celsus, a second-century-ce pagan who attacked Christianity, also influenced assumptions about the social level of the first Christians. Celsus' remarks are preserved in the writings of his contemporary, the church father Origen. In his treatise entitled *Against Celsus*, Origen cites Celsus, who claimed that Christians themselves realized their beliefs were so bogus that they turned intelligent people away, saying,

> Let no one come to us who has been instructed, or who is wise or prudent; for such qualifications are deemed evil by us; but if there be any ignorant, or unintelligent, or uninstructed, or foolish persons, let them come with confidence.

Based on this rather contemptuous projection, Celsus immediately concludes,

> By which words, acknowledging that such individuals are worthy of their God, they manifestly show that they desire and are able to gain over only the silly, and the mean, and the stupid, with women and children.[10]

Scholars took these and other disparaging comments by Celsus describing Christians as boorish, uneducated rustics[11] as a realistic description of the social level of early Christians. Combined with

---

10. Origen, *Against Celsus*, Bk. 3, ch. 44 at *www.newadvent.org/fathers/04163.htm*.
11. Ibid., ch. 55–58.

Paul's remarks, they provided the foundation for the assessment of earliest Christianity as a movement of the lowest classes.

This view prevailed without much objection until relatively recently, when social historical studies of the Pauline communities by various New Testament scholars produced a different assessment.[12] In each study, scholars looked beyond 1 Corinthians 1:26–28 and Celsus' polemical remarks to examine a wider swath of evidence. For example, in his influential study, Wayne Meeks considered the profiles of the nearly eighty persons associated with Paul's churches named in his letters and in Acts of the Apostles. He noted some had financial means and were able to travel (e.g., Prisca and Aquila and Apollos). Some, such as Lydia, were from the merchant class (see Acts 16:14). Others had homes sufficiently large to accommodate the Christian assembly for its weekly meetings; for example, Prisca and Aquila (see Rom 16:4), Gaius (Rom 16:23), and Philemon (Phlm 1). Phoebe, a female deacon, helped finance Paul's mission (see Rom 16:1). Crispus was a synagogue ruler, a position usually held by a person of some means (see Acts 18:8). Erastus, named at Romans 16:23, was the *oikonomos tēs poleōs*, that is, the "treasurer of the city" of Corinth, a position of status and perhaps some wealth. Some members of the community were slaves, as evident from Paul's letter to Philemon, which concerns his slave Onesimus (see Phlm 1–25), and also from the passage at 1 Corinthians 7:21–22. Meeks also noted that Paul's expectation that his communities would take up a collection for the poor suggests some had the means to support others (see, e.g., Rom 15:22–28; 1 Cor 16:1–4; 2 Cor 9:1–7; Gal 2:10). Meeks also detected economic differences at 1 Corinthians 11:17–22, where Paul upbraids the "haves" for sating themselves at the Lord's Supper, while the "have-nots" arrive to find nothing and go hungry. Meeks' study cemented the scholarly consensus that Paul's first communities comprised people from across the various social strata, with no evidence of people from the absolute lowest

---

12. See, e.g., Gerd Theissen, *The Social Setting of Pauline Christianity: Essays on Corinth* (Philadelphia: Fortress Press, 1982); Abraham J. Malherbe, *Social Aspects of Early Christianity* (Philadelphia: Fortress Press, 1983), 31–59; Wayne A. Meeks, *The First Urban Christians;* Edwin A. Judge, *The Social Pattern of Christian Groups in the First Century* (London: Tyndale, 1960); Rodney Stark, *The Rise of Christianity* (San Francisco: HarperCollins, 1998).

Fresco of Terentius Neo and his wife, Pompeii, National Archeological Museum, Naples. Social-historical studies of Paul's communities indicate that members came from across the social strata.

or highest rungs of society. This continues to be the consensus, notwithstanding occasional challenges to it.[13]

Beyond the evidence pointing to a socially mixed group, Meeks also used modern sociological categories to hypothesize that the first urban Christians experienced "status inconsistency."[14] This occurs when the various measurements of status do not agree. In other words, status inconsistency arises when a person's achieved status— what one is able to gain through education or hard work—is not consistent with one's accredited status, which is based on birth,

---

13. See, e.g., Justin J. Meggitt, *Paul, Poverty and Survival* (Edinburg: T & T Clark, 1998), esp. 97–154, who contends that the earliest Christians, en masse, were destitute. But see the critique of his method and conclusions by Dale B. Martin, "Review Essays: Justin J. Meggitt, *Paul, Poverty and Survival," Journal for the Study of the New Testament* 84.4 (2001): 51–64.

14. Meeks, *First Urban Christians,* 72–73.

race, or ethnicity. This is exemplified in the case of a person who is wealthy but of "low" birth, educated but "only" a slave, or in a powerful position but "only" a woman.

Status inconsistency may explain why some people were more attracted to the gospel and open to conversion than others. It is conceivable that women of means such as Lydia and Phoebe, as well as slaves such as Onesimus, and other members of Paul's churches suffered from status inconsistency. If so, they may have found Paul's gospel preaching, with its message of freedom and equality in Christ, extremely attractive. However, many other reasons beyond the leveling of social status could explain the attraction of Christianity. Paul's gospel offered a vision of life rooted in a wisdom that went beyond the wisdom of the world. Most importantly, it promised eternal life to those in Christ.

From Faith to Baptism

Those who responded to the gospel with faith were incorporated into Christ and the community of God's holy ones through baptism, a special initiation rite that marked believers from outsiders. Paul did not introduce the practice of baptism, a word that derives from the Greek *baptizein,* meaning to dip or immerse. According to Acts, he was baptized soon after his encounter with the Risen Lord (9:18) and baptized others as part of his ministry (see 1 Cor 1:17).[15] In his letters, Paul does not explain baptism or its origins.[16] He seems to assume all Christ-believers had a common experience of baptism (see 1 Cor 12:13) and uses that fact to argue other points (see, e.g., Rom 6:1–11 and Gal 3:26–29). Because Paul's letters contain few direct references to baptism, only a few deductions can be made about the actual rite. First, all believers were baptized into

---

15. On whether Paul's baptizing ministry was as limited as he claims at 1 Cor 1:17, see Maria Pascuzzi, "Baptism-based Allegiance and the Divisions in Corinth: A Reexamination of 1 Corinthians 1:13–17," *Catholic Biblical Quarterly* 71.4 (2009): 813–29.

16. Some scholars think Christian baptism derived from Jewish proselyte baptism, others from the tradition of John the Baptist (see Mark 1:4). Nonetheless, it is distinct from both in at least these two ways: Christian baptism was in/into the name of Jesus (see 1 Cor 1:13 and further Acts 2:38, 19:1–9) and it is associated with the reception of the Holy Spirit (see 1 Cor 12:13 and further Acts 2:38, 19:1–9).

the name of Jesus (see 1 Cor 1.13, 15).[17] Second, baptism entailed a washing with water or perhaps a full immersion (see 1 Cor 6:11 and 10:1–2). Third, in baptism believers each received the same Spirit, which solidified their unity in Christ (see 1 Cor 12:13). Beyond that, it is uncertain what form the baptismal rite actually took in Paul's day.[18] More than likely, there were a variety of ways to administer baptism rather than a single rite practiced by all. At Corinth, the living even received baptism on behalf of the dead (see 1 Cor 15:29). What form that baptism rite

© Erich Lessing / Art Resource, NY

Baptismal scene on a sarcophagus, third-century relief, National Museum of Rome, Italy. In the fresco, a naked youth stands in water with the baptizer's hand resting on his head.

for the dead took and its purpose remain an enigma. However, it serves as a reminder that baptismal practice was not necessarily uniform in Paul's day. What is certain is that over time the rite evolved, along with the theological understanding of baptism.[19]

Paul's few direct references to baptism should not be taken as an indication of its unimportance. On the contrary, Paul understood baptism as signifying the radical reorienting of one's existence. He provided one of the earliest and most profound theological interpretations of baptism at Romans 6: 3–11. For Paul, Christian baptism was not

---

17. In addressing the factious situation at Corinth where community members seemed to have aligned themselves in rival groups behind the minister who baptized them, Paul poses the rhetorical question, "were you baptized in the name of Paul?" (1:13). "No, you were baptized in Christ's name," is the expected, but unstated, answer.

18. See Meeks, *First Urban Christians*, 150–57.

19. Chapter 7 of "The Teaching (Grk. *didachē*) of the Twelve Apostles," usually referred to as "The *Didachē*," ca. 50–150 ce, contains a brief description of the baptismal rite, see Michael W. Holmes (ed.), *The Apostolic Fathers: Greek Texts and English Translations* (Grand Rapids, MI: Baker Books, 1999 rev. ed). See further, Justin, 1 *Apology* 61 at *www.ccel.org/ccel/schaff/anf01.viii.ii.lxi.html*.

reducible to a purification rite or even an act of repentance and conversion for the forgiveness of sins, as preached by John the Baptist (see Mark 1:4). Rather, he conceived it as a real and personal participation in the death, burial, and Resurrection of Christ. In baptism, Paul says, the believer undergoes co-crucifixion (6:6) with Christ and is co-buried (6:4) with him into death. Paul prefixes the preposition *syn* (with) to the Greek verb *stauroō* (to crucify) and *thaptō* (to bury) to reenforce the believer's assimilation into Christ's death and burial. As New Testament scholar Robert Jewett notes, Paul was apparently the first person to connect baptism and burial and, by doing so, to communicate an absolute finality with regard to one's former life of enslavement to Sin.[20] Since Sin, understood as a cosmic power, exercises control over humans only when they are alive, if a believer is dead and buried, Sin's dominion is over. Thus having experienced death to Sin's power, the believer comes forth from baptism able to choose to resist Sin's power. With that new freedom, the believer can begin living for God as Christ does, in order to also participate in a resurrection like his.

The Social and Ethical Implications of Baptism

In addition to this theological exposition of baptism, Paul considers its social and ethical consequences elsewhere in his letters. For Paul, beyond dying to Sin, baptism also entailed dying to all the old religious, cultural, and social distinctions that no longer had any place in the new union of believers in Christ. Paul makes this explicit at Galatians 3:26–28, where he states,

> for in Christ Jesus you are all children of God through faith. As many of you as were baptized into Christ have clothed yourselves with Christ. There is no longer Jew or Greek, there is no longer slave or free, there is no longer male and female; for all of you are one in Christ Jesus.

Pauline scholars recognize that these verses contain a pre-Pauline baptismal formula that may have been recited during the baptismal

---

20. Robert Jewett, *Romans: A Commentary* (Minneapolis, MN: Fortress Press, 2007), 398.

rite.[21] In the context of his argument in Galatians, Paul cites this formula to refute the opposition's claim that circumcision was a requisite for salvation. Thus the statement serves primarily as a soteriological statement, affirming that all have equal access to salvation through faith in Christ. But it is also widely recognized as a socially inclusive statement with revolutionary consequences. In a hierarchical world where social distinctions mattered, this statement asserts the relative unimportance of ethnicity, social status, and gender and establishes union with Christ as the one requisite for sharing in the promises God made to Abraham. Wayne Meeks characterized this baptismal formula as a "performative utterance,"—not mere words, but words that "make a factual claim about an objective change in reality that fundamentally modifies social roles."[22]

Scholars debate to what degree social roles and structures were actually modified. Certainly regarding the relationship between Jewish and Gentile Christ-believers, which constituted Paul's chief concern in Romans and Galatians, he expected ethnic differences to be overlooked so that a community of equals in Christ could take shape. As one practical demonstration of this new common life in Christ, Paul apparently expected Jews and Gentiles to eat together. This can be inferred from Galatians 2:11–14, where Paul recounts his confrontation with Peter, who backtracked on eating with Gentiles. The practical implications regarding slaves are less clear. Paul had something to say about the status of slaves at 1 Corinthians 7:20–22, but what he intended remains an enigma.[23] Elsewhere, Paul

---

21. Paul uses the same formula, minus the terms "male and female," at 1 Corinthians 12:12–13, which contains a direct reference to baptism, and there serves his argument about unity.

22. See Wayne A. Meeks, "The Image of Androgyne," *History of Religions* 13.3 (1974): 165–208.

23. The problem centers on v. 21, which abruptly concludes with the words *mallon chrēsai,* literally, "rather make use of." But it is uncertain what Paul commands slaves to "make use of." Should they make use of freedom if they can gain it, or make use of their present condition of slavery? Various translations have been proposed, such as "Were you a slave when you were called? Do not be concerned about it. Even if you can gain your freedom, make use of your present condition now more than ever" (NRSV); "Were you a slave when you were called? Do not be concerned but, even if you can gain your freedom, make the most of it" (NAB rev. ed.); "Were you a slave when you were called? Don't let it trouble you—although if you can gain your freedom, do so" (NIV); "Were you called while a slave? Do not be concerned about it; but if you can be made free, rather use it" (NKJV).

intervenes on behalf of the slave Onesimus, exhorting his master Philemon to receive him back "no longer as a slave but more than a slave, a beloved brother" (Phlm 16). Whether Paul intended their new fraternal relationship in Christ to override or even annul their master-slave relationship remains a matter of debate. In any event, neither text suggests that Paul had the abolition of the slave system in mind. Also unclear are the practical social implications regarding women.[24] Unfortunately, Paul did not provide a blueprint outlining changes to the status quo or their practical implementation. However, he did expect that the working out of this new state of affairs resulting from baptism would require changes in believers' attitudes and behavior. Paul communicates this at 2 Corinthians 5:15–17, where, alluding to baptism again, he states,

> And He died for all, so that those who live might live no longer for themselves, but for Him who died and was raised for them. From now on, therefore, we regard no one from a human point of view; even though we once knew Christ from a human point of view, we know Him no longer in that way. So if anyone is in Christ, there is a new creation: everything old has passed away; see, everything has become new!

In addition to social consequences, baptism also had ethical implications. Baptism was not just a ceremony at the beginning of one's faith journey. Believers were "clothed" in Christ (Gal 3:27), an expression used to communicate neither superficial nor temporary identification with Christ but the adoption of a new lifelong identity and manner of life consistent with it. By their daily choices, believers were expected to grow into that identity, which came with both freedom and obligation. As those washed, sanctified, and justified in the name of the Lord Jesus (1 Cor 6:11), believers had to renounce the behaviors from their pre-Christian lives (1 Cor 6:9–11) and use their freedom to make choices that strengthened the unity and holiness of the new community to which they now belonged. Because Christian life was a call to communal existence, realized and affirmed in

---

24. Women's status and roles will be examined in chapter 9.

baptism, a member's individual actions always affected the life of the whole. There was no retreating into solitary existence.

Freedom and the Spirit

Notwithstanding the fact that Sin, understood as a power, had been dethroned, and its stranglehold on humans broken by Christ's death and Resurrection, Sin remained an ever-present reality. It stood ready at any moment of human weakness to transform the gift of freedom into a license to sin (see Gal 5:13). Some people did not consider freedom without any exterior constraints a gift. In Galatia, it apparently became a source of fear and fretting. How could one know right from wrong and avoid falling into Sin's grip, apart from laws? But Paul solemnly declares to the Galatians, "For freedom Christ has set you free. Stand firm, therefore, and do not submit again to a yoke of slavery" (Gal 5:1). Paul did not want believers relying on laws. Rather, they were to rely on the Spirit, the empowering presence given at baptism precisely to guide and enable them to live Christian lives. This is why Paul exhorts believers, "live by the Spirit" (Gal 5:16).

In his letters, Paul focuses on the Spirit primarily with regard to its dynamic presence in the lives of believers. The Spirit prevents believers from falling back into fear (Rom 8:15), reminds them of their identity as children of God (Rom 8:16), helps them in their weakness, and intercedes for them before God (Rom 8:26). Most importantly, believers are imbued by the Spirit. Paul says the Spirit dwells in believers (Rom 8:9; 1 Cor 3:16), in their hearts (Gal 4:6), and in their minds (1 Cor 2:6–16). Unlike the law, which was an exterior constraint on humans, the Spirit resides within and moves believers from the very depths of their being. Thus to "live by the Spirit" does not mean to follow a new set of laws. It means to be indwelled by an empowering presence that assists believers to do the good they desire but were incapable of doing when they were slaves to Sin (see Rom 7:14–25). Empowered by the Spirit, they can finally lead lives pleasing to God (Rom 8:1–4; 1 Thess 4:1).

Paul assured believers that Spirit-led freedom, though admittedly fragile, was not without content or direction. Rather, it is freedom to perform every deed that begins and ends with love and produces the fruits that confirm that one is Spirit-led (see Gal 5:13–14, 22–23). Paul was a realist and recognized that falling back under the power of Sin into old patterns of individually and socially destructive behavior was always a possibility. However, he was more convinced that, with the Spirit as their strength from within, believers could walk in the newness of life.

Paul's Key Ecclesial Images

Appreciating Paul's key images to describe the church requires understanding a significant difference between his cultural context and today's. Individualism is characteristic of contemporary Western culture. It is the patrimony of Enlightenment thinkers and their conceptual forebears, who stressed individual rights and promoted the notion of the individual as a bounded, distinct self. Highly individualistic societies such as the United States encourage people to be self-reliant and to pursue personal fulfillment from an early age.[25] As a first-century Jew, Paul was heir to the scriptural stress on the primacy of community and group solidarity. Individuals derived their identity from the community, and their actions affected the community, either positively or negatively (see, e.g., Josh 7:1–26). Thus the notion of an autonomous self, functioning apart from and without impact on the community, was inconceivable to Paul. For him a Christian was a Christian precisely insofar as he was a member of the saved community in Christ. As Pauline scholar J. P. Sampley observed, there is "no evidence that Paul ever conceived of a solitary, isolated believer."[26] In fact, the texts referenced throughout this chapter indicate that Paul never speaks about becoming Christian from the point of view of the individual. Rather, he consistently employs the first- or second-person plural. For example, "we" were buried with him by baptism (Rom 6:4); Christ became for "us" wisdom, righteousness,

---

25. On how individualism became the defining characteristic of American society see, Thomas F. Schindler, *Ethics: The Social Dimension: Individualism and the Catholic Tradition* (Wilmington, DE: Michael Glazier, 1989), esp. 1–45.

26. See J. Paul Sampley, *Walking Between the Times: Paul's Moral Reasoning* (Minneapolis, MN: Fortress, 1991), 37.

sanctification, and redemption (1 Cor 1:30); "you" (plural) were washed, sanctified (1 Cor 6:11). Thus being a Christian entailed incorporation into the body of believers in Christ through baptism. Paul's conviction of the realism of this union is especially evident in the images he uses to describe the church.

The Church as the Body of Christ

The dominant image Paul employs for the church is "body of Christ." He speaks of believers as "one body in Christ and individually members of one another" (Rom 12:5). In 1 Corinthians 12:12–26 he compares the church to a body and then declares, "now you are the body of Christ" (v. 27). No one knows for sure how Paul came up with the "body" concept as a designation for the church. Scholars have advanced a variety of backgrounds, ranging from the notion of "corporate personality" in the Jewish Scriptures, to a Gnostic primal man myth, to the Eucharistic tradition of sharing in the body of Christ.[27] While it is possible to detect various influences in Paul's use of the body image, many scholars think it most likely that Paul adopted this concept from the arena of ancient political discourse. The metaphor of the "body" for society was common in ancient political literature from the fifth century bce through the second century ce, and its influence on Paul is detectable even in the details of 1 Corinthians 12:12–20.[28] Paul's contemporary Seneca often used this analogy, referring to members of society as "parts of one great body."[29]

Three salient features of Paul's use of this image prove significant. First, "body" allows Paul to express both the organic unity and the dynamic interaction that takes place within the church. Body is not a static image. It conjures a variety of movable parts, each diverse and all essential. Just as a body consists of various parts,

27. Hypotheses are succinctly outlined by R. K. Y. Fung, "Body of Christ," in *Dictionary of Paul and His Letters,* ed. Gerald F. Hawthorne, Ralph P. Martin, and Daniel G. Reid (Downers Grove, IL: InterVarsity Press, 1993), 76–82, esp. 77–78.

28. See Margaret Mitchell, *Paul and the Rhetoric of Reconciliation*, 157–64.

29. See Seneca, *Moral Epistles*, 95.52: "all that you behold that which comprises both god and man, is one—we are the parts of one great body." An extensive comparison between Paul's and Seneca's use of this metaphor is provided by Jan N. Sevenster, *Paul and Seneca* (Leiden, The Netherlands: EJ Brill, 1961), esp. 167–218.

each functioning for the good of the whole, so is the church com-posed of members who fulfill a diverse range of functions (see 1 Cor 12:27–30). Second, the diversity in the community is the work of the Spirit, who gives each person different *charisma*, or spiritual gifts, not for self-promotion but for the "the common good" (1 Cor 12:4–7). Paradoxically, the Spirit who is the source of diversity is also the source of unity: "For in the one Spirit we were all baptized into one body . . . and we were all made to drink of one Spirit" (1 Cor 12:13). Third, diversity, not uniformity, is of the essence of the church. However, diversity that does not promote unity destroys the whole, which is the source of life of each of its parts. Applied to the community, this means that without mutual interdependence and shared responsibility, neither Christian community nor individual Christian existence is sustainable.

In the context of 1 Corinthians where Paul addresses the extensive factionalism that threatened to destroy the church, the body image provided him with an apt analogy to exhort unity in diversity. Paul uses the phrase in a similar fashion in his exhortation at Romans 12:4–5. This figurative use of "body of Christ" does not preclude the possibility that Paul attached a deeper significance to the phrase. In light of the various expressions (e.g., "in Christ") Paul used to communicate the intimate union of Christ and believers,[30] it seems reasonable to assume that Paul understood "body of Christ" to express a vital, intimate, and perhaps mystical union with Christ.

The Church Is God's Temple

Shrines and temples to a variety of gods and goddesses were part of the urban landscape in the cities where Paul preached. In his travelogue, the ancient geographer Pausanius reports that Corinth was home to a variety of temples.[31] The remains of the temple of

---

30. On the significance of Paul's prepositional phrases, "in Christ," "with Christ," and variations, see James D. G. Dunn, *The Theology of the Apostle Paul* (Grand Rapids, MI: William B. Eerdmans, 1998), 390–408.

31. Pausanius' *Description of Ancient Greece: Books 1 and 2*, trans. W. H. S. Jones and H. A. Omerud (London: G. P. Putnam's Sons, 1918), Bk. 2 "Corinth." Book 2 can also be accessed online at *archive.org/details/pausaniasgreece01pausuoft*.

Apollo, built ca. sixth century bce, still dominate what was once the Roman forum.

On their way to the forum, Corinthians of Paul's day would have passed the temples of Apollo and Hera, as well as another large temple overlooking the forum, which may have been erected within a decade or so of Paul's arrival in Corinth ca. 50 ce.[32] Paul limits his use of the term *temple* (Grk. *naos*) to the Corinthian correspondence, where he employs it as a metaphor for the whole community.[33] At 1 Corinthians 3:16–17, he writes, "Do you not know that you are God's temple and that God's Spirit dwells in you? If anyone destroys God's temple, God will destroy that person. For God's temple is holy, and you are that temple." Then at 2 Corinthians 6:16b, he states, "For we are the temple of the living God . . ." Paul knew the temple imagery would resonate with the Corinthians, given their surroundings, but beyond environmental links, Paul's choice of the metaphor was certainly influenced by Jewish tradition. When a Jew thought of the temple, there was only one referent: the temple in Jerusalem. In Jewish life, liturgy, and memory, the temple occupied a place of unparalleled significance. This was the one place on Earth where God chose to live. The very fact that God dwelled within it made the temple holy. Jewish tradition also believed that the establishment of a new temple where God would dwell permanently would signal the dawning of the new eschatological age (see Ezek 37:26–28).

By using the unitary image of temple to describe the Corinthian Christ-believers, Paul was not asking the community there to think of itself literally as a brick-and-mortar building. Rather, as the new eschatological community of God gathered in Christ, they were to understand themselves via this metaphor as that living place where God now dwells. As all Paul scholars recognize, in this

---

32. It is unsure to which deity this temple, referred to as Temple E, had been dedicated. On its history and construction, see *corinth.sas.upenn.edu/ad150templee.html*.

33. Paul uses the term *temple* one more time at 1 Corinthians 6:19, in what is often interpreted as a reference to an individual. However, Paul's phrasing "the body" (singular) of "you" (plural) is awkward and could be construed to refer to the whole community. See, e.g., Nijay K. Gupta, "Which Body Is a Temple (1 Corinthians 6:19)? Paul Beyond the Individual/Communal Divide," *Catholic Biblical Quarterly* 72.3 (2010): 518–36.

Remains of the Temple of Apollo, Corinth, built ca. 540 BCE.

one metaphorical use of the word "temple," Paul communicates and underscores both the unity and the holiness of the church. Wherever the Lord dwells is his holy temple (see Psalm 11.4) and Paul tells the Corinthians: "you are that temple" (1 Cor 3:17).

Paul was not the only Jew of his day to adopt the image of the temple as a metaphor for God's holy community. The Essenes also believed they were the living temple of God, a holy gathering in the midst of which God dwelled.[34] In contrast to Paul, however, the Essenes rejected Israel's religious establishment, preeminently symbolized in the temple, saw themselves as a counter-temple movement, and withdrew from society.[35] Apart from the fact that Paul appears to have recognized the continuing validity of the temple, he expected his communities to be living temples in the midst of society, not separate from it.

The *ekklēsiai* Paul addressed in his letters were local assemblies scattered throughout the Mediterranean. When he used images such as the body of Christ and temple of God, he had these small

---

34. See, e.g., 1QS 8:1–10, 9:1–6.

35. See Bertil Gärtner, *The Temple and the Community in Qumran and in the New Testament: A Comparative Study in the Temple Symbolism of the Qumran Texts and the New Testament* (Cambridge, MA: Cambridge University Press, 1965), esp. 16–44.

local communities in mind. In time, the church developed into a worldwide, universal reality and remains so. Regardless of its size and extent, the church's vocation never changes. It is called to unity and holiness. Absent these essential hallmarks, the existence of the church as God's people in Christ is in jeopardy. The Christian church, marred by sin and disunity, has been around so long that today this can easily be forgotten. Paul made sure the people he converted and ministered to did not forget.

Summary

This chapter has examined Paul's understanding of the church and various aspects of his thought related to its nature and composition. By stepping back from each particular point examined to consider the whole, one can see that all of Paul's insights revolve around his central conviction that the church is God's new eschatological community, called into being in Christ, in unity and holiness. Paul's theology of baptism; his insights about the sanctifying, unifying, and empowering presence of the Spirit; and his images of the church as the body of Christ and temple of God all converge to reinforce the holiness and unity of God's end-time community. Paul retains the stress found in the Jewish scriptures on the primacy of community and group solidarity with his emphasis on the common life of God's people, their common sharing in the one Spirit, and common participation in Christ's death in order to share in his Resurrection.

Paul's insistence that God called into being a new people not based on social class, gender, or ethnicity, but on a shared faith in Christ raised questions he could not ignore: What about God's chosen people Israel, Paul's fellow Jews, who had not believed in the gospel proclamation and were not baptized into Christ? Would God simply abandon the people He had called his own? If so, how could God be trusted? Paul tackles these questions in Romans, his final letter, which he addressed to a largely Gentile community. In his long and sometimes tortuous argument at Romans 9–11, Paul defends the trustworthiness of God, explains the role of unbelieving Israel in God's redemptive historical plan, and declares that in the end, "all Israel will be saved" (Rom 11:26). As with the social consequences of baptism, so also here, Paul does not provide a blueprint detailing when Israel will be saved or how. Will it be by coming to faith in Christ or through fidelity to the historical covenant God had made with Israel? This remains an open question.[36]

Questions for Review and Reflection

1. In what ways do you see the Exodus story influencing Paul's portrayal of baptism and its effects?
2. Why would Paul be uncomfortable with the description of Christian life as a "personal walk with Jesus"?
3. What are the ethical consequences of baptism?
4. In your opinion, how well or poorly does the church exhibit the kind of holiness and unity that Paul believed were the necessary hallmarks of the church?
5. Where do you see Sin continue to exercise its power today?
6. Why could people find freedom without restraints frightening?
7. In your view, what aspects of contemporary society pose the greatest threats to the survival of church, as Paul understood church?
8. Where do you see the church today as especially tolerant/intolerant of diversity?

Opening Other Windows

Banks, Robert J. *Paul's Idea of Community: The Early House Churches in Their Cultural Setting*. Grand Rapids, MI: Baker Academic, 1994.

Fee, Gordon D. *God's Empowering Presence: The Holy Spirit in the Letters of Paul*. Grand Rapids, MI: Baker Books, 2009.

Ferguson, Everett. *Baptism in the Early Church: History, Theology and Liturgy in the First Five Centuries*. Grand Rapids, MI: William B. Eerdmans, 2009. See especially "Baptism in the Pauline Epistles," ch. 9, pages 146–64.

---

36. For the scholarly debate on this question, see Christopher Zoccali, "'And so all Israel will be Saved': Competing Interpretations of Romans 11:26 in Pauline Scholarship," *Journal for the Study of the New Testament* 30.3 (2008): 289–318.

Gorman, Michael J. *Cruciformity: Paul's Narrative Spirituality of the Cross.* Grand Rapids, MI: William B. Eerdmans, 2001.

Harrington, Daniel J. *Paul on the Mystery of Israel.* Collegeville, MN: Liturgical Press, 1992.

Jensen, Daniel J. *Living Water: Imagery, Symbolism and Settings of Early Christian Baptism.* Leiden, The Netherlands: Brill, 2011.

Longenecker, Bruce W. *Remember the Poor: Paul, Poverty, and the Greco-Roman World.* Grand Rapids, MI: William B. Eerdmans, 2010.

O'Brien, P. T. "Church," in *Dictionary of Paul and His Letters*, ed. Gerald F. Hawthorne and Ralph P. Martin. Downer's Grove, IL: InterVarsity Press, 1993, 123–31.

O'Connor, Jerome Murphy. *Becoming Human Together: The Pastoral Anthropology of St. Paul.* Wilmington, DE: Michael Glazier, Inc., 1982. See esp. Part 3: Community.

Still, Todd D., and David G. Horrell, *After the First Urban Christians: The Social-Scientific Study of Pauline Christianity Twenty-Five Years Later.* New York: Continuum, 2009.

Chapter 8

Living as Members of the Saved Community

Overview

This chapter considers the ethical behavior that Paul believed was appropriate to communities of believers. A careful examination of Paul's views on sexual morality follows a consideration of what other Hellenistic Jews and pagan moralists said on this subject. The comparison shows that Paul's views were quite consistent with those of his peers. In the final section of this chapter, the focus turns from the narrow concern over sexual morality to Paul's insistence on cruciform ethics as the essence of Christian living.

Recommended Reading

Genesis 1–2

Wisdom 13:1–14:31

1 Thessalonians 4:2–8

Romans 1:18–3:20 (especially 1:18–32)

1 Corinthians 5:1–7:40

1 Corinthians 8:1–14:40

Not Like the Gentiles: Paul on Sexual Issues

As noted in chapter 7, according to Paul, God's new eschatological community in Christ was supposed to manifest its unity and holiness in its manner of living. Paul expected believers to model their lives on the example of Christ and distinguish themselves from pagans by their morally superior behavior. He inherited the latter concern from Judaism, which insisted on its moral superiority over pagans who did not know God or his will and behaved immorally.[1] Jews were especially enjoined to avoid sexual immorality, considered the hallmark vice of pagans. Paul instructed Christians to do likewise. In fact, the heading of this section, "not like the Gentiles" comes from 1 Thessalonians where Paul advocates sexual self-control, exhorting believers not to act "with lustful passion, like the Gentiles, who do not know God" (4:5).

Because Paul considered sexual morality an important manifestation of the holiness of God's people, this chapter begins by examining his vision of Christian living regarding sexual behavior. Paul never addressed the subject of human sexuality in a systematic way. In fact, he makes few references to sexual matters. Concentrated mostly in 1 Corinthians, they are responses occasioned by the particular circumstances in that community. In reply to questions, he comments on sex within marriage, divorce, and other related matters in 1 Corinthians 7:1–40. He responds to a reported case of incest at 1 Corinthians 5:1–13 and discusses whether fornication with prostitutes is permissible at 1 Corinthians 6:12–20. At Romans 1:26–27, and perhaps again at 1 Corinthians 6:9–10, he writes with same-sex relations in view. Apart from these instances, Paul's only other explicit statement about sexual behavior is found in his earliest extant letter at 1 Thessalonians 4:3–8.

Today, many people find Paul's views on marriage and sexual relations repressive. The low esteem for marriage in later Christian tradition, with its emphasis on the excellence of virginity,[2] is usually traced to 1 Corinthians 7. As one scholar observed, this chapter "was to determine all Christian thought on marriage and celibacy for centuries."[3] Paul's views are also seen as the basis of some churches'

---

1. It is a commonplace in both biblical and postbiblical Jewish texts that Israel was to distinguish itself from foreign peoples by its sexual conduct (see, e.g., Lev 18:24–30).

2. In Roman Catholicism the superiority of virginity was expounded until the Second Vatican Council. See, e.g., Pope Pius XII, "Sacra Virginitas," *Acta Apostolicae Sedis* 46 (1954): 161–91, esp. 70–74.

3. Peter Brown, *Body and Society: Men, Women and Sexual Renunciation in Early Christianity* (New York: Columbia University Press, 1988), 54.

negative attitude toward sexual expression, especially homoeroticism. Indeed, in the contemporary controversy over homosexuality, Paul is the New Testament writer appealed to most on this matter. However, as this chapter and the discussion on women in chapter 9 will show, in many instances Paul's views were consonant with contemporary Jewish writers and pagan moralists. Therefore, understanding the cultural reality and the views of his contemporaries should help in assessing what Paul said about sexual matters. Before considering that reality, it is important to recognize that there was no uniform sexual culture in the vast Roman Empire—just as there isn't one in places such as the United States or Asia today. Thus the discussion of first-century sexual culture is based on what is known from certain texts written by educated males. The considered thoughts of non-elite Jewish and pagan men and women, and even elite women, about their sexual lives, or sexual mores in general, are virtually unknown.

Sex and the City: Greco-Roman Sexual Culture and the Moralists

Soon after becoming the uncontested ruler of Rome ca. 27 bce, Caesar Augustus announced his plan to clean up Roman society and restore the *mores maiorum*, that is, the time-honored morals of the ancestors. He had broad support for this plan. Many had already expressed disapproval of the widespread immoderate living, sexual licentiousness, and marital infidelity that characterized Roman society.[4]

Augustus pledged to renew Rome's venerable status by restoring conjugal unity and rehabilitating family life. In the early imperial period, neither mattered much to aristocratic men and women, who considered marriage and children restrictive and burdensome.

---

4. Sallust, the historian, blamed Roman soldiers for bringing home Greek vices, cf. *The War with Cataline,* esp. chs. 1–12. Text available at *penelope.uchicago.edu/Thayer/ E/Roman/Texts/Sallust/Bellum_Catilinae*.html.* Horace, the poet, worried that marital infidelity threatened not only the institution of marriage but also the survival of Rome. See Horace, *Ode* 3.6. Note how Horace blames women for this state of affairs. The text is available at *www.poetryintranslation.com/PITBR/Latin/HoraceOdesBkIII. htm#_Toc40263851.*

The reform was intended to encourage marriage, procreation, and the rearing of legitimate children. Augustus did not consider these merely private matters. Ultimately, they were matters of state, since Rome's survival depended on population growth and on the goodwill of the gods, whose favor might turn to disfavor if noble virtues were not restored. Augustus reinforced his reform program with a series of laws designed to curb adultery, grant privileges to the married, penalize celibacy, and reward childbearing.[5] He expected the elite to become models of moral rectitude and comportment for everyone under Rome's dominion—a kind of trickle-down morality that would make its way to the farthest reaches of the empire.

Though Augustus bragged about restoring ancestral customs and virtue, his attempts to promote moral living and curb licentiousness were ineffective overall. Certainly, there were many examples of marital fidelity and stable family life from the aristocratic to the lower classes, as attested by inscriptional and archeological evidence. However, sexual decadence continued, as evident in Pompeii, a city full of brothels, vulgar graffiti, and sexualized art on public walls and in private homes. Though Pompeii cannot be used as the exclusive measure of sexual mores across imperial society in the first century ce, this type of activity was apparently not confined to Pompeii.[6] Evidence

© Erich Lessing / Art Resource, NY

Fresco from the House of Caecilius, Pompeii ca.50–79 ce, National Archeological Museum, Naples. In Pompeii and nearby Herculaneum, erotic encounters were typical subjects of wall paintings in public and domestic spaces.

---

5. Augustus enacted the *Lex Julia* (18 bce) and the *Lex Papia Poppaea* (9 ce). The Augustan legislation is discussed in *Women in the Classical World: Image and Text*, ed. Elaine Fantham, et al. (New York: Oxford University Press, 1994), 302–6.

6. Excavations of Pompeii and surrounding cities buried in the eruptions of Vesuvius in 79 ce have turned up thousands of examples of graffiti. Some recovered and translated can be read at *archaeology.uakron.edu/pompeii_site/Topics/graffiti/graffiti_frameset.html*.

elsewhere of sexually explicit art and graffiti, as well as the ubiquity of both heterosexual and homosexual male and female sex workers, suggests adultery and fornication were a reality in the urban centers of the empire.[7]

Though Augustus did not achieve all he intended, his attempt created a sense of urgency about sexual mores among the Greco-Roman moralists, who advocated strict sexual ethics. They expected that men and women would marry and attached to that expectation the ideal hope that harmony and partnership would characterize marriage.

The moralists considered marriage the only appropriate context for sexual intercourse. Also, they considered the purpose of sexual intercourse to be the procreation of legitimate children.[8] However, men had many options for both heterosexual and homosexual activity outside of marriage, which they could take advantage

On Marriage

But in marriage there must be above all perfect companionship and mutual love of husband and wife, both in health and in sickness and under all conditions . . . Where, then, this love for each other is perfect and the two share it completely, each striving to outdo the other in devotion, the marriage is ideal and worthy of envy, for such a union is beautiful.

—Musonius Rufus, Lecture XIIIA on
"The Chief End of Marriage"

---

7. See Thomas A. McGinn, *The Economy of Prostitution in the Roman World: A Study of the Social History of the Brothel* (Ann Arbor: University of Michigan Press, 2004), esp. 78–111.

8. Voicing a view shared by other moralists such as Epictetus and Seneca, Musonius declared, "The primary end of marriage is community of life with a view to the procreation of children," see Cora E. Lutz, *Musonius Rufus: The Romans Socrates* (New Haven, CT: Yale University Press, 1947), 90–92, Lecture 13A; the book is now available at *sites. google.com/site/thestoiclife/the_teachers/musonius-rufus*. See further, Suzanne Dixon, *The Roman Family* (Baltimore, MD: Johns Hopkins University Press, 1992), 61–97.

of with impunity.[9] For example, in addition to male and female prostitutes, a man was free to use his slaves, and some women not protected by law, for his sexual pleasure.[10] The moralists agreed that all such sexual activity outside marriage was driven by excess and self-indulgence. The position of the renowned Roman Stoic Musonius Rufus (ca. 32–62 ce) is representative of the views of first-century-ce moralists:

> Not the least significant part of the life of luxury and self-indulgence lies also in sexual excess; for example those who lead such a life crave a variety of loves not only lawful but unlawful ones as well, not women alone but also men; sometimes they pursue one love and sometimes another, and not being satisfied with those which are available, pursue those which are rare and inaccessible, and invent shameful intimacies, all of which constitute a grave indictment of manhood. Men who are not wantons or immoral are bound to consider sexual intercourse justified only when it occurs in marriage and is indulged in for the purpose of begetting children, since that is lawful, but unjust and unlawful when it is mere pleasure-seeking, even in marriage. But of all sexual relations those involving adultery are most unlawful, and no more tolerable are those of men with men, because it is a monstrous thing and contrary to nature. But, furthermore, leaving out of consideration adultery, all intercourse with women which is without lawful character is shameful and is practiced from lack of self-restraint.[11]

---

9. A man could be prosecuted for incestuous sex; sex with a boy or girl from a good family or with a widow; or for adultery, that is, sex with another man's wife or his concubine; see Aline Rousselle, *Porneia: Desire and the Body in Antiquity,* trans. Felicia Pheasant (Oxford: Blackwell, 1993), esp. 78–92. As is well known, a double standard existed for men and women regarding extramarital sex; it was expected of men and condemned in women.

10. Slaves could not legally marry. They had de facto marriages and offspring, but parents and offspring were the sexual property of their masters, who used and abused them at will; see Jennifer A. Glancy, *Slavery in Early Christianity* (Minneapolis, MN: Fortress Press, 2006).

11. See Lutz, *Musonius Rufus,* Lecture 12, "On Sexual Indulgence," 85–89.

Though prostitution was legal, Musonius indirectly condemns it in the text just cited. Seneca does likewise.[12] Dio Chrysostom openly condemns those paying for sexual services, as well as the state for permitting prostitution.[13] Roman society attached no deep religious significance to marriage, which could be dissolved for any number of reasons. However, even though Roman law permitted divorce, the moralists complained about it and blamed women for its frequency, as clear from the following remark:

> Is there any woman who blushes at divorce now that cer-
> tain . . . ladies reckon their years, not by the number of
> the consuls, but . . . husbands . . . ? They shrank from
> this scandal as long as it was rare; now since every gazette
> has a divorce case, they have learned to do what they used to
> hear so much about.[14]

The moralists severely condemned homoeroticism and pederasty in particular.[15] They considered homoeroticism contrary to nature,[16] an affront to marriage and procreation, and hence a threat to the stability of society.[17] Plutarch blamed the Greek gymnasium, where athletes went about naked, for male effeminacy and pederasty.[18]

---

12. "A man does wrong in requiring chastity of his wife while he himself is intriguing with the wives of other men; . . . as your wife should have no dealings with a lover, neither should you." See *Seneca Ad Lucilium Epistulae Morales*, trans. Richard M. Gummere (New York: G. P. Putnam's Sons, 1925), vol. 3, *Epistle* 94.26. Also available online at *archive.org/details/adluciliumepistu03seneuoft*.

13. Dio Chrysostom, *Discourses 1–11*, trans. J. W. Cohoon (Cambridge, MA: Harvard University Press, 1932), 7.133–37. Text available at *penelope.uchicago.edu/Thayer/E/Roman/Texts/Dio_Chrysostom/Discourses/7*.html*.

14. Seneca, *On Benefits*, trans. John W. Basore (Cambridge: Harvard University Press, 1935), 3.16.2.

15. The term *pederasty*, from Greek *pais, paidos* (male child or boy) + *erastēs* (lover), from *eraō* (to love passionately), refers to sexual intercourse between men and postpubescent boys. On the origins of pederasty, see Thomas F. Scanlon, "The Dispersion of Pederasty and the Athletic Revolution in Sixth-Century bc Greece," in *Same-Sex Desire and Love in Greco-Roman Antiquity and in the Classical Tradition of the West*, ed. Beert C. Verstraete and Vernon Provencal (Binghamton, NY: Haworth Press, 2005), 63–86.

16. See Plutarch, *Amatorius*, 5, available at *www.perseus.tufts.edu/hopper/text?doc=Perseus%3Atext%3A2008.01.0314%3Asection%3D5*.

17. Ibid.

18. See Plutarch, *Moralia*, trans. Frank Cole Babbitt (Cambridge, MA: Harvard University Press, 1936), vol. 4, *Roman Questions*, 40. Also available at *penelope.uchicago.edu/Thayer/E/Roman/Texts/Plutarch/Moralia/Roman_Questions*/B.html*.

Seneca also considered male same-sex activity to be against nature and especially pitied slaves who had to service their masters' lust.[19] Dio Chrysostom shared the view that homoeroticism was exploitative and driven by excess lust.[20] Homoerotic sexual acts were considered against nature because of the understanding of appropriate gender roles of the time.[21] Males were active, or penetrators. Females were passive, or penetrated. Thus males who allowed themselves to be penetrated were effeminized and, with the penetrator, acted against nature.

Hellenistic Judaism on Sex and Marriage

Whether living in Palestine or scattered throughout the empire, first-century-ce Jews, with few exceptions, believed that God required them to marry and procreate (Gen 1:28, 2:18–24). Arranged marriages between teenage girls and boys began with a period of betrothal, after which they formalized the marriage union. As Jewish historian Josephus authoritatively declared, marriage was between a man and woman; intercourse was licit only within marriage and only for the procreation of children.[22] The Hellenistic-Jewish philosopher Philo agreed.[23] He also condemned as a mere pleasure-seeker any man who knowingly married a barren woman and, contrary to nature, wasted his procreative power.[24] Even apart from barrenness, Philo condemned all immoderate pleasure with one's own wife.[25]

---

19. Seneca, *Ad Lucilium Epistulae Morales*, vol. 1, *Epistle*, 47.7. Also available online at *archive.org/details/adluciliumepistu01seneuoft*.

20. Dio Chrysostom, *Discourses*, 7.151–2. This text is also available at *penelope. uchicago.edu/Thayer/E/Roman/Texts/Dio_Chrysostom/Discourses/7*.html*.

21. Jews and pagans shared these assumptions about sex roles. See Bernadette J. Brooten, *Love between Women: Early Christian Responses to Female Homoeroticism* (Chicago: University of Chicago Press, 1996), 1–2.

22. Josephus, *Against Apion*, 2.199.

23. Philo, *On Joseph*, 42–3. All references to Philo are from C. D. Yonge (trans.) *The Works of Philo: Complete and Unabridged* (Peabody, MA: Hendrickson, 1997). This text is also available electronically at *www.earlychristianwritings.com/yonge*.

24. Philo, *Special Laws*, 3.34–36.

25. The accent here is on "immoderate." See Philo, *Special Laws*, 3.9. Elsewhere, Philo recognizes the importance of pleasure between spouses, see *On the Creation*, 161.

Adultery was unequivocally condemned and, according to Philo, merited death.[26] Divorce, on the other hand, was permitted and could be initiated only by the husband. The Book of Sirach even counsels husbands to divorce wives who do not follow their directives.[27] In Jewish literature of this period, a series of illicit sexual unions were condemned, including relations with prostitutes.[28] Harshest condemnation was directed to homoerotic relations, especially pederasty. Across the literature, one finds the same few core reasons for the condemnation.[29] First, it was against nature. Jews also assumed sexual activity "according to nature" took place between heterosexual spouses who fulfilled their respective active and passive roles. Second, beyond the fact that male-to-male sex "wasted seed" and could not be procreative—the agreed-upon purpose of intercourse—it also perverted the male nature of the penetrated partner, who was made effeminate.[30] Elsewhere in Hellenistic Jewish literature, the perversion of male nature is linked to idolatry. For example, in the Jewish writing "The Testament of Naphtali," the patriarch Naphtali warns his sons not to become like Sodom, "who changed the order of its nature" (T. Naph 3:3–5). This seems to be an implicit reference to same-sex relations. It is what the Gentiles do who have "changed the order" (3:3), by forsaking the Lord and following after sticks and stones. The implication is just as idolatry is the denial of God's true nature, male same-sex acts are the denial of a male's true nature. Another widespread reason for condemning male same-sex relations was their association with excessive drink and insatiable lust.[31]

This review of representative Hellenistic Jewish literature reveals that although Jews claimed to be superior to pagans in sexual

---

26. Philo, *Special Laws*, 3.11

27. Ibid., 3.30; Josephus, *Ant.* 4.253; Sirach 25:26.

28. Philo, *Special Laws*, 3.2.12–3:6–35, 3.9.51; *On Joseph*, 9.43.

29. Jewish texts of this period that refer to same-sex relations are collected in William Loader, *Philo, Josephus and the Testaments on Sexuality: Attitudes towards Sexuality in the Writings of Philo and Josephus and in the Testaments of the Twelve Patriarchs* (Grand Rapids, MI: William B. Eerdmans, 2011).

30. Philo, *Special Laws*, 2.50, 3.37–40.

31. In *On Abraham*, 135–37, Philo discusses same sex-activity in reference to the excesses that characterized Sodom. See further, Josephus, *Ant.* 3.275.

conduct, their views on sexual behavior were actually quite similar to those of contemporary pagan moralists. Jews shared the expectation that men and women would marry. They shared the view that marriage was the only valid context for sexual intercourse and then only for procreation. Both cultures accepted divorce. Jews, like the pagan moralists, condemned same-sex relations because they were not procreative, were driven by unbridled lust, and were against nature. Separately, Jews also linked same-sex relations to idolatry as another basis for condemnation.

Sexual Issues in Paul

Because 1 Corinthians 5–7 contains most of Paul's comments about sexual issues, a brief consideration of what occasioned the letter will help to contextualize his teaching. Paul evangelized Corinth over an eighteen-month period (see Acts 18:11) spanning either 50–51 or 51–52 ce. By then, Corinth was a major urban center of the eastern Mediterranean and capital of the Roman province of Achaia.[32]

Its strategic location at the isthmus linking the Peloponnese to mainland Greece and its control of two harbors, Lechaeum and Cenchreae, made Corinth a hub of commerce and communication.

---

32. Corinth's history is explored in Jerome Murphy-O'Connor, *St. Paul's Corinth: Texts and Archaeology* (Collegeville, MN: Michael Glazier/Liturgical Press, 2002).

Though once a proud and prosperous Greek city, it had become thoroughly Roman and thoroughly cosmopolitan. Merchants, immigrants, athletes, teachers, and preachers arrived at Corinth's ports, bringing ideas and customs that contributed to the city's sophistication, vitality, and appeal.

The Corinthian populace was known to be fiercely competitive and driven by the desire for status, wealth, honor, and power. In 1 Corinthians, Paul had to negotiate the fallout from that competitive spirit, which carried over into the community. He also had to deal with libertine sexual behavior, specifically incest and illicit sexual relations with prostitutes (1 Cor 5:1–13 and 6:12–20), which the Corinthians failed to see as incompatible with Christian life. At 1 Corinthians 7:1, however, Paul addresses what seems to be a current of sexual asceticism with its own peculiar problems.[33] Information about matters related to sex and all the other unity-destroying behavior going on at Corinth came to Paul through both oral and written communication (see 1 Cor 1:11, 5:1, 7:1). The receipt of this news occasioned Paul's writing of 1 Corinthians, which, more than any of his other letters, provides some insight about the sexual attitudes and practices of one Christian community in one large urban center of the empire. First Corinthians is not Paul's first letter to that community. This is clear from 1 Corinthians 5:9, where he mentions having already written to them. However, it is designated "first" because it is chronologically prior to the letter designated 2 Corinthians in the New Testament.[34]

---

33. Scholarly proposals about the ideological source(s) of the Corinthian's sexual behavior, both libertine and ascetic, are numerous and varied. Concise presentations of these proposals are available in critical commentaries; for example, Anthony C. Thiselton, *The First Epistle to the Corinthians* (Grand Rapids, MI: William B. Eerdmans, 2000).

34. Second Corinthians may also have been preceded by other correspondence (see 2 Cor 2:1–4). In fact, no one knows for sure how many letters Paul sent to the Corinthians or whether only two remain. Abrupt transitions in 2 Corinthians have convinced most scholars that it is not one single letter but a composite of two or more separate letters, or letter fragments that an editor joined to form what is now canonical 2 Corinthians. For a concise presentation of the issues related to the compositional unity of 1 and 2 Corinthians, see S. J. Hafemann, "Letters to the Corinthians," in *Dictionary of Paul and His Letters*, ed. Gerald F. Hawthorne and Ralph P. Martin (Downer's Grove IL: InterVarsity Press, 1993), 175–77.

First Corinthians 5:1–13: Incest

Paul's treatment of incest at 5:1–13 and his discussion of fornication at 6:12–20 bracket his argument against community members litigating with each other in pagan courts at 6:1–11. Within that argument, Paul reminds the Corinthians that no *"pornos,"* a Greek generic term for a sexually immoral person, has any place in the kingdom of God (6:9–11). That reminder sheds lights on the urgency accompanying Paul's treatment of the case of incest and topic of fornication.

Paul is irate that a gross case of sexual immorality was taking place within the Corinthian community and no one was doing anything about it. A community member was "having" (*echein*) his "father's wife" (5:1). In Hellenistic literature, this kind of "having" referred to an ongoing sexual relationship. In the Jewish scriptures, one's "father's wife" meant one's stepmother, not biological mother (see Lev 18:7–8). Jewish and Roman law prohibited a sexual relationship with one's stepmother, even if the father was dead.[35] It was considered incest. Paul did not identify either the brother or woman involved. His complete inattention to her suggests she was not a community member.

Why the community not only tolerated but also boasted in this relationship, rather than mourned as Paul expected (5:2), remains a matter of speculation. Whatever their reasons, Paul is not interested. In his view, nothing could justify the countenancing of an incestuous relationship not even heard of among pagans (5:1). Believers—who were supposed to be morally superior—had fallen below even the pagan low-moral mark! The comparison with pagans served as a rhetorical tool allowing Paul to shame the Corinthians, which was intended to motivate them to take action.[36]

---

35. Civil law prohibited incestuous marriages, including marriage to one's father's wife, see *Institutions of Gaius,* Bk. II.63. The text is available in English at *faculty. cua.edu/Pennington/Law508/Roman%20Law/GaiusInstitutesEnglish.htm.*

36. In ancient rhetoric, appeals to the emotions were considered a very important part of argumentation; of all the emotions, shame was considered one of the strongest incentives to change, since no one wished to be disgraced. See Cicero, *On the Divisions of Oratory,* trans. H. Rackham (Cambridge, MA: Harvard University Press, 1976), 26–91.

Paul prescribes excommunication (vv. 3–5), a disciplinary action he invokes nowhere else in his letters. The severity of the measure underscores the gravity of this situation. In Paul's mind, the incestuous relationship imperils the whole community, which is his chief concern throughout this passage. This man, even if he calls himself a "brother," is no more than a rank sinner—a point Paul underscores at 5:11. He contaminates the whole community and compromises its holiness. Paul illustrates this point with a maxim: a "little yeast leavens the whole batch of dough" (5:6). He has to go.

The heart of Paul's argument follows in 5:7–8. Paul uses the two main rituals of the Jewish Passover—the slaying of the paschal lamb and the feast of unleavened bread, when all old leaven had to be removed from the house (see Exod 12:14–20)—to explain why Christians are sinless and how this has come about. He says that on account of Christ's sacrifice (v. 7c.) believers are yeast-free, that is, sinless. This state of sinlessness, the result of a past action of God in Christ, is both individual and corporate, which explains why the community must act to protect its status.

The demands of new sinless life in Christ overlap the demands of the Mosaic law code, which also condemned incest and required the community to "Drive out the wicked person from among you," (Deut 17:7; 1 Cor 5:13b). However, adherence to the law is not why the sinner must be expelled. Rather, the community's corporate identity in Christ demands the cleansing of what is incompatible with their new life in Christ. This "Christological" motivation sets Paul's instruction apart. In Christ, a new sinless reality, the *ekklēsia*, has come into being. Each member must behave in a way that preserves the integrity of the community. Together, the community must act against any believer who threatens that integrity.

Paul's concern to protect the holiness of the whole community is clearly central. He does not address the "brother" or offer him help to correct this situation and avoid expulsion. Rather, Paul addresses and instructs the community so it can protect and preserve its holiness. Here, as elsewhere in his writings, the lens through which he views problems and responds to them is always the community. This is not to say Paul disregarded the individual. In fact, he expected the offender's spirit to be saved (5:5). Nonetheless, his primary concern and context for reflection was the community.

First Corinthians 6:12–20: Casual Sex with a *Pornē*

The same concern comes to the fore in 1 Corinthians 6:12–20. Although Paul directs his argument here against a specific practice, it is uncertain whether he addresses a hypothetical or a real situation of fornication. He does not indicate that there were reported cases of fornication, nor does he expect the community to take any specific action. Rather, he includes only the general admonition to "shun fornication" (6:18). Paul deals with the matter by setting up a dialogue with an imaginary dialogue partner (IDP) who holds what can be called a libertine position, as reflected in the statements at 6:12a, 6:12c, and 18b. At various places in this letter, Paul indicates that some Corinthian Christians saw themselves as spiritually and intellectually superior to other community members (see, e.g., 1 Cor 4:8–10, 18; 8:1–7). Many scholars connect the libertine views Paul opposed in 6:12–20 with these elites. Because the Greek New Testament was written without punctuation, including quotation marks, no one can say with certainty which views were Paul's and which belonged to others. This is further complicated by the possibility that Paul, who preached a law-free gospel, may have used the expression "All things are lawful for me" in his own preaching. If so, he may have been responsible for the misunderstanding that he now attempts to correct.[37] Many scholars who agree that 6:12–20 should be understood as a dialogue find the following assignment of views reasonable:[38]

IDP	v. 12a	"All things are lawful for me"
Paul	v. 12b	"but not all things are beneficial."
IDP	v. 12c	"All things are lawful for me"
Paul	v. 12d	"but I will not be dominated by anything."

37. According to John C. Hurd, "All things are lawful" is Pauline in principle. Hurd believes Paul stopped proclaiming this once he saw how the statement could be misunderstood, cf. *The Origin of 1 Corinthians* (London: SPCK, 1965), 279.

38. This arrangement was proposed by Jerome Murphy O'Connor, "Corinthian Slogans in 1 Cor 6:12–20," *Catholic Biblical Quarterly* 40.2 (1978): 391–96. Though some scholars remain skeptical, more and more now recognize that slogans typical of some Corinthians are contained in 6:12–20, and hence not all views expressed in this passage are Paul's. On this issue, see further, Denny Burk, "Discerning Corinthian Slogans through Paul's Use of Diatribe in 1 Corinthians 6:12–20," *Bulletin for Biblical Research* 18.1 (2008): 99–121.

IDP	v. 13ab	"Food is meant for the stomach and the stomach for food, and God will destroy both one and the other."
Paul	v. 13cd	"the body is not meant for fornication but for the Lord and the Lord for the body. And God raised the Lord and will also raise us by his power."
Paul	vv. 15–16–17	"Do you not know . . . ?" Paul introduces a series of rhetorical questions
Paul	v. 18a	**Conclusion:** "Shun fornication."
IDP	v. 18b	Objection: "Every sin that a person commits is outside the body"
Paul	v. 18c	Counter: "but the fornicator sins against the body itself"
Paul	v. 19	"Do you not know . . . ?" New rhetorical question
Paul	v. 20	**Conclusion:** "therefore, glorify God in your body."

Paul begins by citing a well-known slogan of philosophers who cherished the inner freedom that came with the attainment of wisdom.[39] This attainment enabled one to distinguish between morally significant things and those that were *adiaphora*,[40] that is, of no moral significance. Paul does not reject the slogan's basic claim that "all things are lawful for me," but adds two qualifiers: "not all things are beneficial;" and "I will not be dominated by anything." The first qualifier underscores that not everything licit is good, and here Paul has in mind the good of the whole community. For Paul, it is not enough that something is licit and good "for me." The Christian "me" is always "me-in-community" with others. Thus one member's

---

39. See, for example, Dio Chrysostom, *Discourses*, 3.10, available at *penelope. uchicago.edu/Thayer/E/Roman/Texts/Dio_Chrysostom/Discourses/3*.html*. However, Dio Chrysostom also added qualifications to the teaching that all things are permissible. See *Discourse* 14.13–16, also available online.

40. The Stoics especially distinguished between the things that really mattered (*ta diapheronta*) and their opposite (*to adiaphora*). See Epictetus, *The Discourses*, trans. W. A. Oldfather (Cambridge, MA: Harvard University Press, 1985), Bk. 1. 30.1–7.

actions always positively or negatively affect the unity and corporate identity of his or her community.

Apparently, some in the community, influenced by philosophical discourse or perhaps imagining themselves to have attained perfect wisdom (cf. 1 Cor 4: 8–13), likened the satisfaction of the sexual appetite with the need for food. In this view, sex with a *pornē*, or a prostitute, was an *adiaphoron*, an act having no more moral significance than a casual stop at the local tavern to grab a bite to eat. Sex and food were simply looked on as biological necessities,[41] and in Paul's day many a pub served up both. Paul, however, did not see sexual intercourse as a casual activity on par with other physical necessities such as eating. Thus in the course of 1 Corinthians 6:12–20, he offers a series of arguments against fornication grounded in the God-willed future destiny of believers, the indissoluble union with Christ, and the sanctifying presence of the Spirit.

The position of the dialogue partner betrays an anthropological dualism that Paul counters with his theological anthropology. Against a disregard for the worthless body, destined for death and destruction while the soul lives on, Paul established the power and purpose of God who raised Jesus and will raise "us" (v. 14). Paul uses the pronoun "us" interchangeably with the noun body (*sōma*) because, for Paul, there is no human existence apart from embodied existence. Even future resurrected existence will be bodily existence,[42] although Paul recognizes that one's resurrected body will differ from the one interred (see 1 Cor 15:35–42). Thus Christians cannot engage in fornication or any activity that disregards the dignity of the person/ body that God intends to resurrect.

Paul adds a Christological argument at vv. 15–17. Believers' bodies are members of Christ. By this, Paul means that they are indissolubly united with Christ in a relationship as close and intimate as the union of spouses. For Paul, sex with a *pornē* is a real

---

41. In his discussion of the bare necessities the body needs, the Stoic philosopher Epictetus mentions food, drink, and sex in the same breath. Regarding food, he advises consumption of only what one needs; regarding sex, he advises taking advantage of only that which is lawful. See Epictetus, *The Manual*, trans. W. A. Oldfather (Cambridge, MA: Harvard University Press, 1985), 33.7–8.

42. A reality that some Corinthians, perhaps the same people who are Paul's anonymous dialogue partners here, would deny (see 1 Cor 15:12–19).

union, not a casual encounter to satisfy a man's biological need. Paul grounds this argument in Genesis 2:24, where sexual intercourse is that action that makes the two one. In line with Jewish and secular tradition, Paul understands marriage as the only licit context for sexual intercourse, which results in a new reality—not two, but one new being. By uniting himself to a *pornē*, a male Christian not only compromises his own holiness but also the holiness of his community. Paul leaves implicit his belief that only the sexual union dignified by marriage is compatible with one's spiritual union with Christ and other believers, who together form a new reality. Thus any form of illicit sex must be shunned (v. 18a). Apparently, some Corinthians insisted that the physical body had nothing to do with sin (v. 18b). This squares well with the view that bodily actions concerned with biological necessities had no moral significance, as well as the Stoic idea that sin was not in the performance of any particular external act but was a matter of interior intention.[43] However, Paul does not recognize this dichotomy between actions and intentions (v. 18c).

In verse 19, Paul reemploys temple imagery used earlier at 3:16. Whereas in the earlier verse he used "temple" as an ecclesial metaphor, here Paul applies it to the individual, emphasizing the sanctity of each believer indwelt by the Spirit. That individual's personal lifestyle must not render him unfit for this sanctifying presence. Just as the entire community was enjoined to safeguard its holiness, so too is each individual believer since his body/life is no longer his own. The believer is the sacred place of God's dwelling, completely under new ownership. God, the owner, has paid a costly price and thus sealed the deal on the purchase (v. 20). Consequently, the believer is not free to be controlled by anyone or anything else, as Paul noted in his second qualification of the slogan at the beginning of this argument (v. 12).

First Corinthians 7:1–40: Marriage and Divorce

First Corinthians 7:1a makes it clear that Paul's discussion of sex in marriage, and other matters in this chapter, comes as a response to issues raised by the community in a letter sent to him. In the second

---

43. See, for example, Epictetus, *The Discourses,* trans. W. A. Oldfather (Cambridge, MA: Harvard University Press, 1985), 3.10.18.

part of this verse, Paul begins his response by citing, or summarizing, a line from their correspondence to him: "It is well for a man not to touch a woman" (1b). "To touch" (Grk. *haptō*) was a euphemism in Hellenistic literature for sexual intercourse. Although this statement was once thought to reflect Paul's own views, today most scholars consider it a recap of the Corinthian position, which Paul immediately qualifies with a "but" as he did at 1 Corinthians 6:12. Paul did not say why some in the community advocated sexual abstinence within marriage, which leaves scholars to speculate; nor was he interested in the merits of their argument.[44] He is obviously concerned about one thing, *porneia*. Given the discussion at 6:12–20, it seems likely that, among the range of activities covered by *porneia*, he is particularly worried about sex with prostitutes. In fact, it may be that Paul constructed the dialogue at 6:12–20, anticipating that a spouse denied sex by a partner embracing asceticism would likely run off to a prostitute. It was lawful, and there was availability.

If, as most scholars now recognize, the asceticism expressed in verse 1a does not represent Paul's thought, then it is important to acknowledge that a) Paul is not against sexual desire or its satisfaction—in fact, he understands that such feelings can be extremely intense and does not condemn them (7:9, 36); and b) his stated preference *for* celibacy need not be read as a statement *against* sexual pleasure. However, Paul shared the conventional view that marriage was the only licit context for satisfying one's sexual desires. (7:2). Does this mean he saw no purpose for marriage other than a defense against *porneia*? Not necessarily. In this passage, Paul makes it clear that marriage is an experience of mutual self-sharing and sexual fulfillment. As extensively recognized, the gender parity Paul establishes here is remarkable.[45] Each partner bears equal responsibility for engaging in this self-sharing, which is an indispensable part of marriage and belongs exclusively to it, as Paul argued at 6:16 in

---

44. Some married Corinthian Christians may have been inclined to the Cynic position against marriage and, unable to divorce, may have wanted to eliminate at least the burden of sex, as suggested by Will Demining, *Paul on Marriage and Celibacy: The Hellenistic Background of 1 Corinthians 7* (Cambridge, MA: Cambridge University Press, 1995).

45. The exceptional gender equality and mutual responsibility in marriage that Paul promotes closely parallels Stoic views, as noted by Demining, *Paul on Marriage and Celibacy*, 116–21.

view of Genesis 2:24. Paul wants spouses to have sex with each other and to fulfill the responsibility to the other that comes with marriage. Consequently, one partner may not abusively impose on the other. Nor is one partner free to withhold intimate sharing of self under the pretext of virtue or the pursuit of greater spiritual fulfillment. In fact, Paul is reluctant to admit of any abstention and attaches conditions, the foremost being mutual consent, if one spouse desires an abstention (7:5–6). In the event that one partner opts for abstinence and imposes it on the other, Paul's response is clear: sex outside of marriage is not a solution to this problem; it is *porneia* (7:2).

Divorce is not a solution either. This interest in sexual asceticism seems to have pushed at least one female spouse to seek a divorce.[46] That the wife is the initiator here is suggested when Paul addresses the wife first (v. 10) and includes a proviso related to her course of action (v. 11). She may be either the one who wants freedom to pursue an ascetic path or the partner denied her sexual rights by a husband refraining from sexual intercourse. In any event, Paul appeals to Jesus' categorical prohibition of divorce. In doing so, Paul makes it clear that divorce is not a solution to this problem. Yet he recognized that the separation was likely and added the proviso that she not remarry (7:11). Paul is nonjudgmental and does not berate the woman, which is rather remarkable given the nasty comments by some of his peers about divorce-happy women.

After concluding the discussion of sex within marriage, Paul addresses an assortment of issues with great flexibility, giving advice about what he thinks is good and better. In addressing the unmarried, Paul states his preference that they remain unmarried or celibate, as he is (7:8). This preference distances Paul from the thought and practice of both his pagan and Jewish contemporaries. He does not immediately provide a reason for this recommendation, but clearly Paul does not rank celibate life above married life on some absolute scale. He regards both as gifts from God and recognizes that different people have different gifts (7:7b). As one of God's gifts, marriage

---

46. Raymond F. Collins lays out a persuasive case for why the situation Paul addresses in vv. 10–11 is a concrete, real situation in which a Corinthian woman wants a divorce, rather than a hypothetical case about which Paul gives an opinion. See *Divorce in the New Testament* (Collegeville, MN: Liturgical Press, 1992), 22–24.

does not simply provide a context for sexual expression, but is a lifestyle with positive implications for spouses, even an unbelieving spouse. Paul says the unbeliever may be saved and sanctified through the believing spouse (7:14–16); hence divorce is unnecessary unless the unbeliever requests it, in which case Paul approves[47] (7:12–16). He apparently bases the possibility to communicate holiness and salvation on the licitness of the marital union.

The final positive insight about marriage that Paul offers in 1 Corinthians 7 is that marriage is about two people "anxious" for each other's well-being and focused on pleasing each other (vv. 32–34). The NRSV supplies "anxious" for the Greek verb *merimnaō*, regarding both those anxious about "worldly affairs" and those anxious about the "affairs of the Lord" (vv. 32–34). Therefore, the term carries no negative connotations and could simply be rendered "concerned." Married people are concerned about making a living, providing for each other and their families, and pleasing each other. This is altogether good. And if "please his wife" (v. 33) and "please her husband" (v. 34) refer to sexual pleasure, which in light of 7:34 seems a reasonable assumption, then Paul surely had a much more positive view of marriage than normally assumed.[48] However, Paul went on to link these essentially positive dimensions of marriage with "worldly affairs" (7:32, 34) and then subordinated them to the more important "affairs of the Lord." If spouses are concerned with the first set of affairs, they cannot give their whole and undivided attention to "the affairs of the Lord." Paul never specifies what the "affairs of the Lord" are, but he apparently wants everyone to focus on them, given the stressful times (v. 26). He speaks about the present with eschatological exigency, noting that time is growing short (v. 29) and human existence is ephemeral (v. 30). Paul urges believers to distance themselves from the world's structures and mundane daily concerns and focus on what counts. By his best lights, and obviously based on his own present experience, he believes celibacy better enables one to

---

47. This exception to the indissolubility of marriage referred to as the "Pauline Privilege" has been elaborated and remains in effect in the Roman Catholic Church, see the Code of Canon Law, esp. canons 1143–47.

48. This is also the view of William Loader, *The New Testament on Sexuality* (Grand Rapids, MI: William B. Eerdmans, 2012), 212.

stay focused.[49] However, he also knows, perhaps again based on his own experience, that sexual desire can become a distraction (vv. 9, 36). If it does, then he of course expects people to marry.

Summarizing Paul's Teaching in 1 Corinthians 5–7

Though one cannot extract a Pauline theology of sexuality from these three chapters, some important insights can be isolated. First, with regard to sexual desire, Paul admits it is real and powerful. There is nothing inherently sinful about it, but its fulfillment in holiness and honor (see 1 Thess 4:4) belongs within the context of marriage between a man and a woman. For Paul and every other Jew, this was normative and rooted in scripture. Second, in marriage, sexual intercourse was an act of self-giving between equals. This was not a debt owed, but a shared responsibility and a right to be exercised for mutual self-fulfillment and pleasure. Moreover, in 1 Corinthians 7:1–5, and especially in 6:16, Paul emphasizes the union created through intercourse. Notably, he does not mention procreation in any of the texts examined, whereas his contemporaries injected it into almost every passage where sexual relations were discussed. It is doubtful that Paul considered procreation less important than his peers did. His silence in this regard is usually attributed to his urgent sense of an imminent end.[50] Third, Paul believes the bond created by marriage is indissoluble, a position he grounds on an authoritative statement of Jesus. Fourth, as is clear from 1 Corinthians 5:1–13 and 6:12–20, Paul treats sexual morality as more than an individual matter of choice having only individual consequences. He reminds believers that, in their exercise of freedom, they must avoid egocentric behavior that does not consider the benefit or harm to others, disregards the dignity of the body and the relationship with Christ, and is inhospitable to the indwelling of God's Spirit. Fifth, Paul recognized that when it comes to human sexuality, everyone is different.

---

49. Whether Paul was ever married remains a matter of debate. See the recent discussion in Raymond F. Collins, *Accompanied by a Believing Wife: Ministry and Celibacy in the Earliest Christian Communities* (Collegeville, MN: Liturgical Press, 2013), especially 111–38.

50. See, e.g., Victor Paul Furnish, *The Moral Teaching of Paul: Selected Issues* (Nashville, TN: Abingdon Press, 1985), 35–36.

There is no one-size-fits-all lifestyle for Christians. God gifts each differently. The superior life is not the single or the married, but the one lived as a faithful response to the gift and call received. Paul knew this and so insisted, "let each of you lead the life that the Lord has assigned, to which God called you" (7:17).

Homosexuality

Two texts are usually cited as evidence of Paul's explicit condemnation of homosexuality. They appear in different letters, each written for distinct purposes, and must be considered within their separate contexts.

First Corinthians 6:9–10

These verses immediately follow Paul's reprimand of the Corinthian community for tolerating litigation between community members in pagan courts (6:1–8). Paul wants disputes between community members settled within the community, not outside before the unrighteous (6:1–5). More than that, he wants Christians to give up taking each other to court and to endure, rather than do wrong to each other (6:7–8). By means of a list of vices, Paul reminds Corinthian believers of their pre-Christian days of unrighteous living, emphasizing that the "unrighteous" will not "inherit the kingdom of God." Among the vice-doers to be excluded are the *malakoi* and *arsenokoitai.* The debate over whether Paul here condemns homosexuality turns on the meaning of these terms. There is no agreement about their exact meaning or how to translate them.

Malakos is an adjective meaning "soft." Used here in the masculine plural (*malakoi*), it means "soft ones."[51] In Paul's day, *malakos* could be used pejoratively to imply that a person was lazy, decadent, weak, lacking in courage, and other similar defects, all of which were associated with the feminine.[52] Thus *malakos* may mean no more than an effeminate person, and it has been translated simply

---

51. Apart from 1 Corinthians 6:9, *malakos* is used only in the parallel passages of Luke 7:25 and Matthew 11:7–19, where Jesus speaks of "soft clothing."

52. See the discussion in Dale B. Martin, "*Arsenokoités* and *Malakos*: Meanings and Consequences," in *Biblical Ethics and Homosexuality: Listening to Scripture,* ed. Robert E. Brawley (Louisville, KY: Westminster/John Knox Press, 1996), 117–36.

as "effeminate," as one reads in the KJV.[53] Why being effeminate would exclude someone from the kingdom is not clear. Most scholars assume that it becomes clear when *malakos* is taken in conjunction with *arsenokoitai*, the masculine plural of *arsenokoitēs*, a term traditionally understood to mean "someone who has intercourse with males," or a sodomite. The NIV translation conjoins the two terms and renders them with one phrase "men who have sex with men," adding the editorial note that the "soft ones" are the "passive partners" and the *arsenokoitēs* are "active partners."

As far as is known, Paul was the first to use the term *"arsenokoitēs."*[54] He may have invented the term by combining *arsen* (male) and *koitē* (bed).[55] Both terms are used in the Septuagint at Leviticus 18:22 and 20:13, where male same-sex relations are prohibited. If he did coin the term based on Leviticus, then he surely had in mind the scriptural condemnation of same-sex relations.

Given that much of what is condemned in first-century literature, whether pagan or Jewish, appears to be pederasty, some have argued that Paul condemns only the specific vice of pederasty.[56] However, given the additional evidence for non-pederastic, same-sex relations,[57] it may be unjustified to assume that authors, including Paul, limited their condemnation to pederasty.[58] Nonetheless, there is no way to confirm whether *arsenokoitai* ("those bedding down males") refers only to pederastic relations, to all male homoeroticism in general, or perhaps only to male prostitution.

---

53. Recent translations of *malakos* include "boy prostitutes" (NAB rev. ed) or "male prostitutes" (NRSV).

54. There is only one other New Testament occurrence of *arsenokoitēs*, at 1 Timothy 1:10, but it does not appear with *malakos* or shed much light on what is intended at 1 Corinthians 6:9. Literally, *arsenokoitēs* means "male bed" and may refer to a male who takes a male to bed.

55. As suggested by Robin Scroggs, *The New Testament and Homosexuality* (Philadelphia: Fortress Press, 1983), 106–8.

56. See, e.g., Scroggs, *The New Testament and Homosexuality*, esp. 17–61 and 116.

57. Mark D. Smith cites vase depictions of male-to-male sexual intercourse between what appear to be peers, as well as some literary evidence suggesting adult males engaged in non-pederastic same-sex intercourse, cf., "Ancient Bisexuality and the Interpretation of Romans 1:26–27," *JAAR* 64.2 (1996): 224–56.

58. As pointed out by Robert A. J. Gagnon, *The Bible and Homosexual Practice: Texts and Hermeneutics* (Nashville, TN: Abingdon Press, 2001), 162, n. 6.

The only thing that can be said with a measure of certainty is that 1 Corinthians 6:9 contains a negative evaluation of male same-sex activity. Today, most scholars agree that it is anachronistic to import into this text contemporary notions of homosexuality as an inherent sexual orientation toward persons of the same sex and to insist this is what Paul condemns.[59] What he censures here is not an orientation but male same–sex relations.

Two further considerations are important. First, the list at 1 Corinthians 6:9–10 mentions ten vices.[60] Many scholars recognize that stereotypical catalogs of vices, as well as virtues, were important rhetorical tools in ancient speech and writing. In 1 Corinthians 6:9–10, Paul inserted one of these traditional vice lists sandwiched between the phrase "will not inherit the kingdom" of God. Paul rarely uses this phrase,[61] which serves as a clue that he is borrowing a preformed list that includes *malakoi* and *arsenokoitai*. In fact, the list framed by the kingdom of God statements, as well as the formulaic statement in v. 11 referring to the Corinthians as having been "washed" (*apelousasthe*), may have been drawn from a baptism liturgy.

Second, Paul inserts this list in the context of an argument against Christians' suing each other in pagan courts before the unjust. He gives no indication that the litigation had anything to do with same-sex intercourse any more than with any of the other unacceptable vices listed. Paul inserts the list to wrap up his argument in a crescendo of vices that characterize the behavior of the unrighteous, which Paul's Corinthian converts are no longer. This list reinforces that fact and serves a rhetorical purpose in the whole argument of 1 Corinthians 6:1–11. To spotlight and magnify one particular vice, as if Paul's whole purpose was to focus on that, completely misses

---

59. Some astrologers believed that the position of the stars at one's birth preordained one's sexual orientation, but as Brooten points out, these views are hardly representative of Greco-Roman views in general. Moreover, ancient astrologers did not necessarily have modern notions of homosexuality in mind. See *Love between Women*, 124–30.

60. Other vice lists appear at Romans 1:29–31, 13:13; 1 Corinthians 5:10–11, 6:9–10; 2 Corinthians 6:9–10, 12:20–2; Galatians 5:19–21. See further John T. Fitzgerald, "Virtue and Vice Lists," in *Anchor Bible Dictionary*, ed. David Noel Freedman (Garden City, NY: Doubleday, 1992), vol. 6, 857–59.

61. Paul only uses it at 1 Corinthians 15:50 and at Galatians 5:21, where one finds another vice list.

the point of the list in his argument. While male homoeroticism of some kind is mentioned and condemned here, along with a string of other condemnable vices, Paul's focus was clearly not male same-sex relations.

Romans 1:26–27

In Romans 1:18–4:25, Paul develops one long argument in which he demonstrates that all are "under the power of sin" (3:9) and in need of God's righteousness, now manifested apart from the law through Christ and to be received by faith. Paul's comments about same-sex relations belong to the first discrete section of this long argument, which begins at 1:18 and ends at 1:32.

These fourteen verses describe the depraved state of humans who worship idols instead of God. Because even apart from a special direct revelation, God is knowable and perceptible in the material world (1:20), idolatry, in Paul's view, was really not a matter of ignorance, but of willful refusal to recognize God. This explains why he says idolaters "are without excuse" (1:20; cf. Wis 13:1–9). They suppressed and "exchanged" the truth about God, choosing instead to worship handcrafted deities. Thus he presents idolatry as a changing or perversion of the "order of things" or the exchanging of the truth about god for a lie.[62] In good Jewish tradition, which held that idolatry led to moral chaos,[63] Paul illustrates the immoral behaviors issuing from idolatry via a vice list at vv. 28–31. Absent from the list is any vice involving sexual immorality, which Paul has treated separately in vv. 26–27 where he focused on same-sex relations, the perversion that mostly aptly illustrates idolatry.

Presupposed in Paul's references to same-sex relations are beliefs based on Genesis 1–2—namely, that male-female sex is inscribed in the divine order, as are the requirements that men and women marry and procreate. That is the way things should be according to Jewish tradition, which Paul accepts. Also in line with Jewish tradition, Paul

---

62. See, e.g., Jeremiah 2:11: "Has a nation changed its gods, even though they are no gods? But my people have changed their glory for something that does not profit." "They exchanged the glory of God for the image of an ox that eats grass" (see Ps 106:20).

63. See, e.g., Testament of Naphtali 3:3–5; Wisdom 14:12.

construes same-sex relations as evidence of idolatry, of the perversion of God's created order, which finds its concrete social embodiment in the human exchange of "natural relations" for "unnatural." Paul says God allows this perversion to afflict those who willfully pervert who God is by worshipping inanimate human artifacts (1:26). The point is not that God imbued humans with sinful homoerotic passions and forced them to act on these, but rather that one perversion (idolatry) leads to another (same-sex acts), which is then considered proof of the first.

Paul first references women who exchange natural for unnatural relations (v. 26b) and parallels female same-sex relations with male by the use of the Greek term *homoiōs*, "likewise," or "in the same way."[64] Men give up natural relations with women, and women give up natural relations with men.[65] Paul describes same-sex acts as shameless and those who engage in them as "enflamed by lust[66] for one another" (v. 27). This recalls the period literature, which links homoeroticism to insatiable lust. As New Testament scholar Robert Jewett notes, Paul's phrasing "inflamed by lust" implies an irrational bondage to an egoistic, empty, and unsatisfying expression of animalistic sexuality.[67] It is willful and carries its own punishment, which Paul leaves unspecified.[68]

Some have tried to argue that Paul is not condemning male homosexuality here, but rather male heterosexuals who abandon what is natural for them—namely, relations with women—and turn to men instead. That would mean this text does not condemn homosexuality at all, but the perversion of one's heterosexual orientation. Since male-to male sex is natural to homosexuals, this lets

---

64. The parallel created by the use of "likewise" allows his descriptions at v. 27 to apply to female same-sex relations in v. 26.

65. Since Paul does not specify that women gave up sex "with men," it has been argued that Paul had in view unnatural, non-procreative sex between women and men. But as Brooten has persuasively argued, Paul targets female homoeroticism, see *Love between Women*, 232–37.

66. At v. 27 Paul uses the Greek expression "*exekauthēsan en tē orexei,*" literally "enflamed by lust," which the NRSV translates "consumed by passion."

67. Robert Jewett, *Romans: A Commentary* (Minneapolis, MN: Fortress, 2007), 179.

68. Jewett discusses ancient views on the actual physiological consequences of male same-sex relations. See *Romans*, 178–79. Paul may simply be repeating a traditional idea about how suffering afflicts the righteous (see, e.g., Wis 12:23).

homosexuals off the hook.[69] This position can only be sustained by importing into the texts anachronistic notions of determined sexual orientation, which Paul did not have. As previously noted, his criticism does not focus on homosexuals or heterosexuals, but on persons who participate in same-sex relations.[70] The point in this text is that Paul treats all same-sex relations, indeed all the vices listed, as empirical evidence of humanity's alienation from God, whose presence they refuse to acknowledge. The vices, including homoeroticism, do not cause this turning away from God, but are its result.

In Romans, as Jewett notes, Paul's language removes any notion of decency, honor, or friendship from same-sex relationships.[71] Rather, he construes all same-sex relations as prima facie evidence of godless existence, which necessarily carries with it a condemnation of such relations. Paul's position is consistent with the prevailing social-cultural and religious views of his day. He does not comment on the non-reproductive nature of these acts, but he does state that they are against nature and lust-driven. Moreover, with other Hellenistic Jews, he also associates same-sex relations with idolatry. The fact that he includes female homoeroticism indicates a wider focus than just pederasty, which is of course included in his condemnation.

Paul's choice to focus on same-sex relations provided him, at least rhetorically speaking, with the best way to illustrate idolatry. To change the Creator into a creature is to convert order into disorder. This is the precise dynamic Paul sees at work in same-sex relations: it exchanges the natural God-ordained order for what is unnatural. Some have suggested that Paul used same-sex relations as a rhetorical illustration and that it carried none of his personal evaluation of same-sex relations,[72] but this cannot be confirmed. Moreover, Paul makes his ethical views on sexual relations clear at 1 Corinthians

---

69. As proposed, e.g., by John Boswell, *Christianity, Social Tolerance, and Homosexuality: Gay People in Western Europe from the Beginning of the Christian Era to the Fourteenth Century* (Chicago: University of Chicago Press, 1980), 91–118, esp. 109. But see the critique by Richard B. Hays, "Relations Natural and Unnatural: A Response to J. Boswell's Exegesis of Rom 1," *Journal of Religious Ethics* 14.1 (1986): 184–215.

70. As noted by many, see, e.g., Martti Nissinen, *Homoeroticism in the Biblical World*, trans. Kirsi Stjerna (Minneapolis, MN: Fortress Press, 1998), 109.

71. Jewett, *Romans*, 179.

72. See, e.g., Nissinen, *Homoeroticism in the Biblical World*, 111–13.

6:12–20 and 1 Corinthians 7. In both, he insists the proper context for sexual intercourse is within the bond of marriage between a man and his wife.

Does all this translate to a condemnation of the contemporary phenomenon of homosexuality? Surely, Paul's association of idolatry, drunken debauchery, and insatiable lust with same-sex relations is no longer tenable and cannot be taken for granted as an argument against same-sex relations. Same-sex relations do frustrate the procreative function of intercourse, but many heterosexual couples do likewise, even on a permanent basis. Are same-sex relations against nature? In Paul's day, they were considered to be so. Today, there is no unanimity about what "natural" is. Moreover, today homosexuality is seen as a complex phenomenon, not reducible to same-sex acts, which is what Paul undeniably and categorically condemns. As noted, Paul's condemnation is made apart from any consideration of whether such acts are expressions of love and fidelity by persons in long-term monogamous relationships. Paul's own religiously conditioned assumption that same-sex relations signal one's willful refusal to know God—the source of love, goodness, faithfulness, and mercy—would hardly allow him to associate same-sex relations with anything but wickedness and depravity. And that is what he does.

Contemporary believers are not required to privilege Paul's culture and its concepts and biases; nor are they obliged to make decisions about sexual behavior based on Paul's letters understood a-historically, that is, as providing timeless truths applicable to situations and concerns never anticipated. That would be an abuse of Paul's letters and a disservice to the contemporary discussion. While Paul's letters should not be dismissed in the contemporary debate over homosexuality, neither should they define it.

Beyond Sex: Total Body Ethics

Paul's discussion of sexual matters could easily lead to the impression that he understood the church as a fenced-off corporate body or, via the metaphor of the temple, as a kind of fortress of holiness where, like antivirus software, the mission of the holy ones is to search, quarantine, and delete unholy sex polluting the environment. However, this would sell short Paul's vision of the body of Christ and his understanding of holiness. For Paul, the body of Christ is not primarily a metaphor for a unified organism on the defensive, but for an assembly(ies) of diverse people, enjoined to actualize the ethical significance of the life and death of Jesus. Paul's shorthand way of expressing this is to say believers are called to "imitate Christ." Clearly Paul expected Christians to be sexually decent persons, but that was only part of the total-body ethics of the church of God in Christ. Paul wanted local assemblies to totally and radically conform themselves to Christ—to be active "colonies of cruciformity"[73] immersed in society but characterized by nonconformity to its values. Chapter 10 examines some of the ways Paul expected believers to live against the grain of imperial society. Here the focus is on the shape of Christ's life and death as the model for life *within* the community.

Cruciform Living

Many practicing Christians think of the cross as a fixture on the wall to gaze at and be reminded of a past event. Paul never considered the cross something to gaze at, but rather something to look through—a window through which one comes to see the character of God, which confounds human understanding of deity. The cross exposes God as the great subverter of all human values, notions, and institutions by choosing to be known in Christ as a cruciform God of weakness and humility. God's cross-exhibited love reveals a way of loving that does not operate according to human standards. Cruciform love elects the nobodies, the rejects—those the world considers foolish, low, and despised (1 Cor 1:26–31). Those who benefit from God's cruciform love are the socially inferior rather than the socially superior, the last rather than the first. Finally, in the powerless Christ crucified, God reveals himself as one who eschews the world's power structures to manifest power apart from violence: to redeem and reconcile rather than conquer and divide like the imperial rulers of the world. In Jesus Christ crucified, God gets things done not by the conventional exercise of power, but through the weakness of the crucified one. It is in this weakness that Christ is God's power and wisdom.

---

73. Michael Gorman, *Cruciformity: Paul's Narrative Spirituality of the Cross* (Grand Rapids, MI: Eerdmans, 2001), 349.

Cruciform living was life reimagined through the lenses of God known in Christ-crucified. It was paradoxical living that was at once imitation of Christ and imitation of God. As New Testament scholar Michael Gorman observed, in the cross Christ is Godlike and God is Christlike.[74] Paul demanded that believers totally reorient their existences according to the strange story of what God had done in Christ. The small story of each community's life, whether in Rome or Philippi or Corinth, was supposed to mirror the macro story revealed in the cross. In other words, the cross and its values were supposed to be the "new normal" for life in the community. But what would that look like?

Cruciform Ethics at Work

Paul's discussion in 1 Corinthians 8–10 illustrates how Paul expected the "new normal" to play out in community life. The issue at stake is whether believers can eat food offered to idols. Paul used it as a tool to instruct everyone about the demands of cruciform life.

Regardless of their diverse ethnic, educational, and socio-economic levels, all Corinthian converts heard Paul's gospel of freedom. Whatever values they had previously lived, whatever laws they had previously obeyed, whatever food they had previously eaten no longer mattered. In Christ they were a new creation, freed from the law to walk in the newness of life. If the so called elite of this community were wrong when they championed their freedom to engage in sex with prostitutes, they could not be faulted for claiming their right to eat idol meat. They staked their claim to eat what they wanted on theological knowledge. Paul confirms that they are correct: "no idol in the world really exists" (8:4). Thus those who were not yet completely convinced of the nonexistence of idols and who objected to others eating idol meat held a theologically incorrect position.

If the cross were not the new norm, end of story. The theologically informed win; the superstitious lose. But Paul does not respond in view of theological correctness. Rather, he couches his entire long

---

74. Michael J. Gorman, "You Shall Be Cruciform as I Am Cruciform: Paul's Trinitarian Reconstruction of Holiness," in *Holiness and Ecclesiology in the New Testament,* ed. Kent E. Brower and Andy Johnson (Grand Rapids, MI: William B. Eerdmans, 2007), 148–66, here 154.

argument on this subject by qualifying the rationales the elite offer in the course of the argument. Their opening claim is that they have theological knowledge. Paul agrees, but he says, "knowledge puffs up," whereas "love builds up" (8:1). In response to their other rationale, repeated twice, that "all things are lawful" (10:23), Paul adds a first qualification, "but not all things are beneficial" and then a second, "but not all things build up." For Paul, neither knowledge rooted in sound theological principle nor freedom as the prerogative of those in Christ provides sufficient criteria for determining practice. A third criterion must be factored in: the community. Concern for the brother for whom Christ died (8:13) and concern for what benefits and builds up the entire community must take precedence over the exercise even of a legitimate individual right. An ethic of concern that considers the good of others first, based on the model of Christ's self-emptying love, is the new normal in a cruciform community. In fact, in the cruciform community the renunciation of one's rights may at times be the best expression of Christian freedom, as Paul illustrates in 1 Corinthians 9:1–27 via his own life of self-renunciation for the sake of others.

Paul's lengthy argument concerning spiritual gifts (1 Cor 12:1–14:40) illustrates how "cruciform normal" demands the affirmation of diversity and inclusiveness and the rejection of domination and uniformity. The essence of the one body of Christ is its heterogeneity. A diversity of gifts and talents at the service of the body are necessary for its vitality and well-being. In fact, the issue discussed in chapters 12–14 presupposes that the Corinthian body of believers was blessed with an extraordinary diversity of spiritual gifts and talents. Therein lay the problem—not in the gifts, but in their use by some. Rather than affirming the diversity and welcoming the contribution of each for the building up of the community, some viewed the ability to speak in tongues as evidence of superior spiritual status. To the detriment of the assembly, they exercised these gifts for self-glorification. In response, Paul lays out an extended argument affirming that God gives diverse gifts for the purpose of building up the church, and their use must be motivated by cruciform love that values the other members of the community and their gifts.

Paul's response includes the famous body metaphor at 12:12–26. As noted, Paul did not invent this metaphor, which was frequently used in ancient political rhetoric to combat factionalism and restore unity. The metaphor highlights unity in diversity and the inter-dependence of parts, but at verse 22, which no doubt comes as a sting to the elitists, Paul inverts the status quo by insisting on the indispensability of the weaker members of the body and according greater honor to the inferior members. Paul had already referred to God's inversion of the social hierarchy in his choice to call the nothings of this world (1:26–31). But just as the weaker members of the community had failed to be fully convinced of the non-existence of idols, it appears that the elite had yet to be fully convinced that cruciform logic was the new normal. The failure of the weak was a matter of scruples; the failure of the elite was essentially a failure to affirm diversity and inclusivity. In effect, it was a refusal to recognize and accept the body of Christ. This refusal also manifested itself in the abuses at the Lord's Supper, where the elite showed contempt for those with nothing (see 1 Cor 11:17–34). Paul stings the elite again at 12:27–31, where he presents a hierarchical list that places "speaking in tongues" last among the gifts given for the edification of the church.

In 1 Corinthians 13:1–13, perhaps one of the most recognized passages in Pauline literature, Paul describes a "more excellent way." Though often understood as an abstract meditation on love, discon-nected from the discussion of spiritual gifts, this more excellent way serves as a guide for using spiritual gifts and proposes love as the absolute norm that must govern their exercise. It is also a critique of the community for failure to live by this norm.

Without love, the gifts are useless (13:1–3). Paul's first illus-tration of the uselessness of gifts without love targets speaking in tongues. Without love, they are just so much noise, like brass instru-ments struck without purpose. Other gifts are no better. Even Paul's self-denial and life of hardship are of no account. In sum, all gifts and religious practices are equally of no account unless motivated and informed by love.

After Paul establishes the necessity of love, he lists what love is and is not (vv. 3–7). Paul had already called attention to the Corin-thians' jealousy, boasting, arrogance, rudeness, and so on, at various places in the letter, and here he indirectly critiques their behavior. It was completely unChristian, motivated by self-interest and compet-itiveness. The more excellent way—the only way to transcend this morass and jump-start Christianity at Corinth again—is through the practice of cruciform love. The gifts, no matter how great, provide only partial knowledge of God and are temporary. Unfortunately, the Corinthians boasted in their possession of such gifts, believing that they offered complete access to divine mysteries. The complete understanding they desire, however, is a future reality associated with the end-time, when the perfect replaces the partial. Paul illustrates his point by means of two analogies. One is based on human maturation (v. 11); the other is based on indistinct images produced by a mirror (v. 12). In each case, there is a movement from the partial and incomplete to complete spiritual knowledge and understanding. What the Corinthian elite desired was essentially good, and Paul does not criticize them for that desire. However, their present boasting in and privileging of what is incomplete and temporal—just as their boasting in and preferring certain ministers (see 3:1–4)—indicates their spiritual immaturity and failure to embrace cruciform life. The supreme norm of cruciform life is love, which is eternal. Motivated by love, they can use all the Spirit's gifts for the end toward which God has ordained them: the building up of the body of believers, which exists to re-embody the cruciform story of divine love. Paul concludes this long discussion with practical advice on the use of spiritual gifts at the prayer assembly, which includes a famous censure of women at 14:34–36, an issue considered in the next chapter.

These examples from 1 Corinthians illustrate the type of cruciform ethics that were supposed to be the norm for communities everywhere. Without living cruciform lives, there is no Christianity. Paul understood that well and feared for the survival of the church at Corinth. He was concerned not simply in view of their sexual ethics, but because the total body ethics at Corinth showed little sign that believers had embraced cruciform life as the new normal. The church exists everywhere so communities of men and women actualize in their individual and corporate life the ethical significance of what God had done in Christ. While the churches may do good things, essentially they are called to retell the story of God's love revealed in Christ-crucified. To borrow Michael Gorman's words, "This people, the 'Church' lives the story, embodies the story, tells the story. It is the living exegesis of God's master story of faith, love, power and hope."[75]

75. Gorman, *Cruciformity: Paul's Narrative Spirituality of the Cross*, 379.

Summary

In many respects, Paul's views on sexual morality prove to be rather conventional views prevalent both in Hellenistic Jewish and Greco-Roman society. The chapter considered sexual morality first not because Paul established sexual comportment as the acid test for Christian living, but because in debates on sexual morality, recourse is most often had to Paul's views. An examination of those views shows that Paul formulated them within a cultural context that no longer exists—a milieu with assumptions and biases that differ greatly from those of contemporary society. Thus in the debates today, whether about homosexuality or premarital cohabitation, Paul's texts must be used with caution and awareness of their cultural conditioning. Moreover, if Paul actually had an acid test for true Christian living, its concern was the degree to which the community as a whole, and each member individually, lived a cruciform existence, with cruciform ethics and logic as the new normal.

Questions for Review and Reflection

1. What values are promoted in contemporary society that are opposed to cruciform life and logic and make it difficult for Christians to be Christian?

2. Many people feel that churches are fixated on sexual ethics and could do a better job in emphasizing what this chapter has referred to as "total body ethics." What are your views on this?

3. How does Paul's understanding of Christian freedom and individual rights differ from what most people today think about freedom and individual rights?

4. Do you agree/disagree with Paul that a person is not a Christian apart from membership in a community and responsibility for that community's life?

5. What are the positive aspects of marriage illustrated in 1 Corinthians 7?

6. Do you think Paul's prohibition of sex outside of marriage should apply to unmarried cohabiting adults today? Why or why not?

7. Why might it be considered inappropriate to use Paul's texts (1 Cor 6:9 and Rom 1:18–32) to condemn the contemporary phenomenon of homosexuality?

Opening More Windows

Browning, Don S., M. Christian Green, and John Witte (eds.), *Sex, Marriage and Family in World Religions*. New York: Columbia University Press, 2006.

Gorman, Michael J. *Cruciformity: Paul's Narrative Spirituality of the Cross*. Grand Rapids, MI: William B. Eerdmans, 2001.

Hays, Richard B. *The Moral Vision of the New Testament: Community, Cross, New Creation, A Contemporary Introduction to New Testament Ethics*. New York: Harper Collins, 1996, esp., 16–59 on Paul's ethics.

_____. "Crucified with Christ. A Synthesis of the Theology of 1 and 2 Thessalonians, Philemon, Philippians and Galatians," in *Pauline Theology, Vol. 1 Thessalonians, Philippians, Galatians, Philemon*, ed. Jouette Bassler. Minneapolis, MN: Fortress Press, 1991, 227–46.

Loader, William. *Making Sense of Sex: Attitudes towards Sexuality in Early Jewish and Christian Literature*. Grand Rapids, MI: William B. Eerdmans, 2013.

_____. *The New Testament and Sexuality*. Grand Rapids. MI: William B. Eerdmans, 2012.

_____. *Sexuality in the New Testament*. Louisville, KY: Westminster/John Knox Press, 2010.

Meeks, Wayne A. *The Moral World of the First Christians*. London: SPCK, 1986.

_____. *The Origins of Christian Morality: The First Two Centuries*. New Haven, CT: Yale University Press, 1993.

O'Toole, Robert F. *Who Is a Christian? A Study of Pauline Ethics*. Collegeville, MN: Liturgical Press, 1990.

Winter, Bruce. *After Paul Left Corinth: The Influence of Secular Ethics and Social Change*. Grand Rapids, MI: William B. Eerdmans, 2001.

Chapter 9

Paul and Women

Overview

This chapter examines Paul's attitude toward women. It begins by considering how women functioned in Paul's communities and the extent to which Paul's theology influenced his attitudes about women's status and roles within earliest Christianity. Contemporary Jewish and Greco-Roman views on women are then examined, after which the chapter takes up two Pauline passages considered offensive to women. Finally, the chapter addresses the question of how contemporary readers might appropriate the texts today.

Recommended Reading

Roman 16:1–27

1 Corinthians 3:5–15

1 Corinthians 11:2–16

1 Corinthians 14:1–36

2 Corinthians 5:11–21

2 Corinthians 11:23–33

Philippians 4:2–3

Acts 18:1–28

Genesis 2:4–25

It's More Complicated than You Think

When Christians debate the status and roles of women, Paul's views are usually at the center of the controversy. Most of the statements considered offensive to women—such as the command that women be subject to their husbands (Col 3:18; Eph 5:22; see further

Titus 2:3–5) or that they be silent and prohibited from teaching and having authority over men (1 Tim 2:11–14)—are found in the deutero-Pauline letters. Most scholars concede that Paul did not write these six letters, even if he is named as author.[1] However, two of Paul's teachings, found in one of his seven undisputed letters, are frequently perceived as devaluing women and have been repeatedly cited to argue for women's subordinate status. At 1 Corinthians 14:34–35, Paul commands women's silence and subordination to their husbands. In the same letter, at 11:2–16, part of Paul's convoluted argument about women's hairstyles depends on the view that women are subordinate to men because of the order of creation. Paul states, "Indeed, man was not made from woman, but woman from man. Neither was man created for the sake of woman but woman for the sake of man" (11:8–9).

For many, such statements confirm that Paul deviated from Jesus' approach to women and initiated Christianity's perennially repressive posture toward women by reinscribing within Christianity the patriarchal standards and structures of his day.[2] Others maintain that when all the evidence is examined, not merely a few passages, a truer picture of Paul as a radical egalitarian emerges.[3] So who was Paul? Was he a patriarch and misogynist or simply a man who has been misunderstood and whose views have been exploited by advocates of women's subordination?

These questions can never remain purely academic as long as Paul's words continue to influence or determine how individuals and

---

1. In antiquity, disciples were known to write in a deceased teacher's name in order to advance his legacy. Many believe that Paul's disciples engaged in this practice, known as pseudonymous writing, to continue his teaching for later generations. The distinction between Paul's genuine letters and the deutero-Paulines was noted in chapter 1. See further Bart D. Ehrman, *Forged: Writing in the Name of God—Why the Bible's Authors Are Not Who We Think They Are* (New York: Harper Collins, 2011), esp. 79–114 on texts written by others in Paul's name.

2. See among others, Leonard Swidler, *Yeshua: A Model for Moderns* (New York: Rowan & Littlefield, 1988); Luise Schottroff, *Lydia's Impatient Sisters: A Feminist Social History of Early Christianity* (Louisville, KY: Westminster/John Knox, 1995); Todd D. Still, "Paul: An Appealing and/or Appalling Apostle," *Expository Times* 114.4 (2003): 111–18.

3. See, e.g., Elizabeth Schüssler Fiorenza, *In Memory of Her: A Feminist Reconstruction of Christian Origins* (New York: Crossroad, 1983). Schüssler Fiorenza, however, recognizes that Paul was not consistent, see esp. 236.

churches understand the status and role of women in the domestic, social-political, and especially ecclesial spheres. However, answering them in a balanced way requires a consideration of a number of factors: first, how women actually functioned in the Pauline mission; second, whether and to what extent Paul's theological thought framed his understanding of women's status and roles within the Christian community; third, how women were viewed in contemporary Greco-Roman and Jewish society; and finally, Paul's teaching about women in the Corinthian passages just referenced. Over the course of the chapter, it will become clear that Paul's posture toward women is complex, and the evidence does not lend itself to facile categorizations of Paul as either irredeemably misogynistic or uncompromisingly egalitarian.

Women and Their Roles
in the Pauline Communities

Paul refers to more individual women than any other New Testament author. Most are mentioned by name; two are mentioned in relation to males.[4] These references are concentrated in Romans 16:1–16, where Paul provides most of the available information about the women associated with his mission. Before considering their roles, it is worth noting that Paul mentions more than three times as many male associates as female in his letters.[5] This statistic could suggest that men played a greater role in the Pauline mission. However, because Paul provides scant supplemental information about what most of his named associates did—whether male or female—it would go beyond the evidence to claim that men bore the greater responsibility for the Pauline mission or exercised more important roles.

If one takes the named women about whom Paul provides some information, one finds, comparable to the findings among named

---

4. Evodia and Syntychē (Phil 4:2); Apphia (Phlm 2); Prisca (Rom 16:3; 1 Cor 16:19); Phoebe (Rom 16:1); Mary (Rom 16:6); Junia (Rom 16:7); Tryphaena, Tryphosa, Persis (Rom 16:12); Julia (Rom 16:15); Chloe (1 Cor 1:11); see also, the "mother" of Rufus (Rom 16:13) and the "sister" of Nereus (Rom 16:15).

5. Paul names about forty-two men (some more than once) associated with his mission. Most references are concentrated in Romans 16 and 1 Corinthians.

men, that only a few key individuals come to the fore.[6] They are Prisca (aka Priscilla), Phoebe, Junia, Evodia, and Syntechē.

Prisca

Prisca is always mentioned along with her husband, Aquila. As one of a number of important missionary couples in earliest Christianity, Prisca and Aquila played significant, probably founding, roles in major centers of earliest Christianity such as Corinth and Ephesus.[7] They were also prominent in the community at Rome, but were expelled under Emperor Claudius, ca. 49 ce (cf. Acts 18:2) and migrated to Corinth. When Paul arrived in Corinth, about a year later, he worked with this couple in their tent-making business and enjoyed their hospitality (cf. Acts 18:3–4). By the time he wrote Romans, ca. 57–58 ce, the couple had apparently returned to Rome and were first among the long list of people to whom Paul sent greetings in Romans 16. In greeting them and the members of their house church, Paul describes Prisca and Aquila as his "coworkers"(*synergoi*) in Christ Jesus "who risked their necks for my life, to whom not only I give thanks, but also all the churches of the Gentiles" (16:4). Paul's comments speak to the esteem enjoyed by Prisca and Aquila, who hosted "house-churches" in their home wherever they were located (see also 1 Cor 16:19).

Whether Prisca was the more prominent member of this missionary couple or enjoyed a higher social status than her husband is not certain. At least from the time of John Chrysostom, (d. 407 ce), the fact that, at Romans 16:3, Paul greets Prisca before her husband has been cited as an indication of her preeminence. However, in the only other place in his letters where Paul speaks of this couple, he names *Aquila* first (1 Cor 16:9). If any significance was attached to the order of names, Paul seems to disregard it.[8]

---

6. Among named male associates, Timothy, mentioned eleven times in the seven undisputed letters, and Titus, mentioned ten times, stand out as Paul's key collaborators.

7. Other couples Paul names are Junia and Andronicus (Rom 16:7) and Julia and Philologus (Rom 16:15).

8. Outside Paul's letters, the couple is mentioned three other times (Acts 18:18, 26; 2 Tim 4:19), with Prisca's name first.

More important than establishing Prisca's preeminence over her husband is recognizing her indisputable preeminence as one of Paul's most strategic allies in the development of the Gentile mission. She and her husband traveled with Paul to Ephesus, where they remained to start the mission while he traveled on (see Acts 18:18–19:10). Some time later, Paul rejoined them at Ephesus (1 Cor 16:19). He found a flourishing community there, which must be attributed to Prisca and Aquila's evangelizing efforts. They instructed many in the faith, including Apollos, whom they encouraged on his mission to Corinth (Acts 18:24–7). Moreover, despite Paul's insistence that he laid the foundation for the community in Corinth (1 Cor 3:10)—a comment best understood as directed against factionalism and the favoring of Apollos by some Corinthians—most probably, Prisca and her husband introduced Christianity to Corinth, where Paul eventually played a significant role in the community's development.[9]

In brief, Prisca appears to have been an indefatigable and courageous collaborator (*synergos*) with Paul in the spread of the Gentile mission. She traveled with him to set up a new mission base and instructed others in the faith. She and her husband were well-respected figures within Gentile communities. Along with her husband, she was responsible for house-churches in at least three major cities: Rome, Ephesus and Corinth. It is tempting to assume that because the churches met in homes managed by women that women such as Prisca must have necessarily had prominent leadership roles in the local communities. However, knowledge about women's roles in house-churches is too limited to draw any certain conclusions about what someone like Prisca actually did when the assembly gathered in her house.[10] In any event, Prisca appears to have been a permanent member of Paul's evangelizing team and must certainly be counted among those who exercised a leading role in advancing the work of the gospel within the context of the Pauline mission. Whether her activities were typical of all Paul's female collaborators, though, cannot be known with certainty based on the scarce evidence.

---

9. Prisca and her husband were already Christ-believers when they came to Corinth in ca. 49 ce. Paul does not mention them among those whom he converted or baptized (see 1 Cor 1:14, 16 and 16:15).

10. See the caution in Carolyn Osiek and Margaret MacDonald, *A Woman's Place: House Churches in Earliest Christianity* (Minneapolis, MN: Fortress, 2006), 3–4, 33.

Phoebe

Before Paul sends his greetings to those named in Romans 16, he introduces Phoebe to the community there (16:1). Phoebe, from the port city of Cenchreae, just east of Corinth, was about to arrive in Rome bearing Paul's letter and laying the groundwork for his upcoming visit to the imperial capital. In asking the Romans to give her a fitting reception, Paul introduces Phoebe as "our sister . . . , a deacon (*diakonos*) of the Church at Cenchreae . . . , a benefactor (*prostatis*) of many and of myself as well" (Rom 16:1–3). The two key Greek terms used in reference to Phoebe, *diakonos* and *prostatis*, are frequently mistranslated: the first as "deaconess," and the second as "helper." In the first case, Paul uses the term *diakonos*, the same masculine singular noun used with reference to men. It should be translated "deacon." The term "deaconess" (*diakonissa*) came into use well after Paul's time to designate a new third-century ce ministry whose functions were much more limited than those of the first-century "deacon."[11] Regarding the second term, *prostatis*, which appears nowhere else in the New Testament, the lexical information indicates that the term signified a protector or patron in the sense of a financial backer. The rendering "benefactor" (NAB rev. ed.; NRSV) is appropriate. Renderings that carry a servile connotation, such as "helper" (NJB; KJV), betray bias. This bias is also discernible whenever commentators on this passage begin with the qualifier "as a woman," after which Phoebe's activities are usually limited to caring for the sick, the poor, and the needs of other women. Fortunately, most scholars have moved beyond the androcentric framework permitting such bias and now acknowledge that Phoebe functioned in the formal role of deacon. But what did deacons do within the context of earliest Christianity?

Only Acts 6:1–6 provides information about the origin and purpose of the diaconal ministry, which was to oversee the distribution of food. This text also describes the character requirements for

---

11. The office of *diakonissa* originated ca. the third century ce. It is mentioned in the *Didascalia Apostolorum*, a third-century-ce text, and the *Apostolic Constitutions*, a fourth-century-ce text. In both texts, the deaconess' role is restricted to ministry to women. See Margaret Dunlop Gibson, trans., *The Didascalia Apostolorum in English* (Cambridge, MA: Cambridge University Press, 2011), 78–79 and further, the *Apostolic Constitutions*, esp. 8.20 and 2.7.58, accessible at *www.newadvent.org/fathers/07151.htm*.

deacons and mentions the laying on of hands, by which they were formally commissioned for this task. While their task appears limited and menial, two verses later, Acts 6:8 mentions that one of the original seven deacons, Stephen, "did great wonders and signs among the people." This parallels what apostles do according to Acts 5:12: "now many signs and wonders were done among the people through the apostles." Moreover, it was Stephen's preaching about Jesus with "wisdom and Spirit" (Acts 6:10; see further 7:54) that incited the Jewish authorities against him. Evidently deacons did not limit their activities to overseeing food distribution, despite that being the reason given for the institution of this ministry. Further, Paul also refers to himself as a *diakonos,* (see, e.g., 1 Cor 3:5; 2 Cor 3:6), but clearly without intending to communicate any limitation of ministerial activities. Therefore, while it can be reasonably assumed that Phoebe, like other deacons, ministered to the needy, there is no compelling reason to exclude preaching, instruction, or baptizing from her ministerial work. Given both her formal diaconal ministry and prominent status as *prostatis,* she clearly had a leading role in advancing the gospel and was integral to the Pauline mission.

Junia

At Romans 16:7, Paul greets Junia and Andronicus, another prominent New Testament pair. He describes them as his close associates[12] and fellow-prisoners, who are *"episēmoi,"* that is, "outstanding" or "prominent" among the apostles. As New Testament scholar Eldon J. Epp points out, all patristic writers understood the phrase *episēmoi en tois apostolois* to mean that Junia and her husband were distinguished apostles.[13] Though early church writers as far back as Origen (early third century ce) unanimously regarded Junia as a woman, some insist that Junia was really a man named Junias, and that he and Andronicus were not prominent, well-known apostles but only well known *to* the apostles.[14] Junia's "sex-change" was a relatively

---

12. The phrase Paul uses, *syngeneis mou,* literally "my kin," may indicate that the couple was related to Paul or were fellow Jews.

13. See Eldon J. Epp, *Junia: The First Woman Apostle* (Minneapolis, MN: Fortress Press, 2005), 69.

14. See the survey in Epp, *Junia,* 32–35 and further, 79–80.

Praise for Junia

Despite sharing society's overall low assessment of women, Saint John Chrysostom (d. 407 CE), had high praise for Junia. In his comment on Romans 16:7, he wrote, "indeed to be apostles at all is a great thing. But to be even amongst these of note, just consider what a great encomium this is! But they were of note owing to their works, to their achievements. Oh! How great is the devotion of this woman that she should be even counted worthy of the title of apostle!" (*Epistle to the Romans*, Homily 31.2).

recent operation, dating to the late 1800s. Biblical scholars inserted a circumflex accent over the "a" in the Greek *Iouniân*, indicating a contracted form of the male name Junianus; in contrast, the acute accent, *Iounián*, indicating a feminine name, had been used since the Middle Ages, when accents were first inserted into the Greek text.[15] However, all such attempts defy the evidence, which overwhelmingly favors taking the name Junia as a reference to a female apostle.

Since the term *apostle* simply means "one sent," it is important to understand what Paul, who defended his right to be called an apostle (see 1 Cor 9:1–3), means by the term. He implies that an apostle was one who had encountered the Risen Lord (1 Cor 9:1; Gal 1:1.15–17) and received a divine commission to proclaim the gospel. In his four major letters, Paul begins each letter by stressing his apostolic call and status (Rom 1:1–5; 1 Cor 1:1; 2 Cor 1:1; Gal 1:1). It serves as the basis of his authority to preach, baptize, exhort, correct, and command and comes with certain apostolic rights (see 1 Cor 9:1–15). Elsewhere, he indicates that being an apostle is labor-intensive. Physical suffering and various indignities were a daily part of apostolic life and signs of apostolic authenticity (1 Cor 4:9–13; 2 Cor 4:8–9, 11:23–29; 1 Thess 2:1–2). Apparently, Junia and Andronicus, fellow prisoners with Paul, met these criteria; otherwise it is hard to understand why Paul, who rarely uses *apostolos* to designate others,

---

15. See Epp's discussion of the evidence, including the complicated issue of accenting, *Junia*, 3–59.

would use the term for Junia and her husband.[16] Given the significance of *apostolos* in Paul as the basis of authority, Junia the apostle must have exercised not only a leading but also an authoritative role in the early Christian movement.

Evodia and Syntychē

Paul provides limited information about Evodia and Syntychē. He addresses both women in his letter to the Philippians, urging them "to be of the same mind in the Lord" (4:2). The fact that Paul publicly names them, refers to their disagreement, and calls on a mediator (v. 3) to help them resolve their dispute, indicates that the disagreement was serious and perhaps risked dividing the community. It also speaks to Evodia and Syntychē's high profile in the community. Paul describes them as having "struggled [*synathleō*] side by side with him in the gospel along with Clement and the rest of Paul's fellow-workers"

© Scala / Art Resource, NY

Restored third century CE fresco, Catacombs of Priscilla, Rome, featuring a female figure at prayer. Women were prominent in earliest Christianity, but their contributions were largely overlooked before twentieth-century feminist attempts to recover their history.

---

16. At Philippians 2:25, Paul refers to Epaphroditus as "*hymōn apostolon*," literally "your apostle," which is usually rendered nontechnically as "your messenger" (NRSV; NAB rev. ed.); at 1 Thessalonians 2:7 where Paul states, "though we might have made demands as apostles of Christ . . ." Silvanus and Timothy should probably be included in the "we."

226 PAUL: WINDOWS ON HIS THOUGHT AND HIS WORLD

(v. 3). This description suggests the two women were part of an evangelizing team that included both men and women. While the terms Paul uses to describe the women, "cofighters" and "coworkers," do not refer to formal leadership roles, these women were on the front lines, participating in Paul's struggle to advance the gospel. Though the exact extent and nature of their ministry cannot be specified, they were clearly leading figures in the community at Philippi.

Women Advancing the Gospel

This brief examination of Paul's key female collaborators reveals that apart from Junia and Phoebe, Paul describes no women using terminology that suggests a formal leadership role. However, all of the women examined were key figures in the Pauline mission with whom Paul personally collaborated in varying degrees. In the case of Prisca, the collaboration extended over a number of years. If one adds to these five names those of the women whose contribution Paul mentions only in passing—for example, Mary and Persis "who worked hard" (Rom 16:6,12); Tryphaena and Tryphosa, "workers in the Lord" (16:12); and Apphia, who hosted a house-church (Phlm 2–3)—as well as Lydia and the women of Philippi mentioned in Acts (16:11–40), it appears that a sizable number of women collaborated with Paul to advance the gospel.

Theological Context

Many scholars attribute the inclusion and prominence of women in the Pauline mission to certain of Paul's theological principles, starting with his new creation theology described at 2 Corinthians 5:11–21. This text forms part of a larger argument that Paul carries on with the Corinthians, who found him to be a rhetorically inept, pathetic figure without apostolic gravitas and were not persuaded by his gospel of a crucified messiah.[17] He counters by arguing that the Corinthians' negative perceptions are part of the old age of sin and death. This old age and the perspective it offered on reality are now

---

17. The contempt the Corinthians had for Paul, as seen in 2 Corinthians, is not evident in 1 Corinthians, and reflects the degree to which relations between Paul and the community had eroded in about a year's time.

nullified by what God has done in Christ, through whom a new age has dawned (vv. 14–15). Paul therefore expected that all Christians, including the Corinthians, who were of the "new creation," would view all reality through the Christ-event (v. 16). As many recognize, this radically new point of view conditioned Paul's thought and actions. But did it impel him to radically reevaluate gender hierarchy or women's roles? Were Jewish and pagan women attracted to Christianity precisely because Paul's new creation theology entailed their liberation from oppressive social structures and allowed them previously unavailable opportunities?

To answer these questions, scholars usually turn from the broad new creation theology in 2 Corinthians to Galatians 3:26–28, where, as previously noted, Paul cites an early Christian baptismal formula that included the statement: "There is no longer Jew or Greek, there is no longer slave or free, there is no longer male and female; for all of you are one in Christ Jesus." New Testament scholar Howard Clark Kee declared,

> In ancient literature, pagan, Jewish, and Christian, there is no statement about the place of women more radical than Paul's declaration in Galatians that "in Christ" (his term for the new Christian community) there is no place for the ethnic, social, and sexual differences the wider society maintains . . .[18]

For feminist scholars, this verse constitutes a kind of a Pauline manifesto on women's rights, which, in their view, should be given precedence when assessing Paul's thought on women's status and their roles in ministry.

Many feminists, influenced by Wayne Meek's description of this verse as a "performative utterance"[19] demanding changed attitudes and behavior, believe that the "new behavior" engendered by the baptismal declaration found its concrete manifestation with respect to women in their exercise of new leadership roles in the house-churches and the early Christian movement. In their view, baptism brought about a

---

18. Howard Clark Kee, "Changing Role of Women in the Early Christian World," *Theology Today* 49.2 (1992/93): 225–38, here 230; see further, e.g., Pamela Eisenbaum, "Is Paul the Father of Misogyny and Anti-Semitism?" *Crosscurrents* 50.4 (Winter 2000–2001): 506–24.

19. See the explanation in chapter 7.

fundamental change in women's status not only soteriologically, that is, with regard to their saved status, but also socially in terms of their ecclesial status and functions.[20] Two assumptions usually accompany this understanding of the consequences of Paul's baptismal teaching at Galatians 3:28. First, baptism brought about a real improvement in the lives of women, who had previously lived subordinate, oppressed existences. Second, new egalitarian existence in Christ attracted women to the Jesus movement because it allowed women, whether Jew or Gentile, to function in leadership roles denied them in the patriarchal society at large due to their gender. However, both assumptions oversimplify the situation. Even from the limited evidence, a much more complex and dynamic picture of first-century-ce women's lives, both Jewish and Greco-Roman, emerges.[21]

Women in First-Century CE Judaism

In his assessment of the social position of first-century-ce Jewish women, New Testament scholar Joachim Jeremias painted a bleak portrait of oppressed women stuck in an intensely misogynistic religion.[22] He concluded his appraisal of Jewish women's social status by observing that only against this repressive background can one fully appreciate Jesus' attitude to women. Until relatively recently, many Christian scholars accepted this appraisal and, in light of it, portrayed the Jesus movement as offering Jewish women the opportunity to break with Jewish patriarchy and misogyny by joining a presumably egalitarian movement, free of patriarchy and repressive practice.[23]

Jewish feminist scholars have justifiably objected both to this characterization of first-century-ce Jewish women and the assumption that Christianity provided the liberation Jewish women sought. In their

---

20. See, e.g., Schüssler Fiorenza, *In Memory of Her*, 205–36.

21. Besides the fact that any extant evidence about first-century Greco-Roman women's lives is limited, most of the literary evidence was written by men and is inflected by the prevailing cultural biases regarding women and the behavior expected of them. Further, the authors' descriptions do not necessarily reflect the realities of Roman women, especially lower-class women, about whom almost nothing is written.

22. Joachim Jeremias, *Jerusalem at the Time of Jesus: An Investigation into Economic and Social Conditions during the New Testament Period* (Philadelphia: Fortress Press, 1969), 359–76, appendix on "The Social Position of Women."

23. See, e.g., Ben Witherington, "Women in the New Testament," in *The Anchor Bible Dictionary*, ed. David N. Freedman (New York: Doubleday, 1996), vol. 6, 957–60.

© Zev Radovan / www.biblelandpictures.com

A monumental staircase led to the tomb of Helena of Adiabene in Jerusalem. She was one of Judaism's most illustrious first-century converts. Excavated tomb remains, including the queen's sarcophagus, are stored in the Louvre Museum, Paris.

view, the championing of "liberating Christianity" over "oppressing Judaism" is simply another variation on Christian anti-Judaism.[24] As they point out, the pitiable portrait of Jewish women and accompanying misogynist portrayal of Judaism are caricatures constructed from rabbinic sources that postdated Paul and nascent Christianity by more than two hundred years.[25] Moreover, it is now widely recognized that rabbinic literature did not offer a description of the actual social reality. Rather, it reflected an idealized social order. In fact, other literary and inscriptional evidence shows that women actually found Judaism attractive and converted willingly. Josephus relates events surrounding the conversion of some women of Damascus.[26] He also reports the conversion of Helena Queen of Adiabene, who was famed for her generous support of the Jews and the temple and who retired to Jerusalem, where she died and was buried.[27]

---

24. Judith Plaskow, "Blaming Jews for the Birth of Patriarchy," *Lilith* 7 (1980): 11–13; and more recently, Amy-Jill Levine, "Second Temple Judaism, Jesus and Women: Yeast of Eden," *Biblical Interpretation* 2.1 (1994): 8–33.

25. See Jacob Neusner, *Method and Meaning in Ancient Judaism* (Missoula, MT: Scholars Press, 1979), 83; Ross S. Kraemer, "Jewish Women and Christian Origins: Some Caveats," in *Women and Christian Origins*, ed. Ross S. Kraemer and Mary Rose D'Angelo (New York: Oxford, 1999), 35–49, esp. 35–39.

26. Josephus, *Jewish Wars*, 2.20.2.

27. Josephus, *Ant.* 20.17–19. Fulvia, a Roman aristocrat, was also attracted to Jewish practice, see *Ant.* 18.81–84.

In a pseudepigraphal text, the pagan Asenath freely converts to Judaism in order to marry Joseph. Although a fictional elaboration of Asenath's marriage to Joseph (see Gen 41:45), many believe it reflects real women's conversion experiences.[28]

Inscriptional evidence attests that Jewish women had significant leadership roles within the synagogue as *archisynagōgos* or *archisynagōgissa* (head of the synagogue) and *presbytera* (synagogue elder), and available archeological evidence suggests that they were not segregated from men in the synagogue.[29] Jewish women also managed their own affairs, studied Torah, made authoritative pronouncements based on scripture, and asserted themselves in ways usually presumed impossible.[30] All such evidence challenges the often-repeated claim that Jewish women "would have seen the new religious roles allowed them in Christianity in stark contrast to what had been the case in the Jewish synagogue or home."[31] Clearly, the monochromatic, bleak portrait of Jewish women does not reflect social reality. Nonetheless, there is no denying that first-century Judaism remained a patriarchy. Views of women as inferior, weak, wayward, fit only for the home, and needing male direction also persisted. This gender ideology, meaning the shared beliefs and attitudes about women's status and roles, is reflected in both canonical and noncanonical texts written between 200 bce and 100 ce.[32]

---

28. See the full text with introduction and notes in James A. Charlesworth (ed.), *The Old Testament Pseudepigrapha*, vol. 2 (Garden City, NY: Doubleday, 1985). A summary of the story is available at *jwa.org/encyclopedia/article/asenath-bible*.

29. The evidence is collected in Brooten, *Women Leaders*, esp. 5–33. Women's roles in the synagogue have been scrutinized again recently in Ross Shepherd Kraemer, *Unreliable Witnesses: Religion, Gender and History in the Greco-Roman Mediterranean* (New York: Oxford University Press, 2012), esp. 232–41.

30. Evidence and arguments attesting that Jewish women were more active and self-directing than usually granted are found in, e.g., Tal Ilan, *Integrating Women into Second Temple History* (Peabody, MA: Hendrickson, 2001); Ross S. Kraemer, *Her Share of the Blessings: Women's Religions among Pagans, Jews, and Christians in the Greco-Roman World* (New York: Oxford, 1992); Serena Zabin, "Iudaee Benemerenti: Towards a Study of Jewish Women in the Western Roman Empire," *Phoenix* 50.3–4 (1996): 262–82, esp. 278–80.

31. See Ben Witherington, III, *Women in the Earliest Churches* (Cambridge, MA/New York: Cambridge University Press, 1988), 114.

32. See, e.g., Sirach 9:2–9; 25:19, 22, 24, 26; The Life of Adam and Eve, esp. chs. 18–21; Testament of Reuben 5:1–3.

In his treatise *Against Apion*, Josephus cites scripture, which allegedly says, "a woman is inferior to her husband in all things."[33] Philo agreed and insisted a woman's place was the home. In his view, space was gendered. Women were to manage the smaller or private arena, the home, and to cultivate solitude. Men belonged in the public square, overseeing the larger affairs of the city.[34] Philo and Josephus also reasoned to women's derivative nature and related inferiority, based on their interpretation of Genesis 2.[35] Josephus even believed that their gender rendered women incapable of giving credible court testimony.[36] Thus while opportunities for Jewish women existed within their own tradition, views about the place of women in the social order kept them circumscribed.

Greco-Roman Women

The assumption that Christianity provided possibilities denied women in the patriarchal society at large is also difficult to sustain with regard to non-Jewish first-century-ce women. Many scholars now recognize that the roles carried out by Paul's female collaborators, especially in Romanized cities such as Thessalonica, Corinth, Ephesus, Philippi, and Rome, were not revolutionary developments deriving exclusively from new creation theology. Rather, a broad range of evidence attests that women occupied strong managerial and leadership roles within the private sphere of the household. Married Roman women had rather extensive autonomy and authority in their own households, including oversight of a large workforce, agricultural productivity, and even sales of produce. Even women of lower class status lived active lives and were probably associated on some level with their husbands' businesses. As New Testament scholars

33. See Josephus, *Against Apion*, Bk. 2.200. Text also available at *perseus. uchicago.edu/perseus-cgi/citequery3.pl?dbname=GreekFeb2011&getid=1&query= Joseph.%20Ap.%202.204*. As noted on this website and elsewhere, the text Josephus cites is not found in the Old Testament.

34. See Philo, *Special Laws* 3.169–71. Text also available at *www.earlyjewish writings.com/text/philo/book29.html*.

35. See Philo, *Allegorical Interpretation of Genesis*, Bk. 2.8. Text also available at *www.earlyjewishwritings.com/text/philo/book3.html*. Josephus also believed that the subordinate place of women derived from the order of creation, see *Ant.* 1.1.2.

36. Josephus, *Ant.* 4.8.15.

© Maria Pascuzzi

According to the inscription, this statue was dedicated to Eumachia, veiled as a priestess, by the fullers (textile workers) of Pompeii. This copy stands in place of the original, which is housed in the National Archeological Museum, Naples.

Carolyn Osiek and Margaret Mac-Donald observe, "this social reality predates the Christian era."[37] Moreover, women also wielded influence beyond the domestic sphere as benefactors and patrons.[38] At Corinth, for example, inscriptional evidence attests to the beneficence of Junia Theodora, a non-Christian contemporary of Paul and Phoebe.[39] As an independently wealthy woman and civic patron (*prostatis*) of Corinth, Junia Theodora used her money to welcome exiles from her native Lycia in Southwest Asia Minor. She also exerted her influence in official circles in Corinth to elicit goodwill toward the Lycians. The actions attributed to Junia Theodora indicate that females were not withdrawn from public life. Another contemporary of Paul and Phoebe, Claudia Metrodora, from the island of Chios off the coast of Ephesus, achieved fame and honor as a major city benefactor and also held public office.[40] Eumachia, one of Pompeii's first citizens and benefactors,

---

37. Osiek and MacDonald, *A Woman's Place,* 144.

38. On women's patronage in the Roman world, see ibid., 199–209.

39. See esp., Rosalinde A. Kearsley, "Women in Public Life in the Roman East: Iunia Theodora, Claudia Metrodora and Phoebe, Benefactress of Paul," *Tyndale Bulletin* 50.2 (1999): 189–210; Junia Theodora is also discussed in Bruce Winter, *Roman Wives, Roman Widows: The Appearance of New Women and the Pauline Communities* (Grand Rapids, MI: Eerdmans, 2003), esp. 183–204.

40. On Claudia Metrodora, see Kearsley, "Women in Public Life," 198–201. Though not a contemporary of Paul, there is good documentation for Plancia Magna (ca. late first/early second century ce), civic patron of Perge. See Mary Taliaferro Boatwright, "Plancia Magna of Perge: Women's Roles and Status in Asia Minor," in *Women's History and Ancient History,* ed. Sarah Pomeroy (Chapel Hill: UNC Press, 1991), 249–72.

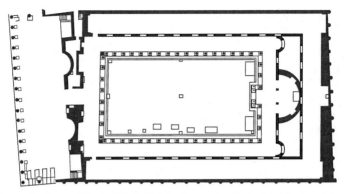

Eumachia financed the building of this large complex, believed to be a commercial center for wool-working and textile production, in Pompeii in 2 CE.

financed a large complex built ca. 2 ce, the remains of which can be seen today.[41]

In brief, as household managers, patrons, and public officials, Gentile women assumed significant leadership roles that brought them into public space. Further, in both the domestic cult and the public arena, evidence indicates that they functioned as prophetesses and priestesses.[42]

The combined evidence makes it difficult to sustain a sharp contrast between a thoroughly egalitarian Christianity and a thoroughly patriarchal pagan cultural environment. Christian women's roles were apparently not all that different from those of their non-Christian peers. Thus to construe them as expressions of a new, improved status for women afforded exclusively by Christianity is probably more than the evidence can bear.[43] In general,

---

41. Eumachia of Pompeii, cf. *www.cnr.edu/home/sas/araia/Eumachia.html*.

42. For primary evidence on women's religions and roles, see Ross S. Kramer (ed.), *Women's Religions in the Greco-Roman World* (New York: Oxford, 2004); Sarolta A. Takács, *Vestal Virgins, Sibyls, and Matrons: Women in Roman Religion* (Austin, TX: University of Austin Press, 2008); with specific reference to Philippian women and their cultic activities, see Lillian Portefaix, "Women and Mission in the New Testament: Some Remarks on the Perspective of Audience," *Studia Theologica* 43.1 (1989): 141–52.

43. See Wendy Cotter, "Women's Authority Roles in Paul's Churches: Countercultural or Conventional," *Novum Testamentum* 36.4 (1994): 350–72. See further, Averil Cameron, "Neither Male nor Female," *Greece & Rome* 27.1 (1980): 60–68.

women—whether Jewish, pagan, or Christian—engaged in activities that did not necessarily conform to the prevailing gender ideology, which stressed women's inferiority, incapacity, and domesticity. Nonetheless, although women ran businesses, financed civic projects, held public office, and were honored with dedicatory statues, inscriptions, and titles[44] attesting their social and political clout, they never received rights equal to those of men, regardless of their economic stratum. This social reality persisted throughout the Roman period. When women attempted to assert themselves beyond appropriate limits, gender discourse was deployed to control, shame, and remind women of their place. Whatever exercise of power and autonomy women enjoyed, it was always within the framework of the male-dominated, hierarchically structured macro-society. In addition, it always took place within the regnant, or dominant, ideology of female inferiority and domesticity.

Paul and Women: Two Difficult Texts

It is within this broader social-cultural reality, where women remained relatively circumscribed in spite of their demonstrated capacity to lead and manage, that Paul's ambivalent posture toward women needs to be considered. This ambivalence is evident in the two texts from Corinthians mentioned at the outset of this chapter. Before looking at them, it is important to repeat that Paul did not create the baptismal formula he cites at Galatians 3:26–29. Moreover, in the context of the letter to the Galatians, the pair crucial to his argument against the necessity of circumcision was the religious-ethnic pair, Jew/Greek. This narrow focus in Galatians does not mean Paul was unaware of the full emancipatory implications of the baptismal formula or that he disagreed with them in principle. However, he did not always agree with how the implications were put into practice, as illustrated by the situation in the Corinthian community. Apparently, certain women interpreted Paul's new creation theology in ways that went beyond what he could countenance. Paul's distress over the liberties taken by some Corinthian women,

---

44. The many titles accorded Plancia Magna are listed in Taliaferro Boatwright, "Plancia Magna," 249–50.

presumably based on Galatians 3:28, may explain why he drops the third pair, male/female, at 1 Corinthians 12:13.

In responding to the women's behavior at 1 Corinthians 11:2–16 and 14:33b–36, Paul employs gender ideology to exert control. His teaching in these texts is far from emancipatory and conflicts with his mission practice, which did not seem to place limits on his female collaborators. To rescue Paul from charges of antifeminism, some argue that these texts were inserted later by unidentified editors who proffered their own views on women. However, 1 Corinthians 11:2–16 is not lacking from any manuscript, and the majority of scholars affirm the authenticity of this passage.[45] Likewise, the two verses commanding women's silence, at 1 Corinthians 14:34–5, are not missing from any known manuscript. Yet some scholars argue that these verses are not authentically Pauline.[46] Among reasons cited are the following: 1) the verses interrupt the flow of the argument; 2) some manuscripts locate verses 34–35 between verses 33 and 36; others locate them after verse 40; 3) the verses appear to contradict 11:2–16, where it is assumed women do pray and prophesy; and 4) the expression "the law says" (v. 34) is un-Pauline. However, as advocates of the authenticity of verses 34–35 point out,[47] in the majority of manuscripts—indeed, in some of the oldest and most reliable textual witnesses[48]—verses 34–35 are found after verse 33. By contrast, few manuscripts have verses 34–35 located after v. 40, and those manuscripts may be traceable to one original.[49] Additionally, the passage is too brief for arguments against its authenticity based on style to be compelling.[50] Despite obscurities, which will be

---

45. See the survey of literature on the authenticity of this passage in Margaret Mitchell, *Paul and the Rhetoric of Reconciliation* (Tübingen, Germany: JCB Mohr, 1994), 261–62.

46. See, e.g., Gordon D. Fee, *The First Epistle to the Corinthians* (Grand Rapids, MI: William B. Eerdmans, 1987), 699–708.

47. See, e.g., Craig S. Keener, *1 and 2 Corinthians* (Cambridge, MA: Cambridge University Press, 2005), 116–20.

48. For example, the Chester Beatty Papyrus, designated P46 (ca. 50–70s ce); the Codex Sinaiticus designated by the Hebrew letter ℵ [aleph] (ca. fourth century ce); the Codex Alexandrinus designated by the capital letter *A* (ca. fifth century ce), and the Codex Vaticanus designated by the capital letter *B* (ca. fourth century ce).

49. See Antoinette Clark Wire, *The Corinthian Women Prophets: A Reconstruction through Paul's Rhetoric* (Minneapolis, MN: Augsburg Fortress Press, 1990), esp. 149–53.

50. Keener, *1 and 2 Corinthians,* 117.

236 PAUL: WINDOWS ON HIS THOUGHT AND HIS WORLD

considered below, these verses can be reasonably attributed to Paul
and presumably reflect his own views.

First Corinthians 11:2–16: Hairdos and Don'ts

At 1 Corinthians 11:2–16, Paul deals with a situation in which men
and women were praying and prophesying in the assembly, hence
publicly. He takes aim at their appearance, although it is unclear
from his language in verses 4–6 whether he refers to head coverings or hairstyles. Many commentators believe Paul was concerned
about hairstyles, which may seem banal to contemporary readers of
Corinthians. However, hairstyles have always figured in discussions
about gender identity.[51] In Paul's day, both pagan philosophers and
Hellenistic Jewish thinkers debated them.[52] Basic to the debate was
the notion that hair was gendered and should be worn in a way that
both reflected and reinforced gender difference. Though apparently
both men and women in the Corinthian community transgressed
gender boundaries regarding hairstyles,[53] Paul's argument focuses
almost exclusively on women's appearance.[54] Paul clearly wants
to maintain gender distinctions, hence his command to women
to observe the conventions that restore and reinforce these distinctions, which he apparently did not consider erased as a result
of baptism.

Paul's anxiety can be understood within the context of ancient
Mediterranean culture, where the pursuit of honor and avoidance of

---

51. See, e.g., Rose Weitz, "Women and Their Hair: Seeking Power through Resistance
and Accommodation," *Gender and Society* 15.5 (2001): 667–86; Anthony Synnott, "Shame
and Glory: A Sociology of Hair," *British Journal of Sociology* 38.3 (1987): 381–413.

52. Ancient views on hairstyles are surveyed in Raymond F. Collins, *First Corinthians* (Collegeville, MN: Liturgical Press, 1999), 396–99.

53. Men may have been wearing their hair effeminately long, and women may
have kept their hair bound up. Archeological evidence relating to hairstyles and head
coverings is discussed in Cynthia L. Thompson, "Hairstyles, Head-Coverings and
Saint Paul: Portraits from Roman Corinth," *Biblical Archaeologist* 51.2 (1988): 99–115;
See further Will Roscoe on the "galli," priests both despised and revered for gender
transgression evident in their long hair and use of make-up, "Priests of the Goddess:
Gender Transgression in Ancient Religion," *History of Religions* 35.3 (1996): 195–230.

54. Women are the focus in vv. 7–16; what nature teaches focuses mostly on
women (vv. 13–15), and the final argument, based on the practice in the churches,
logically relates to what Paul had just said about women and their hair in v. 16.

shame were paramount concerns.[55] In this cultural context, there was more or less a consensus about which behaviors brought honor and which behaviors brought shame. Transgressing gender boundaries fell under the latter category. It brought shame not only to the individual but also to those whose honor depended on that person's behavior. Thus a woman who prayed or prophesied with an inappropriate hairstyle brought shame not only on herself but also on her "head" (v. 5), that is, the man above her in the social hierarchy. Therefore, by insisting that women wear their hair in a manner that observes gender distinctions and avoids shame, Paul reinforces patriarchal notions of gender. He grounds his argument in a hierarchical framework in which God is the head of Christ; Christ, the head of man; man, the head of woman (v. 3). Man is the image and glory of God, while woman is the glory of man (v. 7), because woman was created from man and for man (v. 8). Paul assumes man's preeminence in view of both the larger cosmological order and the creation story (Gen 2), where man is chronologically prior to woman.[56] Because of this priority, woman owes man honor and must avoid whatever would bring shame. In his insistence on the distinction between men and women, as well as women's derivative and therefore subordinate nature based on the order of creation, Paul shares the gender ideology of Jewish contemporaries such as Philo and Josephus. As previously indicated, they reasoned to women's subordinate status in view of Genesis 2. Paul was not beyond upholding the status quo or using traditional arguments to reject behavior that he feared could discredit the church in the eyes of outsiders (cf. 1 Cor 14:23). Some have argued that Paul retracts this whole subordinationist line of argument at verses 11–12, when he states,

> Nevertheless in the Lord, woman is not independent of
> man or man independent of woman. For just as woman

---

55. Bruce Winter believes that by unveiling themselves, Corinthian Christian women risked identification with an emerging group of liberated women in Roman society, who flouted social convention and were known for loose behavior, cf. *Roman Wives*, esp. 77–96.

56. On rabbinic discussions and solutions to the apparent conflict between Genesis 1, where the male and female are simultaneously created, and Genesis 2, where woman is a secondary creation, see Judith R. Baskin, "Women in Rabbinic Judaism: Focal Points and Turning Points," in *Judaism from Moses to Muhammad: An Interpretation* ed. Jacob Neusner et al. (Leiden, The Netherlands: Brill, 2005), 303–33, esp. 307–12.

came from man, so man comes through woman, but all things come from God.

If this is a retraction, then it leaves readers with a confused and incoherent Paul, rather than a Paul who devalues women. Many have sought to resolve the tension by denying either the subordinationist character of verses 3–10 or the egalitarian character of verses 11–12.[57] Rather than resolve the tension, perhaps readers would do well to take these verses as an indication that Paul had deeply ambivalent views about women.

First Corinthians 14:34–35: Women Silent and Subordinate

If Paul sounds confused and contradictory at 1 Corinthians 11:2–16, he seems unequivocally repressive when he states,

> women should be silent in the churches. For they are not permitted to speak, but should be subordinate, as the law also says. If there is anything they desire to know, let them ask their husbands at home. For it is shameful for a woman to speak in church.

There is no end to the scholarly debate about whether these are Paul's words, what exactly he intended, and the text's implications for women in church leadership.[58] Some scholars who accept that Paul made these statements recognize and try to resolve the tension between them and the earlier passage, where he does not object to women's public roles at liturgy but only to their hairstyles (1 Cor 11:2–16). Others who agree that Paul is responsible for this teaching insist that it was addressed to a specific case at a specific time and is

---

57. Various solutions and opinion are discussed in Judith M. Gundry-Volf, "Gender and Creation in 1 Cor 11:2–16: A Study in Paul's Theological Method," in *Evangelium Schriftauslegung Kirche: Festschrift für Peter Stuhlmacher*, ed. J. Ådna, S. J. Hafemann, O. Hofius (Göttingen, Germany: Vandenhoeck & Ruprecht, 1997), 151–71.

58. Discussions of which scholars subscribe to what position and why, as well as the plausibility of each position, are available in major commentaries such as Collins, *First Corinthians*, 511–17, or Anthony C. Thiselton, *The First Epistle to the Corinthians* (Grand Rapids, MI: William B. Eerdmans, 2000), 1150–62.

neither universally nor perennially valid. Still others insist that Paul was actually citing the views of male spiritual elitists, who wanted male-only leadership in the church at Corinth. As the champion of women's equality, Paul cited their position in order to reject it at 14:36 where he says "or did the word of God originate with you?"[59]

As previously noted, the arguments against the authenticity of these verses are not compelling. However, even when accepted as genuine, questions remain. No one can say with certainty whether Paul directed this command to all women or only a specific group.[60] Nor is it clear whether Paul was prohibiting women from talking in public in general or whether he had a particular kind of speech or questioning in mind.[61] The text suggests that the problem concerns location: women asking questions in public, in the assembly, which Paul tells them they must do at home, in private. Paul's reasons are twofold: 1) women are *subordinate* and 2) it is *shameful* for them to speak in public. In light of 1 Corinthians 11:6, the only other time Paul uses the Greek term *aischron*, "shameful," he probably means it would bring shame to the husband.

Despite the obscurities associated with these verses, this much is indisputable: Paul's prohibition and accompanying rationale reflect the gender ideology prevalent in both pagan and Jewish culture at the time. In the Roman historian Livy's (d. ca. 16 ce) account of Cato's speech in favor of the Oppian laws, which Roman women

---

59. According to Charles H. Talbert, Paul employs diatribe here, a rhetorical strategy in which a writer/ speaker quotes his opponent's position and then rejects it, "Biblical Criticism's Role: The Pauline View of Women as a Case in Point," in *The Unfettered Word: Southern Baptists Confront the Authority-Inerrancy Question*, ed. B. James Robison (Waco, TX: Word Books 1987), 62–71. Among others arguing that Paul advocates for women against male elitists, see e.g., Daniel W. Odell-Scott, "In Defense of an Egalitarian Interpretation of 1 Cor 14:34–36: A Reply to Murphy-O'Connor's Critique," *Biblical Theology Bulletin* 17.3 (1987):100–103; and Robert W. Allison, "Let Women Be Silent in the Churches" (1 Cor 14:33b–36): What Did Paul Really Say and What Did He Mean?" *Journal for the Study of the New Testament* 10 (1988): 27–60.

60. Schüssler Fiorenza has argued that Paul directs his prohibition only to married women, see *In Memory of Her*, 230–32.

61. Suggestions vary; see e.g., Terence Paige, "The Social Matrix of Women's Speech at Corinth: The Context and Meaning of the Command to Silence in 1 Corinthians 14:33b–3," *Bulletin for Biblical Research* 12.2 (2002): 217–42; Anders Eriksson, "'Women Tongue Speakers, Be Silent': A Reconstruction through Paul's Rhetoric," *Biblical Interpretation* 6.1 (1998): 80–104.

publically protested (ca. 195 bce) because the laws restricted their use of luxury goods, Cato is said to have begun by remarking,

> If each of us, citizens, had determined to assert his rights and dignity as a husband with respect to his own spouse, we should have less trouble with the sex as a whole; as it is, our liberty, destroyed at home by female violence, even here in the Forum is crushed and trodden underfoot, and because we have not kept them individually under control, we dread them collectively.[62]

Then Cato inserts what he had in mind to say, but did not, to a crowd of women he met in the streets that day who were rushing to the forum to protest:

> What sort of practice is this, of running out into the streets and blocking the roads and speaking to other women's husbands? Could you not have made the same requests, each of your own husband, at home? Or are you more attractive outside and to other women's husbands than to your own?[63]

Cato then continues,

> Our ancestors permitted no woman to conduct even personal business without a guardian to intervene in her behalf; they wished them to be under the control of fathers, brothers, husbands; we (Heaven help us!) allow them now even to interfere in public affairs, yes, and to visit the Forum and our informal and formal sessions . . . Give loose rein to their uncontrollable nature and to this untamed creature and expect that they will themselves set bounds to their licence . . . It is complete liberty or, rather, if we wish to speak the truth, complete licence that they desire.[64]

---

62. Livy, *The History of Rome*. Bks. 31–34, trans. Evan T. Sage (Cambridge, MA: Harvard University Press, 1935), Bk. 34:1–3. Also available at *www.perseus.tufts.edu/hopper/text?doc=Perseus%3Atext%3A1999.02.0164%3Abook%3D34%3Achapter%3D1*.

63. Ibid., Bk. 34:8–9.

64. Ibid., Bk. 34:11–14.

Toward the end of the first century ce, the satirist Juvenal commented on the intolerability of women who went about the city, intruding on men's meetings and talking down to those present, all in the presence of their husbands. Equally intolerable was the woman who dominated the conversation, expressed too many opinions about too many subjects, and corrected the speech or grammar of others.[65]

Plutarch (45–125 ce), a near contemporary of Paul, advised newlyweds, saying,

> Not only the arm of the virtuous woman, but her speech as well, ought to be not for the public, and she ought to be modest and guarded about saying anything in the hearing of outsiders, since it is an exposure of herself.[66]

Two verses later, Plutarch adds,

> if they (women) subordinate themselves to their husbands, they are commended, but if they want to have control, they cut a sorrier figure than the subjects of their control.

Contemporary Jewish writers whose thought was framed by patriarchy expressed parallel views. As previously noted, Philo considered women naturally inferior and fit only for the domestic sphere, where they should be subordinate to their husbands. Women's engagement in public issues amounted to a transgression of gender boundaries. Philo maintained that self-respecting women should stay out of public places and affairs. To do otherwise would be improper and shameful.[67] This evidence attests to culturally prescribed roles regarding speaking in public. Men were expected to hold forth in public; women were not. If they did, they were transgressing the social order and the gendered spaces that determined male and female roles.

---

65. Juvenal, *Satires*, trans. G. G. Ramsay (New York: G. P. Putnam's Sons, 1928), 6. 398–456. Also available at *archive.org/details/juvenalpersiuswi00juveuoft*.

66. Plutarch, *Moralia: Books 1–6*, trans. P. A. Clement and H. B. Hoffleit (Cambridge, MA: Harvard University Press, 1969), 4.31. Also available at *penelope.uchicago.edu/Thayer/E/Roman/Texts/Plutarch/Moralia/Coniugalia_praecepta*.html*.

67. Philo goes on at some length about women's behavior in *Special Laws*, Bk. 3.31.169–75. This text is also available at *www.earlyjewishwritings.com/text/philo/book29.html*.

Apparently some women in the Corinthian congregation did not accept these culturally prescribed roles. Whatever their reasons, Paul is not interested. His concern is with their behavior, which elicits the triple injunction that women be silent, subordinate to their husbands, and limited to acquiring knowledge from their husbands in the home. It again seems clear that Paul was not beyond upholding patriarchal authority and recourse to traditional arguments to squelch behavior he considered objectionable. There is no getting around the fact that this text is offensive to women. By not specifying the type of speech prohibited or whether he had only specific women in mind, Paul's words amount to a categorical prohibition, targeting women as a group. Whether he intended to or not, Paul provided the scriptural authority that generations have used to discriminate against women in both civil and ecclesial contexts. Given the cultural framework within which Paul operated, it is probably not justified to label him a misogynist. Rather, this text again illustrates the tension that existed in Paul's own thought and practice about women's status and roles within the Christian communities he founded.

Appropriating Paul's Texts Today

No responsible approach to the Bible can ignore these two texts that were and remain offensive to women. They are part of the canon. However, no responsible assessment of Paul's views on women can be filtered through these two texts alone, to the neglect of the rest of the evidence. Paul may have been disturbed by certain women's hairstyles, but, that notwithstanding, 1 Corinthians 11:2–16 is prima facie testimony that not every woman sat down and remained silent and subordinate when the community assembled. The fact that the injunction that women be silent in the *ekklēsia* was not even applied absolutely in the church at Corinth should be sufficient caution against applying it universally in any other circumstances or time. Further, the evidence from Paul's missionary practice offers even more reason to see these texts, which envision women as subordinate, as lacking universal applicability. Paul provides indisputable testimony that women did play key, even formal, roles in the life of the church.

Hermeneutics

Hermeneutics, from the Greek *hermēneia* (interpretation), concerns the principles used in the interpretation of a text. Biblical hermeneutics refers to the modes or the interpretive lenses through which one reads and makes sense of the text.

Yet Paul himself was culturally biased when it came to certain women's behaviors. He continued to hold on to the social codes associated with hierarchy and patriarchy, was uncomfortable with the behavior of women that too transparently challenged this status quo, and unequivocally censured that behavior. While Paul proclaimed the wonders of the new creation, he remained to some extent caught up in the structures of the old. In his ambivalence about women, Paul penned texts that remain problematic and have been cited across the millennia as an authoritative basis for censuring women and limiting their roles.

Traditional exegetical questions about what Paul meant or what precise situation he had in mind when commanding women's silence and subordination are important. Equally important are questions about how contemporary readers interpret these texts and what biases inform their interpretation. Feminist hermeneutics, practiced by both men and women, is an interpretive method that seeks to recover the important contributions of women from the earliest days of Christianity.

The scriptural texts, written by men with their androcentric focus, rarely showcase these contributions. Feminist interpretation also concerns how the texts have been traditionally interpreted and applied. In relation to Paul, feminist hermeneutics challenges readers to abandon the lenses of patriarchy and hierarchy (not to mention anti-Semitism) through which Paul has been read throughout the centuries with unfortunate results for many.[68] That the gospel

---

68. On the (mis)use of Paul in the service of shoring up injustice and oppression, see Neil Elliot, *Liberating Paul: The Justice of God and the Politics of the Apostle* (Maryknoll, NY: Orbis Press, 1994), esp. chs. 1–3.

message had yet to fully transform Paul when it came to accepting patriarchy and hierarchy does not excuse contemporary churches that continue to interpret and apply his texts without concern for justice and equality and in ways that intentionally diminish women. Rather than imitating Paul—who was inconsistent in his dealings with women—and justifying women's subordinate status in view of a few Pauline texts, churches can choose to pick up where he left off in the struggle to advance God's work of bringing about the full transformation of creation.

Summary

Paul's attitude toward women is complex and defies neat categorizations. Many women collaborated with Paul to advance the gospel. Women and men served equally as Paul's "coworkers" and "cocontenders" in the gospel; women and men were "deacons"; women and men risked their lives for the sake of the gospel; women and men were benefactors who used their resources to support Paul's mission. Nothing in his descriptions of their work suggests that women were subordinate or their roles were gender specific. Yet Paul, whose mission owed its success no less to women than to men and who paid tribute to women colleagues, also resorted to gender ideology to control women who transgressed traditionally constructed gender boundaries, as well as shored up traditional patriarchal structures.

In the post-Pauline tradition, especially in 1 and 2 Timothy and Titus (known collectively as the Pastoral Epistles), the repressive side of Paul triumphed. More recently, attempts have been made to rescue Paul from centuries of misrepresentation and to stress his liberationist and egalitarian side. In the end, as the evidence suggests, Paul was not exclusively one or the other, but both.

Questions for Review and Reflection

1. What were the prevailing views about women and their status in Paul's day?

2. What are feminist hermeneutics and what is their aim? Some feminists believe that texts susceptible to interpretations that

devalue women should be eliminated from the canon of scripture. What are your views?

3. What are some of the roles Jewish and Greco-Roman women played in their own social and religious settings? What impact does evidence about Jewish and Greco-Roman women's roles have on the contention that Jewish and Greco-Roman women joined the Jesus movement because it provided opportunities denied these women in their own settings?

4. Paul was not entirely consistent in his dealings with women. What is your experience or perception of the Christian church today? Is it free of the patriarchal and hierarchical biases that influenced Paul, or does it continue to operate out of those same cultural biases?

5. If Paul taught the fundamental equality of men and women in Christ, are there any ecclesial roles from which women should be barred? What roles, if any, should be gendered in your view and why?

Opening More Windows

Brooten, Bernadette J. "Jewish Women's History in the Roman Period: A Task for Christian Theology," *Harvard Theological Review* 79.1–3 (1986): 22–30.

Campbell, Joan Cecelia. *Phoebe: Patron and Emissary.* Collegeville, MN: Liturgical Press, 2009.

Cohick, Lynn H. *Women in the World of the Earliest Christians: Illuminating Ancient Ways of Life.* Grand Rapids, MI: Baker Academic, 2009.

D'Ambra, Eve. *Roman Women.* New York: Cambridge University Press, 2007.

Elliott, Lynn H. "Jesus Was Not an Egalitarian: A Critique of an Anachronistic and Unrealistic Theory," *Biblical Theology Bulletin* 32 (2002): 75–91.

Gillman, Florence M. *Women Who Knew Paul.* Collegeville, MN: Liturgical Press, 1992.

Illan, Tal. *Jewish Women in Greco-Roman Palestine.* Tübingen, Germany: JCB Mohr, 1995.

Keller, Marie Noël. *Priscilla and Aquila: Paul's Coworkers in Christ Jesus.* Collegeville, MN: Liturgical Press, 2010.

Kraemer, Ross Shepherd. *Unreliable Witnesses: Religion, Gender and History in the Greco-Roman Mediterranean.* New York: Oxford University Press, 2012.

Lefkowitz, Mary, and Maureen B. Fant. *Women's Life in Greece and Rome: A Sourcebook in Translation.* Baltimore, MD: Johns Hopkins University Press, 1992.

Wire, Antoinette Clark. *The Corinthian Women Prophets: A Reconstruction through Paul's Rhetoric.* Philadelphia: Fortress Press, 1990.

Internet Resources

"Roman Portrait Busts with Professor Eve D'Ambra," YouTube video, 57:54, *www.youtube.com/watch?v=GoDfac8Z5kk.*

Chapter 10

Reading Paul's Letters in the Context of the Roman Empire

Overview

This chapter considers the political implications of Paul's gospel within the Roman imperial gospel. The chapter begins by resituating Paul within the world of first-century-CE politics. Then it considers the evidence from Paul's writings, mission practice, and his expectations for community practice, usually cited to support the claim that Paul's gospel had serious political implications. An examination of Romans 13:1–7, a passage that poses an obstacle to a liberationist reading of Paul's letters, concludes the chapter.

Recommended Reading

1 Thessalonians 1:1–5:25   1 Corinthians 8:1–10:33
Roman 13:1–7   2 Corinthians 8:1–24
1 Corinthians 1:18   Philippians 1:1–3:21
1 Corinthians 2:16   Acts 16:6–17:15
1 Corinthians 6:1–9

Paul and First-Century CE Politics

In 1 Thessalonians, written ca. 49–50 ce, Paul refers to the intense opposition he and his coworkers encountered when evangelizing in Thessalonica, the capital of the Roman province Macedonia. The opposition seems to have forced their premature departure from Thessalonica. When they arrived in Athens, Paul sent Timothy back to see whether this nascent community of former pagans was persevering in their newly adopted faith (1 Thess 3:1). Paul feared that trials and suffering would dishearten them (1 Thess 2:13–14, 3:1–3). When Timothy returned with the good news of their steadfastness, Paul immediately penned 1 Thessalonians, a letter urging believers to remain firm in their faith.[1]

According to Acts 17:1–9, Paul's success among pagans so riled the Jews of Thessalonica that they brought accusations against him to the city's administrative officials. The Jews indicted Paul in political terms, saying he and his coworkers were "acting contrary to the decrees of the emperor saying that there is another king named Jesus" (v. 7). The magnitude of the perceived affront to the social and political order was such that they accused Paul of "turning the world upside down" (v. 6). The Acts account complements the information Paul provides in 1 Thessalonians. There is good reason to believe the account has a solid base in history. The reasons Jews would have been particularly wary of seditious speech will be examined later. For now, suffice it to say that, according to Acts, Paul's preaching was perceived as having serious political implications.

Until relatively recently, few thought of Paul as having any interest in politics. Over the millennia, the feisty historical Paul who boldly preached the messiahship, which is to say, the kingship of Jesus, began to fade from view. In order to guarantee Paul's relevance to generations who never met him, he was recast in ways that divorced him from his world and pastoral concerns. He became the model defender and transmitter of orthodox teaching (2 Tim 1:8–14); a mystic who revealed the inscrutable mysteries of the gospel (Col 1:25–27; Eph 3:1–13); and the prototype of the true Christian martyr.[2] By the fourth century ce, Paul was presented as the archetype of

---

1. According to Acts 16:11–12, on what is considered his second missionary journey, Paul sailed across the Aegean, from Troas to Neapolis. He then traveled overland ten miles north to Philippi, where he began his mission in Greece, eventually working his way down the coast to Corinth by 50–51 ce. See map depicting Paul's second missionary journey on page 38.

2. See Ignatius, *Letter to the Ephesians*, 12.2 "You are the route for God's victims. You have been initiated into the [Christian] mysteries with Paul, a real saint and martyr, who deserves to be congratulated." Accessed at *www.ccel.org/ccel/richardson/fathers. vi.ii.iii.i.html.*

Christian perfection.[3] Paul's transformation continued in the Middle Ages, especially among the reformers of the eleventh through thirteenth centuries. They variously portrayed him as the defender of purity against clerical concupiscence; of the church against internal and external foes; as the champion of church order; and as a systematic theologian who ordered the divine truths revealed to him.[4] The interpretive tradition that emerged during the Renaissance, associated with Martin Luther, featured Paul as exclusively concerned with the justification of the individual sinner. Texts such as Philippians 3:12–20 convinced interpreters that Paul saw the kingdom as a heavenly future reality with little or no political implications for the present.

By divorcing Paul from the social, cultural, and political world in which he carried out his ministry, the churches over the centuries portrayed Paul in ways that accommodated their own needs and assumptions. The Paul of history who was jailed multiple times, beaten up, stood up to detractors, collected money for the poor, and shared his ministry with women faded from view.

Chapter 6 examined new perspective scholarship's efforts to separate the interpretation of Paul from Luther's legacy and to read his letters not in the context of Reformation polemics, but in the context in which Paul actually lived. Once scholars resituated the study of Paul within the framework of his own sociopolitical and religious world, new questions pertaining to that world naturally arose. How did the Roman imperial context of Paul's mission impact his thought, preaching, lifestyle, and expectations for the communities he founded? Were Paul's interests broader than simply the justification and salvation of the sinner? Did his concerns extend to the social and political conditions of his world? Questions such as these belong to a current in Pauline studies that one scholar has referred to as the "fresh perspective" on Paul.[5] Just as the questions asked in new

---

3. See Margaret M. Mitchell, "The Archetypal Image: John Chrysostom's Portraits of Paul," *Journal of Religion* 75.1 (1995): 15–43.

4. On the various ways Paul was portrayed and brought to bear on church polemics, see the essays in Steven R. Cartwright (ed.), *A Companion to Saint Paul in the Middle Ages* (Leiden, The Netherlands: Brill, 2013).

5. See N. T. Wright, "A Fresh Perspective on Paul," *Bulletin of the John Rylands Library* 83.1 (2001): 21–39. "Fresh perspective" is not as commonly used by Pauline scholars as the designation "new perspective"; however, it is a convenient title to distinguish studies that go beyond new perspective concerns to consider Paul in the context of imperial society.

perspective scholarship were stimulated by new information and new ethical concerns in the wake of the Holocaust, so also questions driving "fresh perspective," or political studies of Paul have been stimulated by postcolonialism and concerns about the control exercised by today's imperial-like powers.[6] For some, this amounts to imposing on Paul a contemporary liberal agenda that taints the study of his letters.[7] However, more than one hundred years ago, German theologian Adolf Deissmann claimed that Paul's audiences would have detected anti-imperialism in his preaching. After all, Deissmann remarked, "the New Testament is a book of the Imperial Age," one that applied to Christ terms already in use in the imperial world for the deified emperors. Believers would not have missed the polemical parallelism.[8] Thus rediscovering the political dimension of Paul's message may simply be a case of recognizing that religion and politics have never been separate. In fact, as evident from the discussion in chapter 3, Rome made no pretense that religion and politics were distinct. Rather, it believed and unabashedly proclaimed that the empire was divinely ordained.

Paul and the Imperial Gospel

At Romans 1:16, Paul declares, "For I am not ashamed of the gospel; it is the power of God for salvation." In a homily on Romans 1, John Chrysostom said that he sensed in the comment about not being ashamed Paul's own realization that his gospel of the poor, humiliated, crucified savior paled in comparison to Rome's narrative of

---

6. On postcolonialism, see Robert J. C. Young, *Postcolonialism: A Very Short Introduction* (New York: Oxford University Press, 2003). Briefly, postcolonialism, or postcolonial studies or theory, can be defined as a postmodern current of intellectual discourse that looks at and analyzes the Western cultural impact on areas and people once ruled by Europeans who viewed themselves as racially and culturally superior to those they colonized.

7. Evangelicals are especially wary; see example, Denny Burk, "Is Paul's Gospel Counter-Imperial? Evaluating the Prospects of the 'Fresh Perspective' for Evangelical Theology," *Journal of the Evangelical Theological Society* 51.2 (2008): 309–37. See further, Scot McKnight and Joseph Modica (eds.), *Jesus Is Lord, Caesar Is Not: Evaluating Empire in New Testament Studies* (Downers Grove, IL: IVP Academic, 2013).

8. See Adolf Deissmann, *Light from the Ancient East*, 4th ed., trans. Lionel R. M. Strachan (London: Hodder and Stoughton, 1927), esp. 339–42.

power and victory.[9] Whether or not Chrysostom's insight was accurate, in addressing a letter to communities in the imperial capital, Paul wrote to people surrounded by monuments to Rome's power and glory. It appeared that Rome had brought peace and security to the world and had a much more powerful and persuasive "good news" story than Paul. Nonetheless, he wrote to announce the gospel of God's Messiah, descended from David, Israel's greatest king (Rom 1:3; cf. Rom 9:5). Paul's good news was that God's power to save all people was manifested in the poor, crucified Jesus and all the values of humility and powerlessness associated with his life and death.

Despite the obvious contrast between Paul's gospel and Rome's, Paul never directly stated that he intended his proclamation to be anti-imperial. However, an explicit statement was probably unnecessary. Paul and his addressees shared an existence ordered and structured by imperial Rome and were exposed to its claims and idiom on a daily basis. As Deissmann surmised, Paul's audience would have had no trouble catching his anti-imperial message or recognizing his subversive use of imperial language. Those who disagree that Paul's letters express anti-imperialism usually cite Romans 13:1–7, where Paul appears to advocate social conformity. This text will be examined after the evidence usually cited for Paul's anti-imperial message and practice has been considered.

The Political Significance of the Cross and Resurrection

In considering the political significance of the Christ-event in Paul, it is important to recall Jewish attitudes toward foreign rulers. Pagan rulers were regularly condemned in the Jewish scriptures, which also acknowledged that God used some pagans to do his will in regard to Israel, whether to punish (see, e.g., Jer 25:8–11) or restore (see, e.g., Isa 45:1–6). But as prophetic eschatology gave way to an apocalyptic vision of reality, the ultimate judgment on foreign powers was that God would destroy them (see Dan 7:1–27 and Ezek 38:17–9:16). The Jewish sectarians who lived at Qumran anticipated a holy war

---

9. Chrysostom's homilies on Romans are available at *www.ccel.org/ccel/schaff/npnf111.html.*

between themselves, the "sons of light," and the "sons of darkness," the Romans, who would be completely exterminated.[10] In *2 Baruch*, written to make sense of the disaster that befell the Jews and Jerusalem at the hands of the Romans in 70 ce, Baruch learns via a revelation that God will vindicate his people by completely destroying the foreign empire.[11] Succinctly stated, apocalyptic-minded Jews of Paul's day believed that the inauguration of God's reign of justice and peace would coincide with the complete destruction of the occupying foreign rulers and their forces.

Chapter 4 examined Paul's belief that in the Christ-event God had decisively intervened in history to inaugurate the new age under his rule. This meant not only the subjugation of the cosmic power of evil but also the overthrow and destruction of the rulers of this world who did Sin's bidding through their unjust and corrupt structures. Thus as Wright and others observe, for Paul the cross and Resurrection function not simply as theology but also as history.[12] They symbolize the overthrow of unjust systems under corrupt rulers and the inauguration of a new world order to be completed at Christ's second coming, when every ruler, power, and authority is destroyed, and Christ hands over the kingdom to God (see, e.g., 1 Cor 15:24). Paul elsewhere refers to the destruction of the "rulers of this age," who failed to understand God's wisdom and who crucified God's Messiah, the true "Lord of Glory." By doing so, they unwittingly brought about their own demise (1 Cor 2:6–8). No doubt Paul's addressees heard in his reference to the "rulers of this age" a verdict against imperial Rome. It alone was responsible for Christ's crucifixion.

In the past, as Neil Elliot pointed out, Christian interpretation had depoliticized Paul's preaching on the cross and Resurrection and turned it into a gospel of private spiritual salvation. Yet Paul proclaimed that the cross and Resurrection nullifies all power and

---

10. One of the Dead Sea Scrolls, the "War Scroll" (1QM) describes this war in detail. A concise explanation of the contents and purpose of the War Scroll is available at *www.pbs.org/wgbh/pages/frontline/shows/religion/portrait/scrolltranslation.html*.

11. See *2 Baruch* 35–40.

12. N. T. Wright, *Paul: In Fresh Perspective* (Minneapolis, MN: Fortress Press, 2005), 70. See also, Neil Elliot, "The Anti-Imperial Message of the Cross," in *Paul and Empire: Religion and Power in Imperial Roman Society*, ed. Richard A. Horsley (Harrisburg, PA: Trinity Press International, 1997), 167–83.

rule except the power and rule of God.[13] Paul leveled this political critique against Rome, the last in a series of imperial rulers from whose oppression God would liberate his people. In Paul's view, the liberation had begun and the new age had dawned in the Christ-event. He did not expect believers to be bystanders in the world, passively awaiting their salvation, but to be actively engaged in advancing God's final triumph by working to transform the whole created order.[14]

Anti-imperialism in 1 Thessalonians

In the opening verse of 1 Thessalonians, Paul refers to Jesus by two titles: "Christ," which means the "anointed one" and designates the Jewish King,[15] and "Lord." These were titles also bestowed on the emperor.[16] Paul says here and in the opening salutations of each of his letters that these titles belong to Jesus, the crucified Messiah and the Lord.[17] By applying the emperor's public titles to Jesus, Paul suggests one of two things: Jesus and the emperor were equals or the emperor was neither Lord nor King, because Jesus was. Either way, this was dangerous, if not downright treasonous. The Thessalonians probably detected further polemical intent in Paul's reference to God's "kingdom and glory" (2:12) and likewise in his use of the "gospel" (*euangelion*) of God (2:2) and the "gospel" of Christ (3:2). The Thessalonians had only one gospel, the imperial gospel, and only one

---

13. Neil Elliot's entire book is essentially an attempt to reread Paul as political theology, cf. *Liberating Paul: The Justice of God and the Politics of the Apostle* (Maryknoll, NY: Orbis Books, 1998), see esp. 55–90.

14. As pointed out by J. Christiaan Beker, *Paul the Apostle: The Triumph of God in Life and Thought* (Philadelphia: Fortress Press, 1980), 313.

15. "Christ" (from Greek *Christos*) is not a name but a title. *Christos* is the equivalent of the Hebrew term *meshiach* (messiah), which means "anointed one." In Israel, it was a title of the king who on his coronation day was anointed with oil, thus becoming Yahweh's messiah, or anointed one.

16. On the use of the honorific *kyrios* (Lord) see James R. Harrison, "Paul and the Imperial Gospel at Thessaloniki," *Journal for the Study of the New Testament* 25.1 (2002): 71–96, here 78, and further, Tae Hun Kim, "The Anarthrous *hyiou theou* in Mark 15.39 and the Roman Imperial Cult," *Biblica* 79.2 (1998): 235.

17. In 1 Corinthians 1:1–9, for example, Paul uses the expression, "Lord Jesus Christ" six times.

kingdom, Rome, to which it owed allegiance.[18] Further, Paul's use of the word *parousia* in reference to Jesus' return (4:15) is hardly neutral. The ordinary meaning of this term was "arrival," but it was used technically with royal significance to refer to a visit by an imperial official, above all the emperor.[19] By featuring Jesus as the returning heavenly Lord at 1 Thessalonians 4:13–18, Paul would have easily been heard as subverting imperial eschatology, which proclaimed that Augustus has arrived (*parousia*) as the ultimate Savior.[20] Later, at 5:3, Paul appears to contest an important component of imperial propaganda, the promise of "peace and security." As New Testament scholar Peter Oakes points out, Paul's mention of peace and security powerfully evoked the central platform of Augustan ideology, which was linked to its propaganda about imperial beneficence.[21] Rome, under its emperor, was making the world more peaceful, secure, and

© The Trustees of the British Museum / Art Resource, NY

Silver coin minted at Ephesus ca. 28 BCE, British Museum, London, featuring Caesar Augustus and, on the reverse, the figure of Pax to celebrate the age of Augustan *Pax* or Peace, also referred to as the *Pax Romana*. Such coins were a key medium for the diffusion of imperial propaganda.

18. See Karl P. Donfried, "The Imperial Cults of Thessalonica and Political Conflict in 1 Thessalonians," in *Paul and Empire*, 215–23.

19. See *"parousia, pareimi"* in Gerhard Kittel (ed.), *Theological Dictionary of the New Testament* (Grand Rapids, MI: William B. Eerdmans, 1964), vol. 5, 858–70. At 1 Thess 4:17, Paul also uses *apantēsin*, a feminine noun from verb *apantaō* (to meet). Both terms *parousia* and *apantēsin* were used in conjunction with official visits. See Harrison, "Paul and the Imperial Gospel at Thessaloniki," 82–86.

20. The details of Paul's challenge to Augustan eschatology are discussed in Harrison, "Paul and the Imperial Gospel," 71–96.

21. Peter Oakes, "Remapping the Universe," 317.

prosperous for everyone. This propaganda legitimated the empire and was stamped on imperial coinage. In reality, the imperial program of "peace and security" was accomplished through war and violence and benefited the propertied classes, whose assets and interests were safeguarded.[22] What peace and security the conquered experienced came at the price of colonization and loss of autonomy. Paul rejects Rome's propaganda, referring to the empire as a kingdom of "night and darkness," destined for wrath and destruction (1 Thess 5:5, 9). Since Christians are "children of light and children of the day" they are destined for salvation (1 Thess 5:5, 9) and should put no trust in the empire's promises of peace and security.

These few examples from 1 Thessalonians seem to confirm that Thessalonian Jews denounced Paul and his coworkers for acting against the decrees of Caesar and proclaiming King Jesus because they perceived his message as anti-imperial. Their apprehension is all the more understandable when one considers the "decrees of Caesar" and what was at stake if they were violated. According to Edwin A. Judge, a scholar of earliest Christianity in its Roman context, the "decrees of Caesar" refer to "oaths" imposed on Rome's subjects by which they swore their loyalty to Caesar.[23] In the oath imposed ca. 6 bce on the people of Paphlagonia, a kingdom in north-central Asia Minor, each one pledged to "support Caesar Augustus, his children and descendants throughout my life in word, deed and thought . . . that whenever I see or hear of anything being said, planned or done against them I will report it."[24]

Though there is no way to reconstruct Paul's preaching at Thessalonica, what has just been highlighted from his letter could explain why the Thessalonians heard Paul's preaching as seditious and threatening to their oath of allegiance. The fact that local magistrates administered the oaths as well as enforced them and dealt

---

22. Karl Galinski, *Augustan Culture: An Interpretive Introduction* (Princeton, NJ: Princeton University Press, 1996), 7.

23. Edwin A. Judge, "The Decrees of Caesar at Thessalonica," *Reformed Theological Review* 30 (1971): 1–7, [reprinted in Edwin A. Judge and James R. Harrison (eds.), *The First Christians in the Roman World: Augustan and New Testament Essays* (Tübingen, Germany: Mohr Siebeck, 2008), 456–62].

24. The oath is cited in Judge, *Decrees of Caesar*, 6. In this essay, Judge references other oaths, including the Cypriots' oath to Tiberius, which was similar to the Paphlagonian oath to Augustus.

with violations probably explains why the Thessalonian Jews brought their charges to the city authorities.

Thessalonica was the Roman administrative capital of the province of Macedonia beginning in 146 bce.[25] Prior to Paul's arrival, the Thessalonians understood that their fate was tied to Rome and their well-being depended on their loyalty. By the time Paul visited Thessalonica, a huge statue of Caesar Augustus, standing victoriously with right arm raised, stood north of the temple of Serapis. The statue, erected during the reign of Caligula, or Claudius, is one of the few excavated objects that can be dated with certainty to the period of Paul's visit. New Testament scholar Holland Hendrix has suggested that an outpouring of honors to Augustus, as suggested by the dedication of this statue, may explain Paul's attack on the imperial program of "peace and security."[26]

The political climate in Thessalonica, and its emphasis on royal theology, may also explain Paul's anxiety over the fate of newly converted Thessalonians and concern for whether they would persevere in the faith.[27] By adhering to Paul's anti-imperial gospel, the first Thessalonian believers would have been perceived as enemies of Rome and Caesar. Hence, the violator and his family would be subject to severe disciplinary measures, including "loss of country, safety, and economic fortune"[28] and possibly even death.

Anti-Imperial Strains in the Letter to the Philippians

In 42 bce, on a battlefield just outside of Philippi, the course of Roman history changed when Marc Antony and Octavian defeated

25. Information on Thessalonica during the late Roman republic and early empire is based on the essay by Holland Hendrix, "Thessalonica," in *The Anchor Bible Dictionary*, ed. David N. Freedman (New York: Doubleday, 1992), vol. 6, 523–27.

26. Ibid., 524.

27. Donfried argued that some Thessalonian believers had already been martyred. See "The Imperial Cults of Thessalonica," esp., 219–23.

28. On various punishments, see Harrison, "Paul and the Imperial Gospel at Thessaloniki," 79–80. The author notes that "loss of country, safety and fortune" were specifically cited in the oath of allegiance sworn to Caligula from 37 ce. On economic loss, see Peter Oakes, *Philippians: From People to Letter* (SNTMS, 110; Cambridge, MA: Cambridge University Press, 2001), esp., 77–102.

Brutus and Cassius, the assassins of Julius Caesar.[29] The Philippians, who had supported Brutus and Cassius, paid a price. Their city was colonized and renamed Colonia Iulia Philippensis.[30] Settlers, including many Roman veterans, were sent to populate the city. The settlers, along with a new regime consisting of two Roman magistrates, were present to promote Rome and protect its interests. After Octavian vanquished Antony at the Battle of Actium in 31 bce, more Roman veterans settled in Philippi, further cementing relations between the Philippians and the emperor. The imperial cult was practiced there, and excavations have turned up a temple to the imperial family as well as a large cultic center dedicated to Livia, wife of Caesar Augustus. She was deified by Claudius in 42 ce and given the title Diva Augusta.

According to the travel schema in Acts, Paul evangelized Philippi during his second missionary journey, ca. late 49 ce. While in Philippi, he was arrested, beaten, and imprisoned along with Silas.[31] When they were finally freed, Paul forced an apology out of the Roman authorities for treating them, both Roman citizens, so shamefully (16:39).

Some years later, during another of his imprisonments, Paul wrote to the Philippians. Like him, they were suffering on account of their belief in Christ (1:29). Paul reminds them in this letter that they belong to an alternative state (a *politeuma*, see 3:20) and await the arrival of this state's savior (*sotēr*), the Lord Jesus Christ, who will save them and rule over all (3:21).

Many scholars believe that Paul contrasts the character of this Lord and Savior, Jesus, with that of Caesar at Philippians 2:6–11. The text is actually a pre-Pauline hymn about Christ that Paul integrates into his letter for his own purposes. The hymn begins with

---

29. The Roman historian Cassius Dio describes the battle in his *Roman History*, 47.35–49. The text is accessible at *penelope.uchicago.edu/Thayer/E/Roman/Texts/Cassius_Dio/47*.html*.

30. Information on Philippi is based on the essay by Holland Hendrix, "Philippi," in *Anchor Bible Dictionary*, ed. David N. Freedman (New York: Doubleday, 1992), vol. 5, 313–17.

31. The specifics of the charges are not given in Acts 16:20–21, which reads, "These men are Jews and are disturbing our city. They advocate customs which it is not lawful for us Romans to accept or practice."

what is traditionally understood to be a reference to Christ's pre-existence (v. 6),[32] then his incarnation (vv. 6–7), and then his exaltation and enthronement (vv. 9–11). When considered against the background of the imperial cult and the practice of honoring the emperor with special titles, it is also possible to detect a contrast between Christ and the emperor,[33] especially given the presence at v. 6 of the phrase *isa theō*, translated "equality with God."

In the world in which Paul ministered, the pursuit of honors was an obsession. Both men and women sought recognition and used their money and power to gain it and wield influence. Those with resources built theaters, markets, and fountains inscribed with their names to showcase their beneficence. They also received honorary titles and enjoyed the deference of others. The highest honor a benefactor could receive was to be considered "*isa theoi*" (equal with the gods), the expression used, in the singular (equal with God), at Philippians 2:6. In the eastern Roman Empire, this honorific was usually reserved for someone who had demonstrated characteristics normally attributed to gods, such as saving a city from war, pillage, famine, or other natural disasters.[34] However, the emergence of Caesar Augustus and the new political climate soon made it clear that the emperor alone deserved the "equal to the gods" honorific.

The Philippians' hymn may suggest the unwillingness of the first believers to acquiesce to this new reality. It proclaims another Lord, who unlike the emperor does not grasp after divine honors. Yet in the end he receives them from God: Jesus is exalted with the name above all other names; only at his name shall every knee bend on heaven

---

32. Others argue that v. 6 is intended to contrast Christ and Adam. On the latter interpretation, see James D. G. Dunn, *The Theology of Paul the Apostle* (Grand Rapids, MI: William B. Eerdmans, 1998), 281–93.

33. The discussion of the Philippians' hymn is informed by the essay of Eric M. Heen, "Phil 2:6–11 and Resistance to Local Timocratic Rule: *Isa Theo* and the Cult of the Emperor in the East," in *Paul and the Roman Imperial Order*, ed. Richard A. Horsley (Harrisburg, PA: Trinity Press International, 2004), 125–54. In another interesting interpretation, Joseph Hellerman detects in the hymn a critique of Roman social values, especially elitism and classism. See "The Humiliation of Christ in the Social World of Roman Philippi," *Bibliotheca Sacra* 160 (Oct.–Dec. 2003): 421–33.

34. The *isa theoi* honors are discussed in Simon R. F. Price, *Rituals and Powers: The Roman Imperial Cult in Asia Minor* (Cambridge, MA: Cambridge University Press, 1986), esp. 47–52.

and Earth; only he is to be confessed as the Lord. According to this hymn, the divine honors come to Christ, who seeks no honors and asserts no power over others, but obediently submits to death on the cross, the icon of Rome's ruthlessness. Yet neither death nor Rome has dominion over Christ, whom God exalts and enthrones as the true *Kosmokratōr*, or world ruler (2:9–11). As Peter Oakes remarked, the scope of submission to Christ envisioned in this hymn includes and goes beyond the emperor's realm. It refers not just to goings on in heaven; the sovereignty was also about what was going on in the here and now, on Earth.[35]

This political climate would have made it hard to ignore the hymn's anti-imperial key. By insisting that Christ alone was equal to God, in effect, the earliest Christians sang a hymn of protest against the imperial deification practices, the emperor cult, and the social standards used to measure and accord divine status.[36] Moreover, if as the hymn insists, Christ is above the emperor, then for believers Christ's imperatives of humility and unity outweigh imperial society's imperatives, which work against these.[37] The polemical intent of this hymn was not lost on Deissmann, who remarked,

> we cannot escape the conjecture that the Christians who heard St. Paul preach in the style of Phil 2:9, 11 . . . , must have found in his proclamation of Jesus as Lord, a silent protest against other "lords" and against thee Lord as people were beginning to call the Roman Emperor.[38]

Anti-Imperial Practices: Living by Gospel Values

When read within the context of imperial theology and propaganda, both the passages from 1 Thessalonians and the Philippians' hymn

---

35. Oakes, "Remapping the Universe," 306. On Jewish reaction to the Imperial cult, see James S. McLaren, "Jews and the Imperial Cult: From Augustus to Domitian," *Journal for the Study of the New Testament* 27.3 (2005): 257–78.

36. See Heen, "Phil 2:6–11 and Resistance," 139.

37. As pointed out by Oakes, "Remapping the Universe," 305.

38. Deissmann, *Light from the Ancient East*, 355.

point to the anti-imperial character of Paul's gospel. Further evidence is notable in his own practices and the manner of life he expected of the communities he founded. Examining some of Paul's practices and those he advocated in light of imperial values and structures opens new avenues for understanding them.

The Price of Patronage

In his study of imperial patronage, the classicist Richard Saller reminds readers that the emperor distributed benefits with a singular purpose in mind: to bind and obligate to himself the recipients of his favors.[39] No matter the demonstration of gratitude, no one could repay in kind what the emperor, the supreme patron, had provided. Thus all tokens of gratitude were, in the end, acknowledgments of one's inferior status. In fact, the patronage system, whether at the imperial or local level, served essentially to reinforce publicly acknowledged inequality. Attempts to mask the inequality included substituting the less inherently offensive language of *amicitia/amicus* (friendships/friends) for that of *patronus/clientes* (patron/client). But as Saller notes, regardless of the language, there was no leveling of status in imperial society, which was structured according to a strict social hierarchy.[40]

Patronal relations, language, and ideology permeated society at every level via a constant flow of goods and services between patrons and clients, or "friends." Members of the lower classes sought to attach themselves to a patron to gain protection and benefits. Even philosophers, teachers, and other men of arts and letters sought patrons. Satirical accounts of how these "kept men" were reduced to pandering to their hosts abound in Roman writings. Martial, the famous Roman poet and satirist, had no scruples about comparing the patron/client relationship to that of master/slave.[41]

---

39. Saller, *Personal Patronage Under the Early Empire* (Cambridge, MA: Cambridge University Press, 1982), 33.

40. Ibid., esp. 11–17.

41. Martial, *Epigrams*, Bks. I–V, ed. and trans. D. R. Shackleton Bailey (Cambridge, MA: Harvard University Press, 1993), 2.32 and 2.68. Martial's epigrams are also available at *www.archive.org/stream/martialepigrams01martiala/martialepigrams01 martiala_djvu.txt*.

Paul's Self-Sufficiency

The report in Acts that Paul worked as a tradesman (18:1–3) is corroborated by scattered statements in Paul's letters where he mentions toilsome labor with his hands (see, e.g., 1 Thess 2:9; 1 Cor 4:12) or alludes to it when he states, "did I commit a sin by humbling myself . . . because I preached the gospel without cost to you?" (2 Cor 11:7). In the past, scholars assumed that Paul, like other early Christians, was from the lower classes. Today many more agree that Paul was a cultured man. Besides finding evidence of Paul's education in his letters,[42] New Testament scholar Ronald Hock notes that Paul actually betrayed his higher social class by disdainfully referring to his manual labor as *tapeinoun* (abasing; see 2 Cor 11:7).[43] This is precisely the term used by aristocratic Romans to describe manual labor, as Hock illustrated via a charming period story.[44] Paul's word choice suggests he felt a considerable loss of status by becoming a manual laborer, a sentiment that would make sense only if Paul were from a relatively high social class.[45]

Paul suffered this loss and chose self-sufficiency so that he would be under obligation to no one and thus could preach the gospel free of charge to everyone (1 Cor 9:18). Paul's renunciation of the community's financial support, to which he had a right (cf. 1 Cor. 9:4–8), his choice to work with his hands, and even his refusal to present letters of recommendation (see 2 Cor 3:3),[46] can reasonably

---

42. Ronald Hock, "Paul and Greco-Roman Education," in *Paul in the Greco-Roman World: A Handbook,* ed. J. Paul Sampley (Harrisburg, PA: Trinity Press International, 2003), 198–227. According to Hock, Paul's letters betray a person who had completed the three-phase curricula of Greco-Roman education.

43. Ronald Hock, "Paul's Tent-making and the Problem of His Social Class," *Journal of Biblical Literature* 97.4 (1978): 555–64. Paul also refers to his work as enslavement at 1 Cor 9:19.

44. In "The Dream," Lucian of Samosata faces a dilemma: he must choose between erudition and manual labor. In his dream he is warned that manual labor is *tapeinoun* (demeaning). The story is accessible at *lucianofsamosata.info/TheVision.html#sthash.4SHEgxCW.dpbs.*

45. Hock, "Paul's Tent-making," 564.

46. In the Roman world, patrons wielded influence through letters of recommendation. Without them, no doors opened. Other Christian evangelizers obtained recommendations, but Paul apparently ignored the convention when it came to himself, see 2 Cor 3:1–3.

be interpreted as a choice to avoid entanglement in the patronage system that structured civic and social relationships at Corinth.[47] Paul preferred enslavement to physical work, rather than run the risk of compromising the gospel by enslavement to Corinthian patrons. Moreover, Paul already had a patron, Christ, and was under exclusive obligation to him at the service of the gospel (1 Cor 9:16–17)!

Paul's refusal of patronage caused him a great deal of trouble throughout his long ministry at Corinth. Some saw it as proof that he was not an authentic apostle. It seems to have raised suspicion that he was pilfering money from the collection for Jerusalem, while claiming to be self-sufficient. That would explain why he took pains in 2 Corinthians 8:16–23 to assure the community that if they came through on their pledge to collect money for the poor of Jerusalem, he would not touch the money but send emissaries, Titus and an unnamed brother "tested and found eager" (8:22), to collect and deliver it. Paul reminds the Corinthians that he took these steps so that "no one blame us about this generous gift that we are administering" (8:20).

Despite being misunderstood, Paul never caved into societal patronage expectations, but reaffirmed his unique obligation to the Lord at the service of the gospel (1 Cor 9:16–17). Where he sensed no threat of being put under patronal obligation, he accepted some assistance, for example, from Phoebe (Rom 16:1) and also the Philippians. But even in regard to the Philippians, Paul informs them at the end of his letter that although he appreciated their assistance, he did not ask for it. Hence, he makes it clear that he is under no obligation to them either (see Phil 4:14–19).

Paul's "No" to Eloquent Speech

As noted in chapter 3, the carefully crafted rhetoric of the Roman Empire was self-aggrandizing. It was meant to impress audiences with the empire's power and divinely ordained role and win allegiance to the imperial gospel. Paul, on other hand, announced only

---

47. Cf. John K. Chow, "Patronage in Roman Corinth," in *Paul and Empire*, 104–25. On Paul's motives for refusing financial support, see also Dale B. Martin, *Slavery as Salvation: The Metaphor of Slavery in Pauline Christianity* (New Haven, CT: Yale University Press, 1990).

one thing: "Jesus Christ and him crucified" (1 Cor 2:2). His preaching was the public portrayal of "Jesus Christ . . . crucified" (Gal 3:1). He presented baptism as co-crucifixion with Christ (Rom 6:1–15). He had no intention, as he reveals at 1 Corinthians 1:18–31, of repackaging the "good news" in persuasive words. He said God's "good news" is expressed not in the imperial rhetoric of boasting in its own power but in a crucified messiah, God's apocalyptic intervention in history, which no amount of eloquence could make palatable. For Paul, the substance of God's "good news"—that is, wisdom manifested in the absurdity and weakness of the cross—determines two things: 1) the demeanor of the Christian evangelizer, a mere earthen vessel who must do nothing to detract from the message (2 Cor 4:7) and 2) the appropriate style of proclaiming the message. That style eschews the use of persuasive words and strategies and was clearly separate from human boastfulness and power displays. Paul's "cross rhetoric" overturned elite ideals and power relations and reached out to embrace the "not powerful," the "not of noble birth," the not "wise by human standards" (1 Cor 1:26–31). It reached out to embrace all those who could never have been "recommended" according to the patronal conventions of Paul's day. As Elliot observed, Paul did nothing to suppress the politically engineered horror of the cross by mystifying the death of Jesus, just as he did nothing to make it sound less brutal.[48] Christian proclamation begins in the unembellished "word of the cross."

The rhetoric of the empire was smooth and easy to hear. It set before humans a salvation story, a "good news" rooted in awe-inducing power and victory. Its truth was measured in fine form and elegant articulation.[49] But the true "good news," the gospel of what God has done in Christ, confronts humans with a power that seems to be no power, a victory that seems to be only defeat, a story that offends human expectations of who God is and how God should act. Yet Paul proclaimed that God self-revealed in the cross, in weakness and suffering, not in the might and display of Rome.

---

48. Elliot, *Liberating Paul*, 93–139.

49. As Edwin A. Judge notes, it was axiomatic in Paul's day that truth and fine form were synonymous. See David M. Scholer (ed.), *Social Distinctives of the Christians in the First Century: Pivotal Essays by E. A. Judge* (Peabody, MA: Hendrickson, 2008), 164.

Paul's renunciation of seductive speech and displays of power earned him criticism as rhetorically inept and unpersuasive: in sum, not worthy of a hearing (cf. 2 Cor 10–12). In Paul's day, to eschew eloquence was completely inexcusable and incomprehensible. As Edwin Judge succinctly stated, "to reject the very aspiration [to speak with sublime elegance] was to be a catastrophic and bewildering failure."[50] This no doubt explains why some Corinthians disdained Paul and preferred Apollos, who was known for his eloquence (see 1 Cor 1:12; and Acts 18:24–28). Despite this, Paul never catered to societal expectations, preferring to plant the gospel among small cells of believers rather than converting the masses through powerful rhetorical declamation, which he considered a betrayal of the gospel. In the end, Paul's most powerful tool against the rhetoric and ideology of the empire was his own lived example. Living the gospel was ultimately what mattered and what he expected of the communities he founded.

Communities of Anti-Imperial Practice

Certainly a pressing question for Paul concerned how to shape believers into communities of women and men whose lives testified that they were now adherents to the gospel of Jesus Christ and lived by its values. How would they live out this vocation in the world in relation to the dominant society, which remained under Roman imperial rule and pervaded by its values and ethos? These were not theoretical questions but practical ones requiring practical and dramatic changes in how one lived. Three such changes, which are often overlooked, deserve mention.

At 1 Corinthians 6:1–9, Paul advises the community to avoid the Roman court system. In the past, this was understood as a prohibition against "hanging out the community's dirty laundry in public." Granted, Paul must have been concerned about any negative exposure that could compromise the community's credibility, but there was more to it than that. The local civil courts were controlled by wealthy patrons who influenced judicial appointments, ensuring that appointees felt obligated to protect their patron's interests over those of the

---

50. Ibid., 165.

socially and economically poor.[51] An affluent community member who remained connected to elite networks outside the community could continue to manipulate the courts through those networks and take unfair advantage of poor and defenseless believers. Since these courts were structurally unjust and part of the imperial infrastructure, Paul did not see them as having jurisdiction over Christ-believers. Instead, Paul proposes a way of operating that radically departs from the imperial system. Within the community of those in Christ, Paul expected that the believer would not only subject self-interest and personal desire to others within the community, but would in turn judge and reconcile community members with integrity.[52] Rather than operating according to the typical hierarchical system of the empire, Paul encourages community members to adopt a system of mutual critique, undertaken as an act of loving service.

Another less-noted counterimperial practice Paul advocates concerns the eating of meat offered to idols (see 1 Cor 8–10). Cult practice was eminently political; religion was bound up with the politics and socioeconomic structures of the day. While Paul concedes in 1 Corinthians 10:23–31 that Christians may eat meat that had been offered in the pagan temples if it is served in *private homes,* he expressly prohibits eating idol meat in pagan temples (1 Cor 8:10). Why? Is Paul simply inconsistent? If no idols exist, as Paul admits (1 Cor 8:4), then there cannot be any food offered to idols, nor can there be eating of idol meat.

Paul understood that going to a pagan temple was not always about the conscious worship of an idol or even about the nature of the food ingested. Rather, it was about participating in the social and political networking associated with pagan feasts.[53] Ancient temple complexes, such as that dedicated to Asclepius in Corinth, included a temple, a courtyard, and three large banquet halls.[54] Like contemporary

---

51. On this point see Alan C. Mitchell, "Rich and Poor in the Courts of Corinth: Litigiousness and Status in 1 Cor 6:1–11," *New Testament Studies* 39.4 (1993): 562–86.

52. As pointed out by Anthony Thiselton, *The First Epistle to the Corinthians* (Grand Rapids, MI: William B. Eerdmans, 2000), 435.

53. See the observations of Richard A. Horsley, "1 Corinthians: A Case Study of Paul's Assembly as an Alternate Society," in *Paul and Empire,* 247–49.

54. See Jerome Murphy-O'Connor, *St. Paul's Corinth: Texts and Archaeology,* 3rd rev. ed. (Collegeville, MN: Liturgical Press, 2002), esp., 186–90.

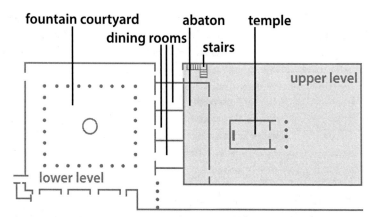

Ancient Corinth was the site of a temple dedicated to the Greek healing god Asclepius. The complex included various altars and a sleeping chamber (*abaton*) for the sick. Like many other ancient temple complexes, it included public dining rooms for hosting banquets. Each of the three dining rooms was lined on three sides by stone couches on which diners reclined to eat and socialize. In 1 Corinthians, Paul urged local Christians to avoid dining in pagan temples.

"power lunches" or "black-tie dinners," pagan feasts also had to do with self-promotion and status, making connections, securing financial or political backing, and being seen with the right people. Many of these were invitation-only dinner parties sponsored by the wealthy and held in a temple, which implicated the gods and suggested their approval.[55]

Given this context, one can understand Paul's insistence that believers renounce the networks of power relations by which imperial society operated. For those in Christ, the only social network that now mattered was the community gathered around the Eucharistic table, where participation was based solely on shared faith in Jesus Christ and unity was strengthened through the sharing of the one bread and cup (1 Cor 10:14–22).

At Corinth the effects of continued participation in pagan social-religious gatherings, where connections counted and status was on display, seem to have carried over with unfortunate results at

---

55. A number of papyrus invitations, e.g., P. Oxy 1755 and 1484, were excavated at Oxyrhynchus, an Egyptian city southwest of Cairo. See Bernard P. Grenfell and Arthur S. Hunt, eds. and trans., *The Oxyrynchus Papyri*, Part I (London: Paternoster House, 1898). This text is digitally available at *archive.org/details/oxyrhynchuspapy05huntgoog*.

the Lord's Supper. Paul laments that those without food or connections were humiliated by elite members of the community who ate and drank without concern for them (1 Cor 11:17–22). Paul aimed to build communities of mutual concern that would stand as alternatives to those in which the quest for honor and status trumped every other concern, but the process would take time.

One final counterimperial strategy to consider concerns Paul's effort to involve believers in an alternative economic system that would render the Christian movement both distinct and independent of Rome. According to Willem Jongman, a scholar of classical antiquity, the story of the Roman economy can be told along two lines: the aggregate income of the empire and the per capita income.[56] Measured by the aggregate income, Roman economy was fairly healthy. All could have enjoyed a respectable standard of living had resources been divided equally. But they were not. Incomes were a function of land ownership, and vast estates remained in the hands of the elite. In both Rome and the provinces, only about two percent of the population became wealthy from tenant rents and taxes. The economic inequality was a major source of social inequality, which worsened as the empire advanced, with an "ever smaller imperial elite controlling an ever larger share of the economy's surplus."[57] Thus as Jongman points out, "the wealth of the elite may not have been a sign of the prospering economy of which Roman historians boasted but instead, of the effective exploitation of the peasant poor."[58] They made up the majority of the population, lived at subsistence levels, and bore a huge tax burden to support the empire, especially its military.[59] These observations serve as a reminder that standards of living never depend simply on the growth of the economy, but on how resources are distributed, to whom, and on what basis. In Paul's day, those decisions were intertwined with the patronage system.

---

56. See Willem Jongman, "The Early Roman Empire: Consumption," in *The Cambridge Economic History of the Greco-Roman World*, ed. Walter Scheidel, Ian Morris, and Richard P. Saller (Cambridge, MA: Cambridge University Press, 2007), 592–618, here 594–95.

57. Ibid., 597.

58. Ibid., 596.

59. Elio LoCascio, "The Early Roman Empire: The State and the Economy," *Cambridge Economic History of the Greco-Roman World*, 618–47, here 632.

Just as it was axiomatic in Pauline studies until relatively recently to assume Paul's disinterest in political matters, it was also axiomatic to assume his disinterest in economic matters.[60] Yet Paul's own letters testify to his involvement in a very ambitious project that he simply referred to as "the collection" (Gal 2:1–10). Besides Galatians, he mentions the collection in his other three major letters (see Rom 15:25–29; 1 Cor 16:1–4; 2 Cor 8–9) and was clearly concerned about the success of this effort. Because collecting money in churches today is so routine, one can easily overlook how revolutionary Paul's collection project actually was.

In a world structured by patronage, with all the inequality and obligation it entailed, Paul asked communities of believers in one city to share their money, without patronage expectations, with the poor in Jerusalem and other communities of believers throughout the Mediterranean whom they had never even met. Biblical scholar Richard Horsley noted that the international character of this system and its economic reciprocity were not only unusual, but probably even unique in the ancient world.[61] This horizontal movement of resources among communities of equals was a powerful social act allowing the Christian community to create a separate economic system based on mutual care and concern.[62]

The purpose of the collection project was to achieve "equality" (*isotētos*).[63] Paul makes this explicit at 2 Corinthians 8:13–15, where he explains that the collection was not intended to ease other people's lives by burdening the Corinthians. Rather, "*ex isotētos*" (v. 13), literally "for the sake of equality," Paul was asking the Corinthians to

---

60. The usual reasons for this assumption are mentioned in Bruce W. Longe-necker, *Remember the Poor: Paul, Poverty and the Greco-Roman World* (Grand Rapids, MI: William B. Eerdmans, 2010), 3–6.

61. Richard A. Horsley, "1 Corinthians: A Case Study of Paul's Assembly as an Alternative Society," in *Paul and Empire*, 242–52, here, 251. See also the comments of Wright, *Paul: In Fresh Perspective*, 167.

62. See Luise Schottroff, "'Give to Caesar what Belongs to Caesar and to God what Belongs to God': A Theological Response of the Early Christian Church to Its Social and Political Environment," in *The Love of Enemy and Non-Retaliation in the New Testament*, ed. Willard M. Swartley (Louisville, KY: Westminster/John Knox Press, 1992), 249.

63. On Paul's use of "*isotētos*" cf. Lawrence L. Welborn, "'That There May be Equality': The Contexts and Consequences of a Pauline Ideal," *New Testament Studies* 59.1 (2013): 73–90.

share their "abundance" with those in need (v. 14). The impetus for this new system came from the example of the Lord Jesus himself (2 Cor 8:9), who voluntarily impoverished himself to benefit others. New Testament scholar Lawrence Welborn sees this as a radically new idea—a deity who impoverishes himself voluntarily and thereby establishes a new paradigm of economic relations.[64] The equality envisioned by Paul implies more than a one-time act of generosity. Rather, the collection project sought to realize the social ideal of the equal distribution and permanent sharing of material wealth based on the imitation of Christ.

Initially only the Philippian community seems to have adopted this proposed system (see Phil 4:15); other communities needed coaxing (see 2 Cor 8:1–15). Nonetheless, this system evolved over time, allowing the early Christians to establish themselves as an independent movement operating apart from the imperial system with its inequitable distribution of resources. The collection was a tangible expression of the unity of the church, which emphasized social obligation on behalf of those with less. Welborn warns that this Christian ideal threatens to be swept away by capitalism and the resurgence of the same type of systemic inequality that prevailed in the Roman Empire.[65]

In brief, in his own practice and in the practices he advocated among believers, Paul expected Christians to stand apart as holy assemblies and live by values that ran counter to the practices and ideals fostered in the imperial society. He expected them to live differently from the society established by the Roman imperial order—to be governed by another vision of reality, another set of values, and another Lord and King, Jesus.

Romans 13:1–7:
Paul the Social-Political Conformist?

Few scholars today would dispute that Paul envisioned those in Christ as communities of faith called to embody a different spirit and live a different set of values than those that prevailed in the

---

64. Ibid., 75.
65. Ibid., 74.

macro-society in which they lived. However, as acknowledged at the beginning of this chapter, not everyone agrees that Paul intended his communities to be "counter-imperial" assemblies or that he intended his teaching to challenge, much less subvert, the Roman imperial system. Perhaps no piece of evidence cited against the anti-imperial reading of Paul is more critical than Romans 13:1–7.[66]

Romans 13 begins with the exhortation, "Let every person be subject to the governing authorities." (v. 1a). Then Paul introduces a few arguments before suggesting a practical application based on them. The brief passage can be outlined as follows:

- Exhortation (13:1a): Let everyone be subject to the governing authorities.
- Argument 1 (13:1b–2): No authority exists apart from God's design. Therefore, since earthly authority is divinely instituted, it should not be resisted.
- Argument 2 (13:3b–5): As God's appointees, the authorities do God's work by rewarding those who do good and meting out God's wrath on those who do bad. Therefore, do the good.
- Argument 3 (13:3b–5): As ministers of God, the authorities are ordered to the good and against evil; thus, what they do ultimately benefits their subjects. Therefore, be subject to them.
- Practical Application (13:6–7): Because they serve as ministers of God, you should pay taxes and tolls and be deferential.

Many believe that this text, which reads as an unequivocal endorsement of imperial authorities, precludes any anti-imperial, liberationist reading of Paul. It lacks even the slightest hint that Paul thought the rulers of this age would be destroyed or that God had inaugurated a new world order in Christ. It contains none of the disdain Paul expresses elsewhere for representatives of the imperial system (see, e.g., 1 Cor 6:1–11). This text certainly seems to fit its description as the "Achilles Heel" of the liberation approach to Paul.[67]

---

66. Other evidence cited against an anti-imperial reading of Paul is discussed in Seyoon Kim, *Christ and Caesar: The Gospel and the Roman Empire in the Writings of Paul and Luke* (Grand Rapids, MI: William B. Eerdmans, 2008), esp. 34–64.

67. Kim, *Christ and Caesar,* esp., 36–43. Kim claims that neither Paul nor Luke presented their gospels in terms of political liberation.

Some have suggested that Paul did not write this text and that a later editor inserted it. While the passage may sound un-Pauline, the arguments in support of interpolation are refutable and do not compel the conclusion that the passage is inauthentic.[68] As New Testament scholar Robert Jewett points out, "distaste for a passage has no bearing on its authenticity."[69]

The sticking point for most scholars lies in the disparity between the apocalyptic hostility against the rulers of this age and the world's institutions that Paul expressed elsewhere, and the presentation here, where Paul portrays Roman rule as God's earthly vehicle for the maintenance of order and justice. Is Paul overthrowing the divine judgment on earthly rulers? Could the Paul accused of "turning the world upside down" be the same Paul advocating subjection to the authorities?

Situational Approaches to Romans 13:1–7

Scholars who accept the text's authenticity generally agree that Paul did not intend Romans 13:1–7 to be the basis of a timeless political ethic with universal applicability. Beyond this agreement, they differ in their attempts to explain what motivated Paul to advocate subjection to the authorities. Despite differences, each attempt aims to absolve Paul of the charge of political conformism or, at least, to show that he was not guilty of what one author calls a "monumental contradiction."[70]

Among the varied proposals, one suggests that Paul wanted to tamp down Gentile Christian arrogance against Jews, whom they believed constituted a doomed race of Torah-observers, by urging them to pay their taxes and do nothing to exacerbate Roman hostility to Jews.[71] Another suggests that he was countering

---

68. Arguments for interpolation are reviewed in Robert Jewett, *Romans: A Commentary* (Minneapolis, MN: Fortress, 2007), 783, n. 17. But as Jewett points out, the thematic transition between Romans 12 and 13 is not implausible; nor does the use of unique vocabulary signal interpolation, as Paul elsewhere uses unique vocabulary. Further, there is no obvious reason why the text would have been inserted.

69. Ibid., 783.

70. See Gordon Zerbe, "The Politics of Paul: His Supposed Conservatism and the Impact of Post-Colonial Readings," in *The Colonized Apostle: Paul through Postcolonial Eyes,* ed. Christopher D. Stanley (Minneapolis, MN: Fortress, 2011), 62–73, here 70.

71. Elliot, *Liberating Paul,* 214–16.

over-realized eschatology—the belief of some Christians that they were already living in the new age and therefore no longer obliged to pay state taxes.[72] Others think Romans 13:1–7 reflects Paul's political shrewdness. He needed to set up a base in the capital from which to expand his ministry westward. In order to avoid any complications in pursuing his goal, Paul expressed loyalty to Rome and advocated submission to authorities, which would have placated imperial bureaucrats. Thus Paul crafted his teaching at Romans 13:1–7 in view of his missionary goals.[73] Others focus on the protests over unjust taxation.[74] Because Paul knew how Rome handled civil dissidents, and because Christians were already a suspected minority, Paul implicitly discouraged them from joining the local protests against unjust taxes and explicitly encouraged them to pay up in order to avoid drawing the negative attention of the authorities.[75] For others, Roman 13:1–7 reflects the ever-pragmatic Paul who recognized that Rome was in charge and Christians had to obey its rules.[76]

These explanations present Paul, at worst, as an opportunist and, at best, as a protector of either Jews or Christians from the wrath of Rome. Regardless of which social context is used to frame Paul's teaching, nothing changes the fact that Paul presents the imperial authorities in a positive light and promotes subordination and obedience to them. Over the course of the centuries, these verses have been cited to enforce obedience to civil authorities that have oppressed and brutalized populations. In the well-known words of New Testament scholar John C. O'Neill,

---

72. Ernst Käsemann, *New Testament Questions for Today*, trans. George Montague (Philadelphia: Fortress Press, 1969), 196–216.

73. See Jewett, *Romans*, esp. 803.

74. Nero wanted to correct the situation by repealing certain taxes but was blocked by the Senate. See Tacitus, *Annals* 13:50, available at *www.sacred-texts.com/cla/tac/a13050.htm*. On Roman taxation policies and resultant civic unrest throughout the empire, see Neil Elliot, *The Arrogance of the Nations: Reading Romans in the Shadow of the Empire* (Minneapolis, MN: Fortress Press, 2008), 91–100.

75. See example, Anthony J. Guerra, *Romans and the Apologetic Tradition: The Purpose, Genre and Audience of Paul's Letter* (Cambridge, MA: Cambridge University Press, 1995), esp. 157–69.

76. James D. G. Dunn, *Romans 9–16*, vol. 38B (Nashville, TN: Thomas Nelson, 1988), 680.

These seven verses have caused more unhappiness and misery in the Christian East and West than any other seven verses in the New Testament by the license they have given to tyrants and the support for tyrants the Church has felt called on to give as a result of the presence of Romans 13:1–7 in the canon.[77]

N. T. Wright has taken another tack, suggesting the text subverts imperial authorities by insisting that they do not enjoy divine status, but are simply appointees of the one true God. According to Wright, "This passage actually represents a severe demotion of the rulers from the position they would have claimed to occupy."[78] Jewett agrees, noting that "if the Roman authorities had understood this argument, it would have been viewed as thoroughly subversive."[79] Despite the possible subversive intent, however, Paul ultimately advocates submission to these authorities.[80] That seems to be his main point here.

Other New Testament scholars find the insights of postcolonial theory useful in fathoming Paul's divergent postures toward imperial rulers.[81] The postcolonial perspective acknowledges that the relationship between the subjugated and their subjugators is complex. The condition of being colonized or subjugated does not elicit only two opposing responses—that one is either for or against the colonizing power. The situation is much more fluid and given to ambivalence. For example, Paul and his contemporaries may have appreciated and used the new roads and the safer seafaring the Romans introduced. They may have marveled at Roman ingenuity. But at the same time, they may have resented Roman/imperial control over city finances.

---

77. John C. O'Neill, *Paul's Letter to the Romans* (London: Penguin, 1975), 209.

78. Wright, *Paul: In Fresh Perspective*, 78.

79. Jewett, *Romans*, 790.

80. According to Victor Furnish, by "subjection," Paul was asking only that Christians "acknowledge" and "respect" the political order under which they lived, which included paying taxes, cf. *The Moral Teaching of Saint Paul: Selected Issues*, 2nd ed. Rev. (Nashville, TN: Abingdon Press, 1987), 126.

81. See, e.g., Jeremy Punt, "Pauline Agency in Post-Colonial Perspective: Subverter of or Agent for Empire?" in *The Colonized Apostle: Paul through Postcolonial Eyes*, ed. Christopher D. Stanley (Minneapolis, MN: Fortress, 2011), 53–61; also Zerbe, "The Politics of Paul," 62–73, esp. 70–72.

In simplest terms, the colonized tend to have what could be termed a love-hate relationship with their imperial colonizers.

Paul and his contemporaries—a mass of diverse, subjugated populations throughout the Mediterranean—certainly shared the imperial or colonial condition. This could explain why Paul elsewhere speaks with hostility of the rulers of this age, while here in Romans 13:1–7 he attempts to regularize Christian praxis in relation to the state authorities, who are ultimately under God's judgment. The postcolonial lens does not absolve Paul of the charge of "monumental contradiction," but accepts his ambivalence as an unavoidable aspect of the condition of being colonized. Viewing Paul through this lens reminds readers again that Paul was not a systematic theologian attempting to offer a coherent, timelessly applicable exposition on every matter he treated. Instead, he was a man of his times caught up in the struggles of daily existence.

Given these tensions in Paul, multiple readings of his views, whether about women or politics, will always be possible. Thus the question again becomes: through what lens does one interpret Paul? Through Roman 13:1–7 alone or in a dialogue with other texts reflecting his vision of that new age inaugurated in the Christ-event when God's reign of justice and peace is established? In the course of history, the churches have tended to focus on the socially conservative side of Paul and used him to legitimate their own socially conservative agendas. However, recent feminist, postcolonial, and liberationist scholarship continues to challenge that (ab)use of Paul. As many have already commented, to claim Paul the social conservative without reclaiming the radical Paul who announced another Lord and Savior and another way to live in this world risks being both exegetically and socially irresponsible.

Summary

Paul was neither the mystagogue, nor the model of perfection, nor the systematic theologian later history made him out to be. He was a man of his times, killed by the same imperial rulers who killed Jesus. Recent scholarship has begun to refocus on the issues and concerns that occupied Paul and his communities as they struggled to become church in mid-first-century-ce imperial society. Most of the scholars cited in this chapter follow the premise that by studying Paul in his own sociopolitical context, one may detect in his letters strains of anti-imperialism. Without direct statements from Paul that implicate Caesar and the imperial system, there is no way to determine with certainty that Paul formulated and presented his gospel as an antithesis to Rome's proclamation. However, the insights scholars have extracted from Paul's letters about his message and practice point to a political dimension in Paul's gospel that can no longer be ignored or negated in view of Romans 13:1–7. This text reveals Paul's ambivalence, and admittedly, dulls the political edge of his gospel. However, it in no way eclipses Paul's radically political understanding of salvation as the Christ-made-possible condition of liberation and participation in the new world order that God has inaugurated and over which he rules.

Questions for Review and Reflection

1. What evidence do scholars rely on to justify an anti-imperial interpretation of Paul's gospel and the practices he advocated?

2. Name three values promoted in American society today that Paul would find antithetical to the gospel of Jesus Christ and explain why.

3. Explain what the patronage system was. Why wouldn't Paul accept the patronage of the Corinthians? Where do you see the patronage system at work in society today?

4. What insights from postcolonial theory do New Testament scholars find useful in explaining Paul's apparently conflicting attitudes toward the imperial authorities?

5. If Paul were alive, would he find anything positive about capitalism as practiced in the world today or would he find it an economic system completely incompatible with the gospel?

Opening Other Windows

Crossan, John Dominic, and Jonathan L. Reed. *In Search of Paul: How Jesus' Apostle Opposed Rome's Empire with God's Kingdom*. San Francisco: Harper, 2004.

Elliot, Neil. *The Arrogance of the Nations: Reading Romans in the Shadow of the Empire*. Minneapolis, MN: Fortress Press, 2008.

Galinsky, Karl. *Augustan Culture: An Interpretive Introduction*. Princeton, NJ: Princeton University Press, 1996.

Horsley, Richard A. (ed.). *In the Shadow of Empire: Reclaiming the Bible as a History of Faithful Resistance*. Louisville, KY: Westminster John Knox Press, 2008.

_____. *Paul and Politics: Ekklesia, Israel, Imperium, Interpretation, Essays in Honor of Krister Stendahl*. Harrisburg, PA: Trinity Press International, 2000.

_____. *Religion and Empire: People, Power and the Life of the Spirit*. Minneapolis, MN: Augsburg Press, 2003.

Lopez, Davina. *Apostle to the Conquered: Reimagining Paul's Mission*. Minneapolis, MN: Fortress Press, 2008.

Martin, Dale B. *Slavery as Salvation: The Metaphor of Slavery in Pauline Christianity*. New Haven, CT: Yale University Press, 1990.

Nugent, John C., and Branson L. Parler (eds.). *Revolutionary Christian Citizenship. Collected Addresses and Articles of John Howard Yoder*. Harrisonburg, VA: Herald Press, 2013.

Vassiliades, Petros. "Equality and Justice in Classical Antiquity: The Social Implications of the Pauline Collection," *St. Vladimir's Theological Quarterly* 36.1–2 (1992): 51–59.

Internet Resources

Goldfarb, Lynn, and Margaret Koval, Producers. *Empires: The Roman Empire in the First Century*. DVD. PBS Home Video, 2001. Available at *www.pbs.org*. Also see PBS's informative website at *www.pbs.org/empires/romans/index.html*.

"Romans," BBC History, *www.bbc.co.uk/history/ancient/romans*.
The BBC website provides solid information on the imperial period.

Epilogue

Closing the Windows on Paul

P aul never wrote a separate account of his key theological insights or a first-person memoir of his life and deeds. In all likelihood, Paul never even imagined that his life and teaching would have had wider importance beyond the small communities of believers he pastored. What remains of Paul, and offers the most direct access to him, are his extant letters to those communities. They were collected by an individual, or perhaps a group of people, who apparently thought them worth preserving.[1] Eventually they were included in the canon of the New Testament.

This book has provided an encounter with Paul's thought through an exposition of select texts from those letters that touch on some of the more advanced and debated topics in Pauline studies today. In the process, it situated Paul's thought within the context of the Jewish and Greco-Roman social and intellectual currents of the first century ce. This study also integrated the contemporary scholarly discussion on the issues treated, which made evident the variety of scholarly viewpoints on almost every topic. Throughout, the study has indicated where scholars have arrived at a consensus and where they continue to disagree. At this point, rather than rehearsing what has been presented, it may be more helpful to conclude by pointing out three broad insights that are important to carry away from this study.

---

1. Scholars disagree on who is responsible for the collection of Paul's letters and why, when, and how they were collected. See the concise discussion in Jerome Murphy-O'Connor, *Paul the Letter Writer: His World, His Options, His Skills* (Collegeville, MN: Liturgical Press, 1995), 114–29.

Key Take-aways

Paul Must Be Studied in Context

Paul is not our contemporary. In fact, the man who emerges from this study was deeply embedded in his own social and religious culture and quite aware of the intellectual currents and issues of his day—not ours. This insight seems so obvious as to require no comment. Yet much of the difficulty of coming to terms with Paul's thought derives from attempts to read and interpret Paul as if he were a contemporary, responding to present-day concerns. He is not. Therefore, attempting to bring Paul into the modern world and apply his thought to it requires one to go back and learn as much as possible about his world.

Today, university students are encouraged to study abroad in order to immerse themselves in a different culture and experience what people in that culture value, what they consider right and wrong, how they express themselves in speech and gesture, and so on. An attentive encounter with another culture's ideas and ethos will necessarily elicit critical reflection on one's own assumptions and culture and how one experiences reality. Studying Paul critically is like a virtual "study abroad" to a past culture. It puts readers in touch with Jewish and Gentile people living in the Roman world with its political, religious, social, and economic history. It brings readers into contact with terminology they think they understand but don't quite. That became clear, for example, in the examination of Paul's use of "Sin" and "flesh," by which he intends a meaning quite different from what contemporary English speakers ordinarily understand by those words.

If one does not make an attempt to understand the world that produced Paul, it will be difficult to understand the texts Paul produced. Moreover, without that sensitivity to his world and the temporal and conceptual distance separating it from the present day, readers risk imposing their concerns on his thought and judging it according to their standards and perspectives. Then Paul is easily reduced to a misogynist, an autocrat, or a grim, sexually repressed moralist. Further, beyond sensitizing against imposing modern concerns on Paul, a critical approach to Paul in context can safeguard against facile appeals to his first-century-ce conditioned teachings to ground authoritative claims about how things should be in the contemporary world.

Paul's Theology: Reshaped by an Encounter and Refocused through an Event

Paul's theology was reshaped by an experience that he interpreted as an encounter with the Risen Christ, which forced him to reconsider the whole Christ-event—that is, the life, death, and Resurrection of Jesus. This event became the lens through which Paul refocused his understanding of God; of Jesus, God's Messiah; and of the Spirit, the sanctifying presence of both God and Christ indwelling believers. Paul believed that his theology—his understanding of who God was in Christ and what God accomplished in Christ—had eclipsed all other ways of knowing God and all other wisdom offered by the various philosophical schools and religions of his day. Thus Paul is not just any man in history whose writings just happened to make it into the biblical canon. Rather, he is a man who had a life-changing experience through which he came to some incredibly important and unique insights that formed the foundation for all subsequent Christian theology.

Many scholars have attempted to isolate Paul's most important theological ideas and then pinpoint a central idea that is alleged to give coherence to all the rest. This study has examined a diversity of ideas, but has steered away from isolating a single central concept for one simple reason: Paul staked his life on a person, not a concept. He had ideas, but he imitated Christ (1 Cor 11:1). He was a man of accomplishments and status, confident in his knowledge. However, once he came to know Christ, everything lost value except for Christ, who was now the surpassing love and value of his life (see Phil 3:7–10). All of Paul's theology emanated from that personal relationship and his experience of the love of God poured out in Christ crucified. What he proclaimed—his gospel—was really nothing other than the story of that love of God for humanity made known in Christ. What he expected of believers was that their lives, individually and corporately, would retell that story.

Responsible Use of Paul's Texts Up to the Reader

Sometimes the meaning of a Pauline text remains indeterminate. For example, the circumstances to which Paul addresses himself may be uncertain or the terminology he used ambiguous. Such texts are open to various interpretations. Depending on the interpreter, they have sometimes become ideological weapons to oppress and even justify violence against certain categories of people. This is "Paul in the Service of Death," to borrow a title from New Testament scholar Neil Elliott, who references the various ways Paul has been useful to systems of domination and oppression.[2]

Today it is widely recognized, thanks especially to feminist scholarship, that there is no such thing as bias-free or assumption-free reading and interpretation of the biblical text. Thus there is a greater awareness that responsible Bible reading and the application of biblical teaching to contemporary situations needs to be done with concern for ethical consequences. To coin an expression that seems appropriate in light of this study, responsible Christian interpretation should employ a "cruciform hermeneutic." This does not mean that one can ignore the plain meaning of the text or reject it simply because the content offends one's own sensibilities. A "cruciform hermeneutic," however, does require that interpretation and application should serve the unity, holiness, and building up of the body of believers. Beyond conveying information about Paul and his world, this book has also stressed the importance of 1) raising questions about the biases and assumptions that condition interpretations of Paul's texts, and 2) thoughtfully weighing authoritative claims based on these interpretations. These are especially important skills, given that so many people continue to have recourse to the Bible to ground religious positions with enormous political consequences.

In writing about his grandfather's desire to meet and converse with St. Paul in heaven, C. S. Lewis remarked that it never even crossed his grandfather's mind that an encounter with St. Paul might be a rather overwhelming experience.[3] Many homilists avoid preaching—and many Christians avoid reading—Paul because they find him "overwhelming," as in too difficult and not awe-inspiring as Lewis intended the word. Finding Paul and his ideas difficult is nothing new. Scripture itself witnesses to the difficulty of trying to make sense of Paul (2 Peter 3:16). This book has aimed to make

---

2. Neil Elliot, *Liberating Paul: The Justice of God and the Politics of the Apostle* (Maryknoll, NY: Orbis Press, 1998), 3–22.

3. C. S. Lewis, *Letters to Malcolm: Chiefly on Prayer* (Boston: Mariner Books, 2002), letter 2.

the encounter with Paul less difficult by providing information and tools to aid in an understanding of what he thought and how he expressed himself. Hopefully, it has paved the way for readers to be "overwhelmed" in the way Lewis meant and come to appreciate Paul not as a relic of the distant past, but as a person who still has something intelligent and meaningful to say to people today who are trying, as he did, to make sense of the world and their own fragile and fleeting existences.

Index

Note: Page numbers followed by *i*, *m*, *c*, *cap*, *n*, *s*, or *t* indicate illustrations, maps, charts, captions, footnotes, sidebars, or tables, respectively.

MacMullan, Ramsay, 112
magic, 80
Malachi, 100*n*9
malakos, 203–4
Malta, 38*m*–39*m*
manual labor, 261
manumission, 87
maranâthâ, 100*n*11
Marcion, 155*n*35
Mark, Gospel of, 21*s*
Mark (Paul's companion during
Roman captivity), 57*t*
marriage, 81, 186. *See also* sexual
issues; *specific topics*, e.g., divorce;
procreation
aristocratic class and, 184–85
Hellenistic Judaism on, 189–91
love in, 186*s*–189
monogamous, 209
"Pauline Privilege," 201*n*47
pleasure between spouses, 187,
189, 199, 201–2
an unbelieving spouse, 201
Martial, 260
martyrs, 256*n*27
Jewish, 102
Paul as martyr, 43*c*, 248
Matthew, Gospel of, 21*s*
Meeks, Wayne, 166–67, 171, 227
messiah
in apocalyptic thought, 96
crucified, Paul's gospel of, 27*n*18,
28, 33, 109, 226, 253, 263
Essenes as awaiting two, 18
as hoped for, 15
Jesus movement and, 18–19,
27–28
Jewish conceptions of, 15–16,
27–28, 33, 100
Paul preaching to Jews, 45
Paul preaching to non-Jews, 40
Paul's acceptance of Jesus, 13,
30, 34

Paul's convictions/message
regarding, 108–9, 151, 248,
251–53, 263, 279
prophetic literature and, 94
ministry of Paul. *See* Paul, ministry
of
miracles, 23, 32, 152
misogyny, 218–19, 228–29, 242,
278
mission of Paul. *See* Paul, mission of
Mitchell, Margaret, 163*n*6
monogamy, 209. *See also* marriage
morally significant things, 196
Moses, 15*n*3. *See also* Law of Moses
Apocalypse of Moses, 119
Musonius Rufus, 83, 186*s*–188
mysteries
of the gospel, 248
of salvation, 98
mystery religions, 79–81

N

Nabatea in Arabia, 40
Naphtali, Testament of, 97, 118, 190
Nazarenes, 16
Nero, 41, 74, 272*n*74
Neusner, Jacob, 152
new age of redemption, 30, 94,
97–99, 101, 108, 227, 252–53,
272, 274
community for, 160
new creation theology, 130, 172,
211, 226–27, 231, 234, 243–44
"new perspective on Paul," 136,
141–55
New Testament, 13, 116*s*, 250, 273
Greek, 195
Paul's letters in, 13, 20–22, 37,
277
nonbelievers. *See* unbelievers
noncanonical literature, 15*n*4, 96*n*5,
118, 190, 230